ENGLISH IDIOMS
AND HOW TO USE THEM

JENNIFER SEIDL
W McMORDIE

D1487777

Oxford University Press

Oxford University Press,
Walton Street, Oxford OX2 6DP

OXFORD NEW YORK TORONTO
DELHI BOMBAY CALCUTTA MADRAS KARACHI
KUALA LUMPUR SINGAPORE HONG KONG TOKYO
NAIROBI DAR ES SALAAM CAPE TOWN
MELBOURNE AUCKLAND
and associated companies in
BEIRUT BERLIN IBADAN MEXICO CITY NICOSIA

OXFORD is a trade mark of Oxford University Press

First edition (by W. McMordie) 1909
Second edition 1913 (reprinted 21 times)
Third edition (revised by R. C. Goffin) 1954 (reprinted 17 times)
Fourth edition (by Jennifer Seidl) 1978
Seventh impression 1985

Paperback edition ISBN 0 19 432764 7

© Jennifer Seidl 1978

Printed in Hong Kong

Contents

I   What are idioms?

general note

We often read and hear the phrase 'language is a living thing', but most of us do not stop to think about *how* and *why* this is true. Living things grow and change, and so does language. One can readily recognise differences between Shakespeare's English and the English of modern authors, but present-day English is also growing and changing, and these tendencies are not so easy to recognise.

Since the general tendencies of present-day English are towards more idiomatic usage, it is important that this book on Idioms should show the learner how the language is developing. Idioms are not a *separate* part of the language which one can choose either to use or to omit, but they form an *essential* part of the general vocabulary of English. A description of how the vocabulary of the language is growing and changing will help to place idioms in perspective.

In this chapter we shall also consider some changing attitudes towards language, several different aspects of idioms, and finally difficulties which learners experience in using idioms.

Growth and change in the English vocabulary

1 One does not need to be a language expert to realise that the vocabulary of a language grows continually with new developments in knowledge. New ideas must have new labels to name them. Without new labels, communication of these new ideas to others would be impossible. Most such words come from the English of special subjects such as science and technology, psychology, sociology, politics and economics.

2 Words which already exist can also take on a particular meaning in a particular situation. For example, *to lock someone out*

usually means 'to lock a door in order to prevent someone from entering'. However, the verb has a special meaning in the context of
industrial relations. It means that the employers refuse to let the
workers return to their place of work until they stop protesting.
The noun *a lock-out* is also used in this special context, and it is,
therefore, a new word in the language. Similar words are *to sit in*,
a sit-in and *to walk out*, *a walk-out*, where the verbs take on a new
meaning in the context of industrial strike and protest and where
the nouns are only used in this context, thus becoming new words.
3 Not only can words which already exist express new ideas and
thus help a language to grow; also, new ideas can be expressed by
the combination of two or three existing words. Here is an example of this: the words *wage* and *to freeze* are well known, but the
idea of *a wage-freeze* came into the language only a few years ago.
To freeze wages is another expression from British politics and
economics and means 'to stop increases in wages'. The same idea
is found in *to freeze prices* and *a price-freeze*.
4 A new word can be formed by changing a verbal phrase into a
noun (as in *a lock-out*), or by changing a noun into a verb. Both
these changes are very popular in American English (AE). British
English (BE) quickly borrows new word formations from AE.
Here are some nouns formed from verbal phrases: *a stop-over*, *a
check-up*, *a walk-over*, *a hand-out*, *a set-up*, all common especially
in informal style. Here are some verbs formed from nouns: *to
pilot (a plane)*, *to captain (a team)*, *to radio (a message)*, *to service
(a motorcar)*, *to air-freight (a parcel)*, *to Xerox (a document)*, *to
pressure (somebody)*. It is easy to give words new grammatical
functions because English is flexible. When the function is
changed, it is not necessary to change the form. Not only nouns,
but also adjectives are made into verbs to show a process, as in
to soundproof, to skidproof, to streamline. All these changes in the
function of words have one purpose, that is, to make the form of
words used shorter and more direct. They are short-cuts in language. These short forms are quicker and more convenient and for
this reason they are becoming more and more popular.
5 There are other short-cuts which BE has borrowed from AE.
Verbs can also be made from the root of a noun, eg *to housekeep*
from the noun *housekeeper*, *to barkeep* from *barkeeper*, *to babysit*
from *babysitter*. *To house-sit* is a new word which has been copied
from *to babysit*, because it includes the same idea, namely, 'to look
after someone's house while he is away'.
6 Another short-cut joins words together in order to form one
adjective instead of a long phrase, eg a *round-the-clock* service,
instead of 'a service which is offered around the clock' (ie 24
hours).

7 New words can be made by adding endings such as *-ise* or *-isation* to adjectives or nouns. This is especially popular in the language of newspapers. Here are some examples: *to decimalise* instead of the long phrase 'to change into the decimal system', *to departmentalise* instead of 'to organise into different departments' and *containerisation* instead of 'the process of putting things into containers'.

8 Prefixes such as *mini-*, *maxi-*, *super-*, *uni-*, *non-*, *extra-* are put in front of words (mainly nouns and adjectives) to indicate the quantity or quality of something in the shortest possible way. Here are some examples: *supergrade petrol* (the best quality), *uni-sex* (in fashion, the same design in clothes for men and women), a *non-stick* frying-pan, *non-skid* tyres, *mini-skirt*, *extra-mild* cigarettes.

9 New words can be made by mixing two words that already exist, i e by combining part of one word with part of another. A well-known example is *smog* (smoke + fog). Others are *brunch* (breakfast + lunch), *newscast* (news + broadcast) and *motel* (motorist + hotel). AE uses more of these words than BE. Here are some from AE: *laundromat* (laundry + automat), *cablegram* (cable + telegram) and *medicare* (medical + care). Here is one from the world of economics: *stagflation* (stagnation + inflation).

Changing attitudes to language

Educated writers and readers of English are becoming more flexible and tolerant about what is considered to be correct or acceptable usage. Some deviations from the grammatical rules of the past are now accepted not only in spoken but also in written English. Such changes of attitude can be observed in several parts of grammar, including case, number, tense and the position of prepositions at the end of a phrase or sentence. A few examples will make this clear. *Who shall I ask?* now appears in written English instead of *Whom shall I ask?* (case). *Neither of them are coming* instead of *Neither of them is coming* (number). *I never heard of her before* instead of *I have never heard of her before* (tense). Prepositions appear now quite regularly at the end of a sentence in written English, where previously this was only common in spoken English and was considered bad style when written. Examples of all the above can easily be found even in newspapers which have a reputation for writing good and correct English.

The attitude of users of the language towards style is also becoming more flexible. Words which were considered to be *slang* in the past may be more acceptable in present-day English; they may now be considered to be *colloquial* or *informal*. The expression *to be browned off with somebody* was in the past a slang expression for 'to be bored with or irritated by somebody'. Since the slang expression of the same meaning *to be cheesed off with somebody* came into the language, *browned off* has generally risen in status and is now considered by most people to be informal and not slang. There are several other cases where a new expression has replaced an already existing one, giving the existing expression a rise in status from slang to informal. This is also partly due to the spread in the use of *taboo* words (or *swear-words*), which much more freely now replace words (like *damn* and *bloody*) which were in the past considered to be *bad language*. The taboo words are now bad language and the other words do not give so much offence as in the past. Both of these sets of words, however, should be avoided by the learner until his mastery of the language is so complete that he knows exactly when, where and how to use such words.

Different aspects of the idiom

We shall now take a close look at some aspects of idioms. An important fact which must be stressed is that idioms are not only colloquial expressions, as many people believe. They can appear in formal style and in slang. They can appear in poetry or in the language of Shakespeare and the Bible. What, then, is an idiom? We can say that an idiom is a number of words which, taken together, mean something different from the individual words of the idiom when they stand alone. The way in which the words are put together is often odd, illogical or even grammatically incorrect. These are the special features of some idioms. Other idioms are completely regular and logical in their grammar and vocabulary. Because of the special features of some idioms, we have to learn the idiom as a whole and we often cannot change any part of it (except perhaps, only the tense of the verb). English is very rich in idiomatic expressions. In fact, it is difficult to speak or write English without using idioms. An English native speaker is very often not aware that he is using an idiom; perhaps he does not even realise that an idiom which he uses is grammatically incorrect. A non-native learner makes the correct use of idiomatic English one of his main aims, and the fact that some idioms are illogical or grammatically incorrect causes him difficulty. Only careful study and exact learning will help.

It cannot be explained why a particular idiom has developed an unusual arrangement or choice of words. The idiom has been fixed by long usage—as is sometimes seen from the vocabulary.

The idiom *to buy a pig in a poke* means 'to buy something which one has not inspected previously and which is worth less than one paid for it'. The word *poke* is an old word meaning *sack*. *Poke* only appears in present-day English with this meaning in this idiom. Therefore, it is clear that the idiom has continued to be used long after the individual word.

There are many different sources of idioms. As will be made clear later, the most important thing about idioms is their meaning. This is why a native speaker does not notice that an idiom is incorrect grammatically. If the source of an idiom is known, it is sometimes easier to imagine its meaning. Many idiomatic phrases come from the every-day life of Englishmen, from home life, e g *to be born with a silver spoon in one's mouth, to make a clean sweep of something, to hit the nail on the head.* There are many which have to do with food and cooking, e g *to eat humble pie, out of the frying-pan into the fire, to be in the soup.* Agricultural life has given rise to *to go to seed, to put one's hand to the plough, to lead someone up the garden path.* Nautical life and military life are the source of *when one's ship comes home, to be in the same boat as someone, to be in deep waters, to sail under false colours, to cross swords with someone, to fight a pitched battle, to fight a losing/winning battle.* Many idioms include parts of the body, animals, and colours (see Chapter 12). The Bible gives us *to kill the fatted calf, to turn the other cheek, the apple of one's eye.*

Idioms take many different forms or structures. They can be very short or rather long. A large number of idioms consist of some combination of noun and adjective, e g *cold war, a dark horse, French leave, forty winks, a snake in the grass*; these are dealt with in Chapter 4. Some idioms are much longer: *to fish in troubled waters, to take the bull by the horns, to cut one's coat according to one's cloth.*

An idiom can have a regular structure, an irregular or even a grammatically incorrect structure. The idiom *I am good friends with him* is irregular or illogical in its grammatical structure. *I* is singular; why then is the correct form in this case not *I am a good friend with him*? This form is impossible although it is more logical; one would have to say *I am a good friend of his.* A native speaker is not consciously aware of this inconsistency. This is, therefore, an example of the kind of idiom where the form is irregular but the meaning clear. A second kind has a regular form but a meaning that is not clear. *To have a bee in one's bonnet* has a regular form, but its meaning is not obvious. It means, in fact, that one is obsessed by an idea, but how can we know this if we have not learnt it as an idiom? There is a third group, in which both form and meaning are irregular. *To be at large*: the form

Verb + Preposition + Adjective without noun is strange, and we have no idea what it means, either! If we talk about a prisoner who is still at large, it means that he is still free. Here are similar examples: *to go through thick and thin, to be at daggers drawn, to be in the swim.*

We find, in fact, that most idioms belong to the second group, where the form is regular, but the meaning is unclear. However, even in this group, some idioms are clearer than others, that is, some are easier to guess than others. Take the example *to give someone the green light.* We can guess the meaning even though we may never have heard it before. If we associate 'the green light' with traffic lights where green means 'Go!', we can imagine that the idiom means 'to give someone permission to start something'.

Other idioms can be guessed if we hear them in context, that is, when we know how they are used in a particular situation. For example, let us take the idiom *to be at the top of the tree.* If we hear the sentence 'John is at the top of the tree now', we are not sure what this is saying about John. Perhaps it means that he is in a dangerous position or that he is hiding. But if we hear the phrase in context, the meaning becomes clear to us: *Ten years ago John joined the company, and now he's the general manager! Yes, he's really at the top of the tree!* The idiom means 'to be at the top of one's profession, to be successful'.

However, some idioms are too difficult to guess correctly because they have no association with the original meaning of the individual words. Here are some examples: *to tell someone where to get off, to bring the house down, to take it out on someone.* The learner will have great difficulty here unless he has heard the idioms before. Even when they are used in context, it is not easy to detect the meaning exactly. We shall take a closer look at the first of these examples. *To get off* usually appears together with *bus* or *bicycle*, as in this sentence: *Mary didn't know her way round town, so Jane took her to the bus stop and then told her where to get off.* But in its idiomatic sense *to tell someone where to get off* means 'to tell someone rudely and openly what you think of him' as in this context: *Jane had had enough of Mary's stupid and critical remarks, so she finally told her where to get off.* For a foreign learner, this idiomatic meaning is not even exactly clear in context.

It was said earlier that we have to learn an idiom as a whole because we often cannot change any part of it. A question which the learner may ask is: 'How do I know which parts of which idioms can be changed?' The idioms which cannot be changed at all are called *fixed* idioms. Some idioms are fixed in some of their parts but not in others. Some idioms allow only limited changes in the parts which are not fixed. We can make this clear with an

example. Take the idiom *to give someone the cold shoulder*. Which
changes are possible? The idiom means 'to treat someone in a cold
or unfriendly way'. We may ask if it is possible to say *to give someone the 'cool' or 'warm' shoulder* or *to give someone 'a' cold shoulder* or
to give a cold shoulder 'to' someone. None of these are possible, but
how can the foreign learner know this? Alternative possibilities
are shown in this book by the mark /. If this mark does not appear
in the arrangement of the idiom, the idiom is fixed. The learner
should note the alternative possibilities and use only these and no
others. *To give someone the cold shoulder* is therefore a fixed idiom.
Here are some more: *to make a clean breast of it*, which means 'to
tell the truth about something'. We can only change the tense of
the verb. The idiom *to take/have/enjoy forty winks* allows a limited
choice of verb but the pair *forty winks* is fixed. We cannot say
'fifty' winks. We cannot explain why this is wrong. We must accept
the idiomatic peculiarities of the language and learn to handle
them. Here are some more examples of idioms which are not fixed
in all parts: *to come to a bad/nasty/sticky/no good/untimely end*; *to
keep a sharp/careful/watchful/professional eye on someone*.

When and where to use idioms

We have now talked about several aspects of idioms: where they
come from, their form, their meaning, if and how we can vary
them. We shall now look at the reasons for the difficulties which
foreign learners experience when they try to *use* idioms.
    One of the main difficulties is that the learner does not know in
which situations it is correct to use an idiom. He does not know
the level of style, that is, whether an idiom can be used in a formal
or in an informal situation. Help is given in this book with the
markings *formal* and *informal*. Unmarked idioms can be used in
any situation.
    Choice of words depends on the person one is speaking to and
on the situation or place at the time. If the person is a friend and
the situation is private, we may use informal or even slang expressions. In a formal situation, when we do not know the person
we are speaking to very well or the occasion is public, we choose
words much more carefully. It would be wrong to choose an informal expression in some rather formal situation and bad manners
to choose a slang expression. This means that we can express the
same information or idea in more than one way using a different
level. Here is an example. If one arrives late when meeting a
friend, a typical informal way of apologising would be: 'Sorry I'm
late!—but I got badly held up.' However, if one came too late to

a meeting with strangers or a business meeting, another choice of expression for the apology would be appropriate, perhaps 'I do apologise for being late. I'm afraid my train was delayed.'

The expressions marked *formal* are found in written more than in spoken English and are used to show a distant relationship between the speakers. Such expressions would be used for example when making a formal speech to a large audience. Expressions marked *informal* are used in every-day spoken English and in personal letters. (*Slang* expressions are used in very informal situations between good friends. Learners should not make frequent use of slang expressions as they usually—but unexpectedly—become out-of-date and sound strange.) It is advisable to concentrate on the expressions which are marked *informal* and on the unmarked expressions which are neutral in style and can be used in any situation.

Another major difficulty is that the learner does not know if an idiom is natural or appropriate in a certain situation. This can only be learnt by careful listening to native speakers or careful reading of English texts which contain idioms. In order to help the learner with this difficulty, examples of usage in typical situations are given where it seems necessary. The learner should take careful note of these examples.

The third major difficulty is that of fixed idioms and only partly fixed idioms, which has already been discussed. It is most important that the learner should be exact in his use of fixed idioms, as an inaccurate idiom may mean very little or even nothing at all to a native speaker. Above all, remember that it is usually extremely unwise to translate idioms into English from one's own native language. One may be lucky that the two languages have the same form and vocabulary, but in most cases, the result will be utterly bewildering to the native speaker—and possibly highly amusing.

As was said earlier, the correct use of idiomatic English should be the aim of every learner. It is an aim which is worthwhile and satisfying. Mastery of idiom comes only slowly, through careful study and observation, through practice and experience, but remember: *practice makes perfect* and *all things are difficult before they are easy*.

Note 1: Stress in idioms

Most English idioms are used in English speech just like any other phrase, clause or sentence, ie the word that is given the main stress (or accent) is the *last* noun (not pronoun), verb (not auxiliary verb), adjective or adverb in the phrase, clause or sentence. For example, in the idioms *on the face of it*, *to take the cake* and *neither here nor there*, the words *face*, *cake* and *there* carry the strong stress.

However, in some idioms the word that carries the strong stress is not the last 'main' word in that idiom. These idioms that have an 'unpredictable' stress pattern are given in this book the special *stress mark* ` in front of the syllable of the word that carries the stress. For example, in the idioms *like a bull in a `china shop*, *a wild `goose chase*, and *a `big shot*, the stressed words are not, as one might expect (or 'predict'), *shop*, *chase* and *shot*, but `*china*, `*goose* and `*big*—therefore these 'unpredictably' stressed words carry the stress mark `.

Note 2: The use of the slant mark / and brackets ( ) in idioms

The slant mark / is used to show *alternative* words in idioms. For example, in *to break fresh/new ground*, the slant mark means that the idiom can be used in either of the forms *to break fresh ground* or *to break new ground*.

The brackets ( ) are used to show *optional* words. For example, in *on board (ship)*, the brackets mean that both the forms *on board* and *on board ship* can be used.

Sometimes an idiom is given with both a slant and brackets. For example, *on (an/the) average* means that any of the forms *on average*, *on an average* or *on the average* can be used.

2   Special uses of words with grammatical functions

general note

There are several words in frequent use which have functions other than the ones with which the learner may immediately associate them. Let us illustrate this. If the learner is asked what he knows about the word 'there', he will most probably say what he knows about its grammatical function as an adverb of place. In the same way, a description of 'shall' or 'should' would certainly include reference to the future and conditional tenses. We therefore call such words 'words with grammatical functions'.

However, several such words can be used in other ways, which need special attention drawn to them. It is the purpose of this chapter to point out some additional uses of 'grammatical' words, as a knowledge of such uses will greatly improve the idiomatic quality of the learner's English.

Explanations have been kept as short as possible. They should not be regarded as 'rules' but as descriptions of what the native speaker expresses when he uses the words in a certain situation. All explanations are followed by an example from everyday usage.

will/would; shall/should

We automatically associate *will* and *shall* with the expression of future time in English. *Would* and *should* are likewise associated with the expression of the conditional tense. These associations are correct, but expression of time is only one use of these words. Also, future time makes use of other means of expression, not only *will* and *shall*. If we examine carefully how the native speaker expresses future thought and action, we find that he makes great use of *to be going to, to be about to*, the present simple tense and the present continuous tense. Let us consider the following examples:

Peter's going to stay here for two more weeks.
I'm about to make a cup of tea.

We leave for Australia in three weeks' time.
I'm leaving soon because my bus goes in half an hour.

In the above, all the actions or events refer to future time but do not depend on *shall* or *will*. However, when the native speaker does use *shall* and *will* to express future events, e g *I'll see John tomorrow*, he does not follow the traditional grammar-book rule which tells the learner to use *shall* with *I* and *we*, and *will* with the other persons. This may be a matter of considerable confusion to the learner. Similarly, grammar books usually tell us to use *should* for the first person in the conditional tense and *would* for the others. If we wish to be realistic about the actual use of *shall/will* and *should/ would* by the educated native speaker, we realise that he usually does not make this distinction in the first person when he speaks. Also, in spoken English, both *shall* and *will* are shortened to *'ll* (e g *I'll, you'll*) unless they are stressed. Additionally, British English (BE) and American English (AE) differ in their use of *shall* and *should* in the first person. The forms *shall* and *should* for the future and the conditional can and do occur in spoken BE, but these forms are rare in spoken AE. *Shall* there appears formal, even unnatural, and *shan't* is almost never heard. *Will* and *won't* replace them respectively. In AE, *shall* is natural only in a question, e g *What shall we do now?* Otherwise, it sounds very emphatic. Similarly, in spoken AE *would* is the usual form in the first person of the conditional tense, shortened to *'d* unless stressed (e g *we'd, she'd*).

To summarise, in spite of what grammar books usually tell us, *will* and *would* are the usual forms for all persons in both spoken BE and AE. *Shall* and *should* do occur in spoken BE, but are very rare in spoken AE. In both BE and AE, the shortened forms *'ll* and *'d* are used informally when not stressed; in the negative, *won't* and *wouldn't* are used.

Let us now look at some special uses of *will/would*, *shall/ should*.

will/would express

I WILLINGNESS OR READINESS

I'll attend the meeting if I possibly can.
Open the door, please, ˋwill you?
I ˋwould attend the meeting but I'm afraid it's impossible.

2 UNWILLINGNESS OR REFUSAL (in negative sentences)

I've asked Bill to lend me his car, but he ˋwon't.
I asked Peter to tell me the secret, but he ˋwouldn't.

3 A PROMISE

I'll lend you the money—that's a promise.
I promise I won't disturb you again.

4 PROBABILITY OR SUPPOSITION

That's the door-bell. It'll be Fred, I bet.
That'll be the lady Mary was talking about; she said she had a
French accent.
Tom would have been about fifty when he moved to London.

5 A HABIT OR FREQUENT OCCURRENCE

She will often play the piano for three hours without a break.
At the weekends we would go to a play or a concert.

6 SOMETHING TYPICAL OR INEVITABLE (*will* and *would* always
stressed)

I keep telling Jim not to talk in class, but he simply 'will do it.
Boys 'will be boys!
The bus 'would come late, just when I'm in a hurry!

7 A REQUEST

Will you give me a ring tomorrow at about three?
Would you let me know at what time you'll be arriving?

would expresses A PREFERENCE TO DO SOMETHING in

*I **would rather** go by train than by bus.*
*I **would sooner** walk than stand in the cold waiting for the bus.*

shall expresses

I A REQUEST FOR THE WILL OF THE LISTENER (in the first and third
persons)

Shall I lend you the book? (ie Do you want me to lend . . .?)
Shall Peter accompany you, or isn't that necessary? (ie Do you
want Peter to accompany you?)

2 THE SPEAKER'S WILL (an order or command in the second and
third persons; *shall* is always stressed)

He says he won't apologize but I say he 'shall!
I know you don't want to go, but I say you 'shall!

3 THE SPEAKER'S PROMISE OR THREAT (in the second and third persons; *shall* is not stressed)

If you're a good girl you shall have an ice-cream.
If Tom is caught stealing again he shall be punished.

4 PROHIBITION

You shall not have your own way, and that's final!

should is not only found in the first person of conditional tenses. Its other, more important, uses are to express

1 DUTY OR MORAL OBLIGATION

Young people should help the old and sick as much as possible.
The rich should be heavily taxed.

2 PROBABILITY OR STRONG SUPPOSITION

I posted the letter two days ago, so it should arrive in New York tomorrow at the latest.
I'll borrow the book from Tom. He should have finished reading it by now.

3 ADVISABILITY OR DESIRABILITY

You should buy a new car before the prices go up.
There should be more copies of this book in the library.

4 THE PAST TENSE OF *shall* (in reported or indirect questions)

Shall I continue reading?
He wanted to know if he should continue reading.

5 A JUDGMENT OR OPINION (in subordinate clauses after *that*)

The speaker introduces his opinion by such phrases as *it is right/wrong/important/desirable/regrettable/strange etc that* . . .

It is surprising that Tom should have failed to win a scholarship.
It is natural that many parents should seek the best educational opportunities for their children.
It is regrettable that such behaviour should be tolerated.

6 OBLIGATION OR EXPECTANCY (following question-words, especially *why* and *how*)

Why should I go and not you?
How should I know what you said? I wasn't there!

7 SURPRISE OR LACK OF UNDERSTANDING (in such phrases as *Why should he say/think/expect etc* . . .? This use of *should* really means *Why does he say* . . .?)

Why should he expect me to do everything he asks?
How should I know?
Why should you have said (= did you say) *that?*

ought to

There are no other forms of *ought* and it is usually followed by a *to*-infinitive.

'*You ought to write to Aunt Sally.*' '*Yes, I know I ought (to).*'

In the negative, it is followed by *not* and can be shortened to *oughtn't to*.

You oughtn't to go outside with that bad cold!

In a question, it stands before the subject.

Ought I to go now?

To indicate past time, *ought* is followed by a perfect infinitive.

I ought to have gone to the butcher's yesterday.

ought to expresses

I DUTY OR MORAL OBLIGATION

Young people ought to help the old and sick as much as possible. The rich ought to be heavily taxed.

2 PROBABILITY OR STRONG SUPPOSITION

I posted the letter two days ago, so it ought to arrive in New York tomorrow at the latest.
I'll borrow the book from Tom. He ought to have finished reading it by now.

3 ADVISABILITY OR DESIRABILITY

You ought to buy a new car before the prices go up.
There ought to be more copies of this book in the library.

used to

The pronunciation of *used* followed by a *to*-infinitive should be carefully noted, ie to rhyme with *roost*, It should not be confused with the *used* that is the past tense of the transitive verb *to use*, which rhymes with *oozed.*

For the negative form of *used to*, there are two possibilities. *Used not to* (and its shortened form *use(d)n't to*) is formal. In informal speech the form *didn't use to* is becoming much more widely used.

used to expresses

1 A REPEATED ACTION OR OCCURRENCE IN THE PAST, OR A HABIT

The postman used to come at 9 o'clock.
Bill used to smoke thirty cigarettes a day, but now he's cut down to ten.

2 A CONDITION WHICH EXISTED IN THE PAST

We used to live in a small house down by the river.
There used to be two cinemas in the town, but now there's only one.

must

Must has no other forms. In a question, it stands before the subject, eg *Must I go?* It is followed by an infinitive without *to*.

must expresses

1 NECESSITY IN THE PRESENT OR FUTURE

I must go now or I shall miss my train.
If you fail your exam you must take it again next year.

2 STRONG LIKELIHOOD OR PROBABILITY

Old Mr Williams must be nearly ninety years old!
John's friend must be German; his name is Hans Müller.

3 OBLIGATION OR NECESSITY (used as a past tense in indirect speech)

The student said that he felt he must work much harder.

must not (and its shortened form **mustn't**) expresses

1 A PROHIBITION

Students must not smoke in the library.

2 ADVICE NOT TO DO SOMETHING

You mustn't miss the bus or you'll be late for work.

may/might

may expresses

1 PROBABILITY OR POSSIBILITY

Tom's late. He may have missed the bus or even decided to walk.
It may be better to buy a good second-hand car, as new ones are very expensive at the moment.

The government fears that the rate of inflation may increase still further.
It's possible that the strike may continue for another week.

2 PERMISSION

May I leave early today?
You may use these books for reference, if you wish.

3 WISHES (for others)

Cheers, Uncle Harry! May you live to be a hundred!
May you be very happy in your new home!

may not is sometimes used to express prohibition, especially in official regulations.

Candidates may not leave the examination room without the supervisors' permission.

might expresses

1 A WEAK POSSIBILITY

You might find John in the library, but I doubt it.

2 A POLITE SUGGESTION

Might I suggest that we start the meeting an hour earlier?
You might give me some advice on this matter, if you have time.

3 THE PAST TENSE OF *may* (in reported or indirect speech)

May we smoke during the break?
We asked if we might smoke during the break.

it

It is a very useful word in English and the student should note the following special uses carefully.

1 As a pronoun, *it* does not only refer to objects, i e lifeless things, but also to animals generally.

Look, there's a mouse. It's just run into that hole.

If the animal is a pet animal which has a name, the pronouns *he* and *she* may be used.

Where's Boxer? I've just seen him chasing the neighbour's cat!

It also refers to a baby when the sex of the child is not important, or is not known.

The mother carefully dressed the baby and laid it in its cot.
(after the birth of a child) *It's a boy! It's twins!*

It is also used to refer to a child in general when what is important is not the sex but the fact that it is a child and not an adult. The child is often referred to as *it* in books on educational psychology etc.

Soon the child begins to identify itself with people around it.

2 *It* is used to refer to a following statement. The statement may begin with a *to*-infinitive.

It is better to try and fail than not to have tried at all.
It was kind of you to come and see us.

The statement may be an indirect question.

It is hard to say what should be done.
It was difficult to decide whether to go.

The statement may be a clause beginning with *that*.

It's a pity you can't come.
It's quite possible that we've met before.

3 *It* is used to describe the weather.

It's been either raining or snowing all the week.
If it's a nice afternoon, we'll go for a walk.
It got darker and darker and then it rained heavily.
It froze hard last night.

4 *It* is used to emphasize one part of a sentence. In this case it is followed by the verb *to be*.

It's Mary who told me the story, not Jane.
It was 'The Times' that published the report, not 'The Guardian'.
It was not until 1928 that women finally got the vote.

5 *It* refers to 'the whole general situation' and not to anything specific. The context makes the meaning clear. The following general phrases occur regularly in conversation:

It doesn't matter
It doesn't make any difference.
It's of no consequence.
So it seems.
It can't be helped.
It was to be expected.
That's the worst of it!
It's for the best.

That's `done it! (in a tone of annoyance, eg when something has been broken, spoilt etc).
Get `on with it! ie Start! Continue!
You've `had it! ie There's nothing more, no more chance etc.
You'll be `for it! ⎤ ie You'll be
You'll `catch it! ⎦ scolded.

6 *It* occurs in a number of phrases where it appears to have no particular meaning at all, although it is the object of the verb. This is because the particular verbs cannot stand without an object.

> *Let them fight it out between themselves!*
> *Are you going to brave it?* ie be brave enough to do something.
> *Jim loves to lord it over people,* ie to dominate them.
> *You'll have to be prepared to rough it on the expedition,* ie to accept the lack of comfort and facilities.
> *I feel inclined to risk it,* ie take a risk.
> *Let's face it, . . .,* ie We must be honest and admit that . . .

Two informal expressions which appear rather strange in their form should be mentioned.

To go it means to carry out any action with vigour or to an exaggerated extent.

> *Mary's really been going it this week! She's spent over £100 on clothes!*

To go it alone means to carry out something without help or support.

> *Tom wanted to enter into a business partnership with Peter, but they quarrelled and now Tom has decided to go it alone.*

Oh, bother/blast/curse/damn it! is an exclamation of impatience, annoyance or anger.

there

1 *There* is not only used as an adverb of place after the verb.

> *I've already been there.*

There can also stand at the beginning of a sentence in exclamations.

> `*There he ˋcomes!* `*There it ˋis!*

It will be noted that in these two examples the subject is a pronoun and the word order is regular. However, if the subject is a noun, the verb stands before the noun. In all these uses *there* is stressed.

> `*There goes my last pound ˋnote!*
> `*There goes the ˋbell!*
> `*There come the ˋothers!*
> `*There comes old Mr ˋScott!*

2 *There* can be used to introduce a sentence together with the verb *to be*. It is unstressed.

There was not a cloud in the sky.
There are always enough jobs to do in a house!

3 *There* occurs in phrases where it has no particular meaning. Here are some common phrases with explanations. *There* is stressed in all of them.

`There you `are! (said when giving something to someone; it means *Here it is!* or *Here they are!*)
`There's a `good `boy/`girl! (said to a child in praise for having done something well, or as encouragement to do something)
`There, `there! `There now! (said in a sympathetic tone to comfort or calm someone)
`There's `gratitude/`thanks for you! (this may be said sincerely or ironically, depending on the situation; it is a comment on the degree of gratitude which a person shows)
`There he/she goes a`gain! (this is meant as a sarcastic comment when someone repeatedly speaks about or does the same thing)
. . . *and* `there you `are! (this is added to an instruction of how to do something; it means 'and there's the solution, desired result etc'; e g *Put the plug in, turn the knob to 'On', press the button for 'Start' and there you are!*)

Possessive adjectives

1 *My/your/his/her/its/our/their* are used with reference to parts of the body or articles of clothing. In this point of usage, English is different from many other languages which use the definite article. Some examples will make this clear.

The man put his hand in his pocket and pulled out a bundle of pound notes.
Careful drivers never take their eyes off the road.
Put your hands behind your back!

However, the definite article is used if the part of the body mentioned does not belong to the subject of the sentence.

Jill took the old lady by the arm and helped her up the steps.
The policeman grabbed the little boy by the collar and told him to stop throwing stones.

2 Possessive adjectives are sometimes used to make a more direct or personal association between the speaker and the object of his attention.

I must run or I shall miss my train!
Have the police caught their man yet?
Our subject today is the poetry of the Elizabethan period.
Fred expected to back a winner at the Derby, but his horse (ie the horse which Fred had put money on) *stumbled and broke its leg.*

Verbs that are active in form but passive in meaning

Some verbs which are usually followed by an object, eg *to sell, to cut, to wash* can be used without an object and take on a passive meaning. In this case, the person carrying out the action of the verb is not referred to.

This book sells very well, ie it is sold to many people.
This dress washes/irons well, ie it is easily washed/ironed.
This material makes up nicely into suits, ie it can be used by the tailor for making suits.
The butter spreads easily, ie it can be spread easily.
The bread is cutting badly because it's very soft, ie to cut the bread is difficult.

Other tenses may also be used, eg *The book sold well. The dress has washed well. The material will make up nicely.* Note that the verbs are followed by adverbs in the above examples. It is also possible to omit the adverb, if the meaning is clear. This is often the case in the question form and in the negative.

The book didn't sell, so it wasn't reprinted.
This dress is very pretty. Will it wash?
The material should make up into a winter dress, shouldn't it?
Butter won't spread when it's been in the fridge.
Will the bread cut? If not, try the other knife.

Here are some other verbs of this sort, with the nouns (subjects) that they are often used with in this construction.

(a car) drives, steers
(a boat) sails
(a clock) winds up
(a door) locks, unlocks
(a book) reads well/easily, ie the book is good/easy to read.

3   Particular words with special idiomatic uses

general note

This chapter deals with a selection of single words which are known to present difficulty to students because of their particular idiomatic meanings. There are three groups of words: 1) adjectives, 2) nouns, 3) miscellaneous words such as *all* and *how*. Special idiomatic uses of verbs are dealt with fully in Chapters 8–11.

Although the learner knows what *dead* means in the phrase *a dead body*, it is difficult to guess what *a dead shot* or *a dead weight* means. In the first example *dead* means 'exact'; in the second example *dead* means 'heavy'. Since many expressions of this kind appear mainly in informal English, it is very important to learn the typical situations in which these idioms are used. Examples of use will help the learner to do this.

Secondly, the chapter deals with adjectives and nouns which have a key position in idiomatic expressions, i e words like *mind* in such idiomatic expressions as *to be in two minds about something*.

Therefore, this chapter has a double purpose. The learner can use its contents to find an explanation for a common word in an unusual context, or he can use it for special study of individual words in their idiomatic uses.

A   Adjectives with special idiomatic uses

dead

Dead can mean many different things when it is used idiomatically. The basic meaning is 'no longer living' as in *a dead body* or *dead flowers*. It also means that something has never had life, as in *dead matter*, e g a stone or metal.

a dead language one which is no longer spoken, e g Latin or Sanskrit.

a dead letter 1 a letter which lies in the post office because the addressee cannot be found, 2 a law which is no longer enforced.

a dead line (in business) an article which a shopkeeper has stopped dealing in because customers have no more interest in it. *Silk stockings have been a dead line for years and years, Madam!*

dead stock goods in a shop which nobody buys. The goods lie 'dead' on the shopkeeper's shelves.

a dead wire one through which no electricity passes.

dead in the eye of the law cut off from the rights of citizenship.

A telephone line can **be/go dead** *The phone's dead/The line went dead* the telephone does not work.

Dead also has the meaning of 'complete' as in the following.

dead beat; dead tired (informal) extremely tired, exhausted.
dead drunk completely drunk.
a dead loss 1 a complete loss for which there is no compensation. 2 (informal) a person who is incapable or no help or use to anyone. *It's no use asking Jack, he's a dead loss at mathematics.*
a dead silence total, unbroken silence. Also, **a dead calm.**
dead slow hardly moving, almost stopped.
to be dead a'gainst something or someone to be completely against or opposed to that thing or person. *My father is dead against my entering college. The office staff were dead against the new proposals of the boss.*
to be in/go into a dead faint to be in/go into a state of complete unconsciousness.
to come to a dead halt to come to a complete stop. Also, **to stop dead.**

Dead can also mean 'exact', as in the following.

dead ahead; dead in front exactly ahead or in front.
the dead centre the exact centre.
a dead heat is applied to the result of a race or competition where two or more competitors are equally as good as each other, ie there is no winner.
dead right (informal) exactly right.
a dead shot a person who hits his target exactly, ie who shoots excellently. It can also mean a shot (bullet, arrow, etc) that hits the target aimed at exactly.
to be on a dead level (with someone) to be exactly as good as, eg runners or horses racing side by side.

Dead can also mean 'blank, monotonous, without brightness', as in the following.

a dead colour a dull colour, without brightness.

a dead sound a dull, heavy sound which does not reverberate.

a dead wall a wall without windows to break the monotony.

'**deadpan** (adjective) (informal) used to describe somebody's face which shows no emotion, and has only the same dull expression.

Other idiomatic expressions with *dead*.

a dead certainty something that is very sure. *The Irish horse will win the 3.30 race; he's a dead certainty.* The phrase is used for either things or people.

a dead end a road, direction, idea etc which does not lead any-where, a *cul-de-sac*.

a 'dead-end job a job without prospects.

to be at/reach/come to a dead end to be at a stage where you cannot make further progress, usually because of problems or difficulties.

a 'dead-line a fixed date for finishing a piece of work, a project etc.

to meet a dead-line to finish the work by the date prescribed.

a 'dead march a piece of slow, solemn funeral music.

a dead sleep a deep, sound sleep. **dead to the world** deeply asleep.

a dead weight something that is very heavy.

the dead of night; the dead of winter here *dead* means 'the mid-dle of'.

to be at/reach/come to a (total) deadlock to fail to agree or to compromise or to settle a dispute etc.

to cut someone dead to ignore someone, treat him as if you do not know him.

to flog a dead horse (informal) to waste one's time or efforts. *Explaining grammar to John is like flogging a dead horse. He just can't take it in!*

to leave someone for dead to believe that someone is dead and therefore to act accordingly.

to make a dead set at someone to make a deliberate attack on someone, often with words.

to wait for a dead man's shoes to wait for an advantage which will result from somebody's death, e g his position.

dead-alive half dead and half alive. If you do something *in a dead-alive fashion* you do it without enthusiasm.

dead and gone; dead and buried used to stress that someone died a long time ago.

dead to all sense/feeling of shame incapable of feeling shame.

hands, fingers or feet can **be/go dead with cold** numbed, unfeel-ing.

flat

(to give someone) a flat denial an absolute, definite denial.

(to give someone) a flat refusal to give an absolute, definite refusal.

a flat tyre a tyre with no or not enough air in it.

beer or lemonade will **be/go flat** when there is no gas in it.

conversation can **be/go flat** uninteresting, dull.

the battery of a car will **be/go flat** when it needs recharging.

to be in/go into a flat spin (informal) to be in or go into a state of confusion, in a mix-up, not knowing which thing to do first etc.

to fall flat on one's back to fall in such a way that you are lying at full length on your back on the floor.

a plan or project can **fall flat** not happen, fail to develop properly.

to go flat out (also with the verbs *to run, to work, to race, to drive*) (informal) to do it with all one's powers or energy, as much or as quickly as possible.

to sing flat not to reach or keep the pitch of the note exactly.

to tell someone flat to tell him in a very positive and definite way, with emphasis.

flat broke (informal) having no money at all.

flat paint is paint without a shiny gloss.

`**flat racing** horse racing on level ground, ie without obstacles.

to knock someone flat to knock him off his feet with a blow.

and that's flat! (informal) used to end an argument, or used when you have told someone what to do or not to do. It means 'And that's my last word on the matter!'

good

Good is an adjective which is used very widely in English and means many different things. It means 'benevolent, friendly' in the following.

a good deed an act of kindness.

a good reception a warm, cordial reception.

good works acts that help the needy, eg the poor, the sick, the old.

to do someone a good turn to do somone a favour in order to help.

Good means 'complete, thorough', as in

a good drink a large quantity. *Bill had a good drink at the pub last night. His wife wasn't at home!*

to give someone a good talking to/scolding to scold someone thoroughly, usually a child, as a punishment. *Johnny's mother gave him a good scolding for pulling up the neighbour's flowers.*

Other idiomatic expressions with *good*:

a good deal often. *I used to go to pop concerts a good deal when I was a teenager.*

a good deal of much.

a good few many.

a good many many.

a good way (from) far away.

good debts debts that will be paid.

as good as gold said of a well-behaved child. *Mary is as good as gold—most of the time.*

as good as almost. *I've hardly worn this coat—it's as good as new. Jim has as good as got the new job.*

as good as one's word true to one's promise. *I said I'd come home for the holidays and I'll be as good as my word.*

to be all to the good to be an advantage.

to be good for to be able or willing to do something, to have the necessary qualities, energy etc. *My old car is good for another two years yet. The old man is still good for a further year's work.*

to be no/not much/some/any good (doing something) to be no etc use or value (in) doing something. *It's no good just thinking about the problem—you must solve it!*

to earn good money (informal) to earn a lot of money.

to have a good mind to do something to have a strong inclination or desire to do something. *I can't stand the cold any more. I've a good mind to emigrate to Hawaii.*

to have a good time to enjoy oneself.

to hold good to continue to be true or valid. *Does your offer still hold good? His promise to return still held good after five years.*

to make good to do well, to be successful in getting a good job and money etc. *Bill went to Australia last year and, as far as I know, he's made good there.*

to make good the loss/damage to compensate for or pay for the loss etc.

to put in a good word for someone (with someone else) to say something favourable about him to some other person. *I hope you'll put in a good word for me with the boss.*

to throw good money after bad to loose more money in an attempt to make up for a loss.

for good permanently, for ever. *Jack lived in Canada for four years but he's come back home for good now.*

for one's own good to one's own advantage.

in good time with plenty of time to spare, early.

good riddance (informal) said when one gets rid of a disagreeable person or an unpleasant piece of work. *Pete is leaving the* *firm Since he was always causing trouble, it's good riddance, I'd say!*

it's a good job that ... a colloquial phrase meaning 'It is lucky that ...' 'It is a good thing that ...'

In conversation, *good* often stands in front of another adjective and intensifies its meaning. *A good hot cup of tea. A good long swim. A good sound sleep. A good strong dose of medicine.*

hard

hard cash actual money, not a cheque etc.

the hard core the centre of or most important part of something.

hard currency stable currency.

hard drinks/liquor strong alcoholic drinks.

hard drugs the strongest drugs, which lead to addiction most easily, eg heroin.

a hard and fast rule a rule that cannot be broken or modified, a rule which applies without exception.

hard lines! (exclamation) bad luck!

hard luck bad luck.

a hard 'nut to crack a difficult problem to solve or a difficult person to deal with.

the hard shoulder the side of the motorway where cars can stop in case of breakdown or emergency.

hard times times of difficulty.

hard words words without sympathy, words which hurt.

to be hard hit to be severely affected by something. *The farmers have been hard hit by the bad harvest.*

to be hard of hearing to be rather deaf.

to be 'hard on someone to treat him in a harsh or strict way.

to be hard pressed (for something) to be under great pressure (of something), or in great need (of something). *I'm hard pressed for time at the moment. I'll do it tomorrow.*

to be hard 'put (to it) (to do something) to have difficulty (doing something). *He was hard put (to it) to give a convincing excuse for his behaviour.*

to be hard to please said of a person who is rather critical or fastidious, ie difficult to please.

to be hard 'up to be short of money, not to have enough money.

to be 'hard up for something to be in want of something. *Jack only said he was ill because he was hard up for an excuse not to go to the party.*

to do/learn something the 'hard way ie with perseverance and practice. *Bill speaks fluent French, as his mother is French. I've had to learn the language in school, the hard way.*

to take a hard line to be uncompromising, not to give in.

as hard as nails 1 very strong and muscular. 2 without feeling.

hard by not far away, near at hand.

high

high life; high living luxurious and pleasurable living.

high noon 12 o'clock in the middle of the day, when the sun is at its highest.

the high sea(s) the water of the open ocean.

high tea (GB only) meal taken in the late afternoon or early evening, instead of dinner.

high tide the time at which the tide is at its highest level.

high treason treason against the State.

a high wind a strong wind.

to be for the 'high jump (informal) to be due to be punished severely.

to be in high spirits to be in a jovial, cheerful mood.

to be high (informal) to be extremely high-spirited after taking alcohol or drugs.

to be/get on one's high horse to behave in a proud or haughty manner. *Jack has been on his high horse ever since he became head of the department.*

to do something with a high hand to do it arrogantly.

to have (a) high colour to have pink, red or flushed cheeks.

high and dry isolated, stranded. *Jim was left high and dry by his girl-friend when he lost all his money.*

high and low everywhere. *Where have you been? I've been looking for you high and low.*

high-handed arrogant.

high-powered of great vitality, dynamic, intense. *A high-powered salesman. When I last saw John, he was having a high-powered discussion with his professor.*

poor

a poor excuse one which is unconvincing, which cannot be fully accepted.

poor soil not fertile, not good for growing.

a poor supply (of something) not much or not many.

poor work bad work.

to be in poor health to be ill.

to be in poor supply to be scarce, to be few. *New potatoes are in poor supply at the moment because of the bad weather during the growing season.*

to have a poor opinion of something or someone to think that something or someone is bad or inferior.

pretty

pretty (informal) fairly, rather.

pretty (informal) often used as understatement and really means 'very'. *I'm feeling pretty awful/rotten/miserable today. That was a pretty nasty thing to do!*

a 'pretty kettle of fish a mix-up, a great state of confusion. It refers to a situation, not a person.

a pretty penny quite a lot of money. *Jack's new house must have cost him a pretty penny to build!*

pretty much almost, very nearly. *Jane's party was pretty much the same as the last one she gave. The result was pretty much to be expected.*

pretty well almost, very nearly. *He's pretty well finished his latest book already.*

to be sitting pretty (informal) to be in a favourable position, usually financially. *Mary's sitting pretty now, since she married that rich American.*

short

short change less money than the correct change one should receive.

a short cut a quicker or easier way of going somewhere or doing something.

a short drink a strong alcoholic drink served in small quantities, eg gin.

short measure; short weight less than the weight of goods (usually food) paid for.

short pastry pastry which is made with a lot of butter or fat.

to be in short supply to be scarce, few, not enough.

to be on short time to work fewer hours or days than usual because the employer has not enough work for the workmen.

to be short (of something) not to have enough (of something) eg of time, money, food.

to be short (with someone) to be short-tempered, curt or abrupt.

to be taken short (informal) to have to make a hurried visit to a lavatory.

to cut something short to bring something to an end before the proper time. *We had to cut short our discussion because the boss had to go to a meeting somewhere else.*

to fall short (of something) to be inadequate, not enough, disappointing (of hopes, expectations). *His profits for the first year of business have fallen short of his expectations.*

to go short (of something) to do without (something), to deprive oneself (of something). *Can you lend me six 12p stamps—or does that mean that you'll have to go short yourself?*

to have a short temper to become angry easily, frequently and quickly.

to make short work of something to deal with something quickly. *Let's make short work of the food and drink!*

to pull (something/someone) up short 1 to stop (a vehicle) suddenly. 2 to interrupt, check or correct (a person) unexpectedly.

to run short (of something) to come to the end of one's supply (of something). *I've run short of sugar. Could you please lend me some?*

to stop short to stop suddenly.

'little/'nothing short of little/nothing less than. *The way he runs his business is little short of criminal.*

the long and the short of it all that there is to be said about a matter.

for short as an abbreviation. *Katherine is always called 'Kate' for short.*

in short briefly, in a few words.

short of except, apart from. *They say he's capable of anything short of murder!*

sorry

a sorry bargain an unsatisfactory bargain.

a sorry excuse an unconvincing excuse.

a sorry fellow a worthless or pitiful person.

to be in a sorry state to be in a pitiful state.

thick

thick (informal, of a person) stupid.

thick and fast many and quickly. *During the boxing match sharp blows fell thick and fast.*

to be a bit thick (informal) to be rather too much, more than is bearable. *Giving us so much English homework is really a bit thick!*

to be as thick as thieves (of two people) very friendly, or sharing the same profitable interests.

to be (in) thick with someone (informal) to be very friendly or intimate with him.

(to go) through thick and thin (to endure) under all conditions, good or bad. *Jack and Jim are old war comrades. They went through thick and thin together.*

to lay it on thick (informal) to exaggerate it, eg praise or criticism.

thin

a thin audience not many spectators.

thin beer weak or watery beer.

a thin excuse an unconvincing excuse.

a thin story, essay, discussion, etc one lacking in substance or interest.

to have a thin time to have an unpleasant time.

to vanish into thin air to disappear without trace.

thin on top not having much hair, rather bald.

B   Nouns with special idiomatic uses

end

to achieve/gain one's end(s) to reach one's aim, purpose.

to be at the end of one's tether to have no possibilities or resources left, to have tried all ways of solving a problem, but without success.

to be at a loose end to have nothing to do in order to occupy one's time. *Bill feels at a loose end, now that he has finished his examniations and has no more studying to do.*

to come to a bad end (of a person) to develop in a criminal way and suffer the consequences, eg prison.

to get hold of the wrong end of the stick to misunderstand the meaning or intention totally.

to go off (at) the `deep end to lose control and become angry.

to keep one's end up means to continue to be cheerful or active even though one is feeling sad or is in difficulties.

to make (both) ends meet to manage with the money one earns. *Julia has spent so much money on new clothes that she's finding it hard to make ends meet again this month.*

to never hear the end of it to have a matter talked about again and again. *My husband is so angry that I threw away his old gardening trousers—I'll never hear the end of it!*

in the end finally, at last.

no end of (informal) many; much. *There was no end of argument at the meeting last night.*

odds and ends various small articles, items, matters, etc. *John always carries lots of odds and ends around with him in his trouser pockets. I have a few odds and ends to attend to in town this afternoon.*

on end continuously. *Bill is a hard worker. He studies for hours on end.*

to no end in vain, for nothing. *He kept proposing marriage to her, but it was all to no end.*

the end justifies the means if the aim is good, it may be achieved by any method, fair or unfair.

line

a hot line a direct telephone line between the heads of governments.

the line   1 the railway line. *Passengers are requested not to cross the line except by the bridge.* 2 a telephone connection.

a 'party line a telephone line which is shared by two or more subscribers.

to be in/out of line (with) to be in agreement/disagreement (with something). *Your suggestions are out of line with my former proposals.*

to be (next) in line (for something) to be (the next person) due for something. *Who's next in line for promotion in your department?*

to bring someone/something into line to persuade someone to obey, to cause something to conform. *He didn't agree with my way of organising the business, but I managed to bring him into line. She must bring her speech fully into line with the firm's policy at the next meeting.*

to choose/take/follow the line of least resistance to choose, etc the easiest or least unpleasant way of doing something.

to come/fall into line (with somebody) to agree with someone, to accept his opinions. *I'm sure Sue will fall into line with us on this matter when she realises how serious it is.*

to do something along/on sound/correct/the right/the wrong lines to use the right, etc method of doing something. *Am I thinking along the right lines, in your opinion?*

to draw the line (somewhere/at something) to set a limit somewhere/at something. *I'll lend you another fifty pounds and no more —I have to draw the line somewhere! I'll have to draw the line at fifty pounds.*

to drop someone a line (informal) to write to someone.

to get a line on someone/something to find out information about someone/something. *Can you get a line on Walker's whereabouts? He hasn't reported to headquarters for two weeks.*

to read between the lines to understand or sense more than the actual words (spoken or written) appear to mean or express. *She didn't tell me directly, but reading between the lines I think she's going to take the job.*

to shoot a line (informal) to lie or exaggerate about one's successes, capabilities etc.

to take a firm/hard/strong line (with someone) (over/on something) to deal decisively (with someone) (over/on a certain matter). *Some of the employees have produced bad work. The management will have to take a firmer line with them in future.*

to toe the line to obey orders, submit to discipline. *If Joe doesn't toe the line in future, he'll be dismissed from the team.*

all along the line at every point, in all matters, with everyone.
*Since he started wearing contact lenses and washing his hair, he's
been a success all along the line.*

hard lines! (exclamation) bad luck!

in line with in agreement with, corresponding to. *The Government
expects all MP's to speak and act in line with party policy.*

mind

to be in two minds about something/whether to do something
to be unsure, unable to decide. *He's in two minds (about) whether
to report the theft to the police or not.*

to be of one mind (about something) means to be in agreement
with someone about something. *My wife and I are of one mind
about the education of children.*

to be of the same mind (as someone) to share the same opinion
or view with him. *I'm of the same mind as Peter on the subject of
religion.*

to be out of one's mind/not in one's right mind to be mad,
crazy.

to call/bring something to mind to recall something to one's
memory.

to change one's mind (about something) to make a new and
different decision or choice. *Mary wanted to go to France for her
holidays but she's changed her mind about that now. She's going to
Italy instead.*

to give/put one's mind to something to give one's attention to
finishing or solving it. *If you really give/put your mind to it, you'll
solve the problem in no time.*

to give someone a piece of one's mind to tell someone exactly
what you think about his behaviour etc, to reprimand someone.
*I'm tired of Jack's excuses. The next time he tells me a lie, I shall give
him a piece of my mind!*

to have half a mind to do something to be inclined to do something but not to be sure that you will do it.

to have a good mind to do something to want to do something
and to be almost sure that you will do it, especially if you are angry
about something. *I've a good mind to send this plate of food back to
the kitchen!*

to have something on one's mind to be worried about something
and think about it often. *Fred is very quiet these days. He must have
something on his mind.*

to keep/bear (something/someone) in mind to remember (some-
thing/someone). *Please bear (it) in mind that I'd like to have your
report by the end of the month. I'll keep you in mind when I want to
sell my car.*

to keep one's mind on something to concentrate on it. *The class are very restless because of the heat. They can't keep their minds on their work.*

to know one's own mind to know exactly what one wants. *Jill is always changing her job. I don't think she knows her own mind.*

to make up one's mind (about something) to take a decision. *He hasn't made up his mind (about) which subjects he wants to study yet.*

to put someone in mind of something to cause someone to remember something. *I had to put him in mind of his promise, otherwise he would have forgotten it.*

to slip one's mind to be forgotten by one. *Maggie said she'd give me her new address, but it must have slipped her mind.*

to speak one's mind to say frankly what one thinks or feels. *My father always speaks his mind, even if it hurts.*

to take one's mind off something to divert one's attention from something unpleasant. *Go to town and see a film. It'll help to take your mind off your troubles.*

in the/one's mind's eye in the/one's imagination. *In my mind's eye I can still see the look on his face—after ten years!*

out of sight, out of mind (proverb) people who are far away or whom we do not see often are soon forgotten.

to `my mind in my opinion.

point

to be beside the point to be not relevant to the matter.

to be on the point of doing something to be about to do something. *I was just on the point of going out when the telephone rang.*

to come to/get to/reach the point to reach the most important thing one wants to say. *Jim is an entertaining speaker, but it always takes him too long to get to the point.*

to fail to see/miss the point (of something) not to understand the purpose of something. *I'm afraid I've missed the point of the argument—could you explain again?*

to get/wander away from/off the point to become vague or lose direction in a discussion.

to get/see the point (of something) to understand the purpose of something.

to make one's point to explain clearly one's argument or idea. *At the meeting last night Jim failed to make his point about more co-operation between teachers and parents quite clear.*

to make a point of doing something to do something because you think it is important. *I make a point of trying to remember my friends' birthdays.*

to see the point (in/of doing something) to understand the purpose or use of something. *I really don't see the point of taking a camping holiday in the middle of winter!*

to stretch a point to go beyond what is usual or do more than is usual. *When it came to the salary rises, I hoped that the boss would stretch a point in my favour—but he didn't.*

to stretch the point to exaggerate or distort the matter.

to take someone's point to appreciate and understand someone's argument or point of view.

a case in point a case that has a (relevant) connection with the case being discussed.

if/when it comes to the point when the time comes, when the matter becomes serious. *Bill says he wants to marry Mary, but when it comes to the point, I don't think he will!*

in point of fact in fact, in reality, actually, indeed. *Chris may have told you that he had paid all his debts, but in point of fact he still owes me two hundred pounds!*

the point of no return the point at which it is impossible to turn back, because the consequences of turning back would be more serious than those of continuing with something, eg a voyage, decision, plan.

there's no/not much/very little/hardly any point in doing something there's no etc use or purpose in doing it.

(what is) more to the point (what is) more important or relevant. *His idea is very good, and, (what is) more to the point, it can be put into practice without extra cost.*

what's the point? what's the purpose? *Why tell me all your troubles? What's the point? I can't help you!*

way

to be in the way to be causing an obstruction.

to be on the way 'out (of clothes, etc) to be going out of fashion, not modern any more; (of a person) no longer effective or needed. *Short skirts have been on the way out for quite some time now—when do you think they'll come back?*

to get one's own way to get what one wants in spite of opposition from others. *Bill says he's strict with his children, but they always seem to get their own way in spite of that.*

to get (something) under way to begin (it), to start (it) moving. *We must get the election campaign under way by next Spring at the latest.*

to go a long way towards (doing) something to be a great help. *The money we won will go a long way towards paying for the new car.*

to go out of one's 'way to do something to do everything possible to help, even if it is inconvenient. *Our neighbours went out of their way to help us when we moved into the new house.*

to go one's own way to act independently, even if it is against the advice of others. *It's a waste of time giving Peter advice. He'll always go his own way in the end.*

to have it 'both ways to have advantages from two things at the same time. *A woman can either become a house-wife and mother or stay working full-time in a profession, but she can't have it both ways.*

to have one's own way to do what one wants. *I offered to pay for the lunch, but she insisted on having her own way and paid her share herself.*

to have a 'way with one to have something charming or pleasant in one's character which is attractive to other people. *Jim's new girl-friend is not pretty, but she has a way with her which is most appealing.*

to mend one's ways to improve one's behaviour, attitudes, etc. *Tom will have to mend his ways if he wants to keep his job.*

by way of through, via. *We travelled through Germany by way of Hamburg, Cologne and Munich.*

down our way in our neighbourhood, where we live.

in any way in any respect, at all. *Can I help you in any way?*

(in) no way! certainly not!

in a small way on a small scale, modestly. *Although they're quite rich, they live in a small way in a cottage in the country.*

in a way/in some ways in a sense, to a certain extent. *In a way you're right, but I can't accept all your arguments.*

a 'long way out inaccurate. *My arithmetic's terrible—my answers are always a long way out.*

out of the way not easy to reach. *They have a lovely house, but it's in the country, and rather out of the way.*

to 'my way of thinking in my opinion.

ways and means methods of doing something successfully. *Sheila is short of money to pay her bills, but she's sure to find ways and means of earning extra money soon.*

where there's a will there's a way (proverb) if you desire something strongly enough, you will find a method of getting it.

word

big words boasting.

hard words strong criticism.

to be word perfect to know a text by heart, eg a poem, a part in a play, and be able to reproduce it perfectly.

to be as good as one's word to do what one says one will do, to be reliable. *Bill is always as good as his word. If he said he would help you, he will.*

to break/go back on one's word to break a promise. *Steve said he'd lend me £100, but he went back on his word so I had to borrow from the bank.*

to coin a word to invent a new word (which may become general usage).

to eat one's words to admit that one was wrong.

to not get a word in edgeways to not get the chance to speak because someone else is talking all the time. *Paul was in a very talkative mood last night. His wife could hardly get a word in edgeways!*

to give someone one's word to make a promise to him. *I give you my word that I won't tell anyone your secret.*

to have the last word to produce a statement or argument to which no one else can make a reply or objection.

to have a word with someone to speak or discuss with someone about a matter. *I can't tell you definitely yet. I'll have a word with my wife about it and tell you our decision tomorrow.*

to have words (with someone) to have a quarrel or disagreement.

to keep one's word to do what one has promised to do.

to mince (one's) words not to speak frankly. *Stop mincing (your) words and tell me exactly what you think of my plan!*

to put in a good word (for someone) to speak in a complimentary way about someone, in order to support, help or defend him. *I put in a good word for you at the meeting last night, but I'm afraid you're going to be asked to resign.*

to take someone at his word to act on the belief that someone will do what he says. *When John said he was going to sell his car, I took him at his word and found him a buyer for it.*

to take someone's word for it to believe him even though there is no proof that what he says is true. *She says she's already paid me back, but I can't remember, so I'll have to take her word for it.*

actions speak louder than words (proverb) what one does is more important than what one says.

by word of mouth in a spoken, not written form. *Most old legends were handed down from generation to generation by word of mouth.*

in a word very briefly.

the last word (in something) the most up-to-date, the best kind, the latest style or fashion.

one's last word one's final statement, warning, offer, advice, etc.

a man of his word a man whom one can trust, who does what he has promised.

mark my words! take note of what I say! listen to me! (used as a warning). *If you don't take my advice now, mark my words—you'll live to regret what you're doing!*

it's my/your etc word against his/mine etc! what I say is true or what he says is true! (when no other person can prove which statement is true).

my word! a polite exclamation of surprise. *My word! You do look pale today!*

not another word! don't say anything more!

not a word! don't speak about it!

a play on/upon words a pun.

that's not the word for it! an exclamation that something is understated. *'It's cold in here today.' 'Cold's not the word for it—it's freezing!'*

there's many a true word spoken in jest (proverb) something that is said as a joke and is not meant seriously often happens, or turns out to be true, etc.

word for word literally, exactly, using all the words used. *to translate a sentence word for word; to copy something word for word.*

a word in/out of season a piece of welcome/interfering advice, which is given at a good/bad time.

words fail me! I am unable to speak because I am so shocked, surprised, angry, etc.

world

the world this phrase is often used in the sense of people generally. *The opinion of the world* therefore means the general or common opinion of men.

to be all the world/to mean the world to someone to be very important to his happiness, etc. *His work is all the world to him—he couldn't care less about his family.*

to be for all the world like someone/something to strongly resemble him/it. *His laugh is for all the world like his father's.*

to be/feel on top of the world to be/feel very happy because of good health, success, etc.

to be (something) out of this world (informal) to be magnificent, remarkable. *Jill's new evening dress is superb! She looks (like something) out of this world in it!*

to come `down in the world to lose one's social and financial position.

to not do something for (all) the world to not do something under any conditions, no matter how good. *I wouldn't leave you on your own for the world.*

to do someone a `world of good/harm to do someone a lot of good/harm. *If this story gets out it could do Jack's reputation a world of harm. Take a month's holiday—the change will do you a world of good!*

to get `on in the world to be successful in one's job and improve one's financial and social standing.

to go 'up in the world to rise to a higher social and financial position, not necessarily through one's own success or abilities. *Since Sally married that rich industrialist she's certainly gone up in the world!*

a man of the world an experienced man, often with a cosmopolitan background.

what in the world am I to 'do? this phrase expresses perplexity and distress. It means 'I don't know what to do to end the trouble, problem, etc.'

C   Miscellaneous words with particular idiomatic meanings

all

to be all 'for something/all for doing something (informal) to be completely in favour of it. *I'm all for selling the car and buying a bicycle!*

to be all 'in (informal) to be completely exhausted. *He was all in after travelling two days and two nights.*

to be all 'there (informal) to be mentally alert, quick.

to be not all 'there (informal) to be mentally deficient.

all along all the time, from the start. *You're telling me nothing new, I've known that all along!*

'all but almost, very nearly. *He all but told me he didn't want me around any more.*

all in all when everything is considered. *All in all, and not forgetting that he is a beginner, he speaks English very well.*

'all the same nevertheless, but, yet. *I'm sure he'll say yes, but I should ask him first all the same.*

and all (informal) in addition, as well. *The thieves stole jewellery, paintings, carpets, fur coat and all.*

for all in spite of. *I wouldn't like to be in his position, for all his wealth!*

for all I know/care (used to express ignorance or indifference) as far as I know/care. *'Where's John gone?' 'I don't know, and for all I care, he needn't come back!'*

it's all one/all the same to someone it makes no difference to him. *It's all the same to me whether we go to the cinema this evening or tomorrow evening. You can either go or stay—it's all one to me what you do.*

it was all someone could 'do not to do something he could hardly stop himself from doing it. *It was all she could do not to laugh when she saw his smart new trousers.*

of all the fools etc/of all the foolish etc things to do! (informal) expresses annoyance when someone has done something which you judge to be foolish.

once and for all for the only or final time. *I'm telling you once and for all, don't play with that dog! She'll bite you!*

how

a how-d'ye-do (short for 'how-do-you-do') (informal) a difficult matter, an awkward state of affairs. *You've lost your passport and all your money! Well, that's a fine how-d'ye-do, isn't it!*

how about something/doing something (informal) this is used to make a suggestion to someone, and to ask someone's opinion about something. *How about inviting Jane and Peter over for dinner this evening? If you can't come before lunch, how about 4 o'clock in the afternoon.*

how come? (informal) why? how does/did it happen that . . .? *How come you never told me about that before?*

how's that? why? what is the reason for that? *'Wendy has just sold her car.' 'How's that? She's only had it four weeks!'*

one

to be at one (with someone) to be in harmony with someone, to share the same view. *Sam and his wife are never at one with each other, no matter what the subject of discussion is.*

to be one 'up (on someone) to have an advantage over someone, to be ahead of someone.

to become one/be made one (formal) to be united in marriage.

(all) in one/(all) rolled up in/into one combined. *Since his wife died, Harry has been mother and father in one to the children.*

it's all one (to me/him etc) it makes no difference, it's all the same.

I/you etc for one to take at least one example (of a person). *I don't think many people will be able to come that night. I, for one, have to be in Madrid.*

for 'one thing for one reason (out of other reasons). *I really don't think we should go on holiday yet. For one thing, we can't afford it.*

number one (informal) oneself, one's own interests. *Don't worry about what other people think. Think of number one and do what is best for yourself!*

one and all everyone.

too

to be one too many (for someone) to be better than, to outwit someone. *I don't think Jim will beat Peter at chess. Peter is one too many for him.*

to carry something/go too far to exaggerate something beyond reasonable limits, eg a joke, trick, style of dress, behaviour.

to have one too many (to drink) to get (slightly) drunk.

all/only too + *adjective/adverb* (as an emphatic assertion or contradiction) very ... *But I'd be only too pleased to help you! This summer's day will be over all too soon.*

none too + *adjective/adverb* (as an emphatic assertion or contradiction) certainly not too ...; not ... enough. *'They've arrived!' 'And none too soon!'*

it's too bad! it's a pity. *It's too bad that you won't be able to take a holiday this year.*

what

to give someone what-'for (informal) to punish him. *Your father will give you what-for if he finds out what you've done!*

to know what's 'what (informal) to be knowledgeable and experienced. *I'm afraid I never quite know what's what with antique furniture.*

I know 'what/I'll tell you 'what (informal) (used to make a suggestion) I suggest ... *I know what, we'll visit Peter, Paul and Mary this weekend!*

so 'what? (informal) what does it matter? *Let him be jealous if he pleases! So what?*

'what about ...? (used to make a suggestion) I suggest ... *What about going out for a drink this evening? What about a drink? What about Nancy?*

(and) what 'have you (informal) (and) all the rest; and so on. *And I've also got to pay the grocer, the greengrocer, the bakery, the dairy and what have you.*

what 'of it? what does it matter?

what's 'up? (informal) what is the matter?

'what with (informal) considering; because of. *What with the visitors and all the extra housework, I've had a very busy week.*

4   Idioms with adjectives and nouns in combination

general note

This chapter deals with idioms consisting of some combination of adjectives and/or nouns. Seven different types of combination are given:

        A Pairs of adjectives
        B Pairs of nouns
        C Collective noun phrases
        D Compound adjectives
        E Adjective + noun phrases
        F Noun phrases
        G Proper names made up of an adjective and a noun

The material of this chapter should prove especially useful to the learner, as much of it is not included either in dictionaries or in grammars of English *in an explicit form*. It is therefore difficult to find this kind of material easily as it cannot always be readily looked up.

If the learner wishes to acquire an active and not merely a passive knowledge of this material, ie if he wishes to *use* these phrases and not simply to be able to *recognise* them, it is advisable to devote time to accurate and intensive learning. Since the changing of any part of the idiom can lead to loss of meaning in most cases, it is best to aim at accuracy from the very beginning.

Examples are given where necessary to indicate the type of context in which the idiom can be used.

A   Pairs of adjectives

English has many phrases which contain two adjectives joined together by **and, but** and **or**. However, the order of the adjectives must not be changed, as it is fixed by usage. The following list includes the most frequently occurring pairs with examples of how they are typically used.

ancient and modern *Throughout history, both ancient and modern, men have been fond of waging war.*

for better (or) for worse whatever may now happen. *For better or for worse, I've bought the train tickets and booked a room at the hotel.*

black and blue (of bruises) *Mary has fallen down the stairs again—she's black and blue all over!*

cut and dried settled, decided. *Jim's a very good speaker. He always has his opinions cut and dried and states them very firmly.*

dead and gone; dead and buried *'What ever happened to old Billy Jones?' 'He's been dead and buried now for at least twenty years!'*

drunk or sober *Drunk or sober, Dave always knows the difference between a good cigar and a bad one!*

by fair means or foul in an honest or dishonest way. *Pete is determined that he will get that promotion, by fair means or foul!*

fair and square (informal) in a fair way. *Let's settle the bill for the damage fair and square. We're both at fault, so we'll pay half each.*

few and far between rare; infrequent. *My visits to my family are few and far between, these days.*

free and easy casual, unworried, unconcerned. *Jack never stays in a job long. He's always been a very free and easy person.*

for good or ill whatever may now happen. *For good or ill—we've done it! We're married!*

great and small (formal) *All creatures of the earth, great and small, need air or water in order to survive.*

good, bad or indifferent *What's your opinion of Robert's latest novel? Good, bad or indifferent?*

high and dry abandoned, without support. *Poor Jim was left high and dry by his so-called friends when he lost all his money and needed help most.*

high and low everywhere. *Where have you been all day? I've been looking for you high and low!*

high and mighty very proud. *Since Lucy's father was made a Lord she does everything in a very high and mighty fashion.*

the long and the short of it all that need be said; the facts. *The long and short of it is, that Jack and Jane have broken their engagement.*

meek and mild *Mike should have defended himself and told Spike what he thinks of him, but I'm afraid he's much too meek and mild.*

more or less almost. *I've more or less finished redecorating the house now. There are only a few small jobs to be done.*

null and void (formal) invalid, without legal effect. *The marriage has been declared null and void.*

past and present *All Presidents of the United States, past and present, have had to undertake to uphold their country's constitution.*

rich and poor *All British students, rich and poor, receive a grant from the government for their studies.*

right and left *Always look right and left before you cross a road.*

right and wrong *Children usually learn the difference between right and wrong at an early age.*

rough and ready not exact, only approximate. *I can't tell you how to use prepositions correctly. I can only give you a few rough and ready rules.*

short and sweet brisk, without delay. *I won't go into a long explanation of the reasons for my leaving, I'll just make it short and sweet.*

slow but sure *He's a slow but sure worker—and the finished product is always first-class.*

through thick and thin through all dangers and difficulties. *Jack and Jim went through thick and thin together in the last war.*

B Pairs of nouns

There are a number of pairs of nouns in English which always occur together, and have a fixed order. It is not easy to explain why one noun always comes first and not the other. Long usage has established the order, which we must not change. Here is a list of some of the most frequent pairs.

Alpha and Omega the beginning and the end; the first and last; God

arts and sciences

babes and sucklings innocent children

bag and baggage (with) all one's luggage

bed and breakfast (at a hotel)

beer and skittles fun and pleasure

body and soul (with) one's entire self

bow and arrow

bread and butter

bread and water

bucket and spade

cloak and dagger like a spy

fire and sword (in war)

fire and water

fish and chips

flesh and blood one's family or relations

friend or foe

hammer and sickle the emblem of Socialism, or of the USSR

hammer and tongs (with) all one's strength

hand and foot (of binding) hands together and feet together

hands and feet

head over heels

heart and soul (with) all one's feeling and spirit
heaven and earth
hill and dale
hole and corner secret
horse and cart
house and home
judge and jury
king and queen
kith and kin
knife and fork
ladies and gentlemen
land and sea
life and limb
life and soul liveliest person
light and shade
lord and lady
for love or money (in a negative sentence) for anything
male and female
man and beast men and animals
man and boy from boyhood
men and women
might and main strength
mother and child
Oxford and Cambridge
part and parcel a part
pen and ink
pen and paper

pins and needles the sensation in an arm or leg after the blood supply has been cut off for a short time and feeling is returning
powder and shot (for an old-fashioned gun)
profit and loss
rack and ruin decay
without rhyme or reason for no understandable reason
sin and misery
skin and bone very thin
son and heir
stocks and shares
stuff and nonsense nonsense
sun, moon and stars
sword and shield
tea or coffee
time and tide the flow of natural events
tooth and nail (of fighting) fiercely
town and country
use and abuse
vice and virtue
wear and tear constant use over a time
wife and children
wind and weather

C   Collective noun phrases

There are several nouns which are idiomatically used when describing collections of certain things. We call these collective nouns. The learner is likely the have difficulty in deciding which is the usual way of describing many sheep or cows in English. Is it usual to say *a herd of sheep* or *a flock of sheep*? The following list gives the conventional collective noun phrases.

animals etc
  a brood of chickens
  a covey of partridges
  a colony of ants

a drove of cattle ie cattle being driven along
a flight of birds
a flock of sheep

a gaggle of geese
a herd of deer
a herd of swine/pigs
a herd of cattle i e cattle pasturing
a litter of puppies
a nest of ants
a pack of hounds
a pack of wolves
a swarm of bees
a swarm of locusts
a shoal of fish
a school of porpoises
a school of whales

others
a bunch of grapes
a bunch of keys
a bunch of flowers

a bouquet of flowers i e specially arranged
a bundle of sticks
a bundle of hay
a chain of mountains
a clump of trees
a cluster of stars
a flight of stairs/steps
a gang of thieves/robbers
a group of islands
a group of people i e not so many
a heap of stones
a heap of sand
a pair of shoes
a pile of books
a range of hills
a series of events
a suit of clothes

D   Compound adjectives

Sometimes in English we find adjectives that are made up of a few words. These are particularly popular in colloquial English and in newspapers. The meaning in most cases is quite clear. These adjectives are always made up of hyphenated words. Here are some typical examples in current use.

a **dog-in-the-manger** *policy* followed by a man who prevents others from enjoying something which is useless to himself or for which he has no interest.

a **happy-go-lucky** *manner* a carefree, easy manner.

a **hit-and-run** *driver* a driver who drives away after causing an accident in which there was material damage or damage to persons.

hole-and-corner *methods* secret, underhand methods.

a **long-hoped-for** *journey*.

a **much-talked-of** *affair*.

a **nine-to-five** *job* a job in which the working hours are from nine in the morning to five in the afternoon.

an **out-of-the-way** *place* far from busy streets.

a **round-the-clock** *service* a service which is offered continuously, all day and all night.

a **run-of-the-mill** *job* an average, ordinary, unexciting job.

stay-at-home *folks*.

E   Adjective + noun phrases

We now look at idiomatic phrases that may cause difficulty to the learner because of their special meaning, which is independent of context. English is full of phrases of the kind *a dark horse*, *an early bird*, *French leave*, consisting of an adjective and a noun. Although the words of these phrases are easily understood by the learner, the total phrase is only readily understood by a native speaker, because long established usage has given the phrase a special meaning. The phrases are listed in alphabetical order of the adjectives. Phrases which have capital letters, eg *the Emerald Isle*, are grouped together in Section G of this chapter.

an able-bodied seaman a trained and certified sailor, classed in the ship's records as A B.

animal spirits (always plural) the natural cheerfulness and love of life associated with youth.

apple-pie order a perfectly orderly arrangement.

an arch look a sly, significant look.

an armchair critic a person who passes criticism without being actively involved.

an armchair job a regular job which is considered easy and well-paid.

the armed forces the military forces, ie the army, navy and air-force.

armed neutrality a condition or policy pursued by a nation that is 'neutral' but armed for defence against agression.

backstairs gossip gossip among servants.

backstair(s) influence influence exerted secretly or underhand.

bad blood unfriendliness *between* two people.

bad language swear-words or taboo words.

a bad shot a wrong guess.

a bad time (informal) a difficult or a miserable experience.

bated breath (ie *abated*) to wait/sit/speak etc *with bated breath* means to do so breathing shallowly because of suspense or anxiety.

a besetting sin a bad habit or characteristic which is often shown.

a 'big shot (informal) an important person

the big top a very large circus tent.

a bird's-eye view an overall view or survey of a thing, place, subject etc.

blank verse poetry in which the lines do not end in rhyming syllables.

a blind alley a narrow street closed at one end, or a job etc without prospects.

a blind date an arranged social meeting of two persons who do not know each other.

a 'blood horse a thoroughbred.

a 'boat-train the train service between a main station and a harbour, for the use of passengers arriving or leaving by ship.

the body politic the state considered as a politically organised group.

a born sailor, teacher etc one who seems naturally gifted for the work.

a bosom friend an intimate, trusted friend.

a brass farthing a worthless thing (mostly found in the phrase *not to care a brass farthing*, ie not to care at all).

broad daylight the full light of day. To do something *in broad daylight* is to do it outside, during the day, and in public.

broken English imperfect English.

a burning question a matter of dispute which should be solved urgently.

a busman's holiday free time in which one is occupied with tasks similar to those of one's regular work.

a capital offence/crime an offence which is legally punishable with death.

the cardinal points are North, South, East and West.

the 'carrying trade the trade which consists of transporting commercial goods, usually by sea.

cast iron iron direct from the smelting furnace.

a casting vote the deciding vote given by the chairman of a meeting when votes for and against a motion are equal.

a 'cat burglar a burglar who enters buildings from the roof or high windows by climbing up drainpipes, balconies, walls etc.

cat's cradle a children's game played by two people using fingers and a loop of string.

a cauliflower ear a swollen ear due to boxing.

a chance meeting a meeting which takes place by chance, without arrangement.

the chief mourner (at a funeral) the nearest relative to the dead person.

circumstantial evidence evidence which does not provide direct proof, but which provides enough information to suggest a person's guilt.

a close-fisted man a mean or stingy man, not spending or giving money willingly.

a close shave a narrow escape from danger, an accident etc.

a close thing something which was almost an accident, failure or misfortune, eg when someone almost misses a train, almost hits another car, almost fails an examination etc.

a close vote a voting result in which the number of votes for and against are almost equal.

'**closing time** the hour at which a shop or public house is closed. Closing time in pubs in Britain is fixed by law.

a cock-and-'bull story an invented story, foolish and hard to believe.

cold comfort poor consolation.

cold feet *to have/get cold feet* to be/become afraid of doing something which is dangerous or which requires courage.

the cold shoulder *to give someone the cold shoulder* to ignore or snub someone, to treat someone in an abrupt and hostile manner.

a cold war a war carried out not by fighting, but by propaganda, economic sanctions, hostile diplomatic relations etc.

a (highly) coloured statement/story an exaggerated one.

a commanding presence an impressive personal appearance.

a commanding view a view from high up, eg from a hill-top.

a confirmed bachelor a man who has decided never to marry.

a cool head *to have a cool head* to remain calm, to think rationally in times of difficulty or excitement.

a cool reception one which is not cordial or enthusiastic.

a corrupt passage a passage in a manuscript or text which is difficult to understand because of mistakes or alterations.

a country cousin a person who is not used to the way of life in towns.

crocodile tears insincere tears which show false sorrow.

a cross examination a close questioning of a witness in a court of law in order to test answers already given.

a crying shame something which is a great shame or a great pity.

a curtain lecture the scolding of a husband by his wife in private.

a dark horse a person who has greater capabilities than he shows or than people are aware of.

a dead-end job a job without prospects.

a diamond wedding the celebration of the anniversary of 60 years of marriage.

a dizzy height a very great height.

a dog-eared book a book with crumpled edges, a book where the corners of the leaves have been turned down to mark particular pages.

a dog-in-the-manger policy a selfish one, in which a person prevents others from getting benefits which he himself, however, cannot profit from.

the 'dog star the star Sirius, the brightest of the fixed stars, in the constellation *Canis Major* (Great Dog).

a double agent a person who works secertly for two opposing sides without either of the two sides knowing of his activity for the other side.

double Dutch unintelligible language.

a ˈdown train (GB) a train from London.

a drawn game a game in which both sides get the same result, and so there is no winner.

Dutch courage courage which is got by drinking alcohol.

a Dutch treat entertainment (a meal, a film etc) where each person pays his own share; they *go Dutch*.

an ˈearly bird a person who gets up early every morning.

an early grave *to come to an early grave* (formal) to die young.

ˈelbow grease hard work, effort.

ˈelbow room room or opportunity to move and act freely.

the eternal triangle a situation of emotional conflict involving two men and one woman or two women and one man.

extra-mural studies studies, lectures etc for students who do not attend the university, i e who study externally.

a Fabian policy a strategy using slow and cautious tactics in order to tire the opposition, a policy of delay.

a fair copy a neat, legible copy.

a fair hand handwriting which is easy to read.

the ˈfair sex women.

a fair weather friend a person who stops being a friend when one is in trouble or difficulties.

a fair weather sailor one who has never encountered a storm at sea.

a falling market one in which prices are declining.

a fancy price an unreasonably high price.

a fast colour a colour which does not fade or wash out of the material.

fast living a way of living which is devoted to pleasure and luxury.

the fatted calf *to kill the fatted calf* (from the Bible, Luke 15, in the parable of The Prodigal Son) to celebrate lavishly and joyfully.

fellow feeling sympathy.

a ˈfield course, ˈfield studies, ˈfield work a course of work undertaken outside the place of study, aimed at practical investigation.

the fine arts the visual arts such as painting, sculpture, architecture.

the fixed stars those which do not change their positions (relative to each other) in the sky, i e not planets.

flying colours *to come through/do something with flying colours* to accomplish it with great success.

a flying jump a jump made with a running start.

a flying visit a very short visit.

a ˈfly leaf a blank page at the beginning or end of a book.

a forced landing an aircraft landing made in an emergency.

a forced march a march made by an army in an emergency at a rapid speed.

a foregone conclusion an obvious or inevitable result.

a foreign body (eg in the eye) a substance (eg a particle of dirt or grit) lodged in or on the body.

a forlorn hope a desperate hope or plan for which there is very little chance of success.

forty winks *to take/have forty winks* (informal) to have a short sleep.

the fourth estate the Press.

a free port a port where customs duties are not levied on imported goods.

free trade trade without the imposition of customs or taxes.

French leave absence without permission.

a French window a double glass door which opens on to a garden or balcony.

a freshwater sailor one who has not made a voyage on the open sea, only on rivers, canals or lakes; a novice or inexperienced person of any profession.

A Freudian slip a speaker's unintentional mistake revealing his true thoughts.

fugitive compositions/verses articles in a newspaper or magazine which are only of temporary interest, of passing value.

further education (GB) full-time or part-time education for persons who are above the compulsory school-leaving age, and who are not in higher education (ie university).

a garbled quotation/statement one which omits much of the original quotation or statement, thus being a misrepresentation or corruption of the original.

the gene'ration gap the failure of the younger and older generations to understand each other's way of life; the difficulties resulting from this.

gilded youth young persons who live fashionable, luxurious lives.

gilt-edged securities/stocks investments which are considered financially safe, ie cannot decrease in value.

a going concern a successful business.

the golden handshake a large sum of money given to a man of high position when he retires from his employment.

the golden mean the middle course between two extremes; moderation.

a golden opportunity a very good opportunity.

golden opinions very favourable opinions.

the golden rule that which Jesus Christ gave to men (in the Bible, Matthew 7) which teaches: 'Treat others as you would wish them to treat you.'

a golden wedding the celebration of the anniversary of 50 years of marriage.

a good address a residence in a fashionable district.

a good hand 1 enthusiastic applause. 2 favourable cards in a card game.

the 'good people the fairies.

a good Samaritan (from the Bible, Luke 10, in the parable of the Good Samaritan) a person who helps another person who is in difficulties, even though he does not know him.

(See also *Good* in Chapter 3)

a Gordian knot a difficult problem or task. *to cut the Gordian knot* to solve a problem by force, by disregarding the difficulties.

a grass widow a wife who is alone because of the temporary absence of her husband.

a gratuitous insult an insult which was not provoked, but given without reason.

the green-eyed monster jealousy.

a green old age a man is said to enjoy a green old age when his outlook on life is fresh and vigorous, in sympathy with the ideas of the young.

a ground swell rough sea-water near the shore or in shallow water.

the 'gutter press those newspapers which specialise in scandalous, sensational and salacious stories.

a hair's-breadth escape an escape which almost failed or ended in disaster.

the happy medium the middle course which avoids two inconvenient extremes.

a happy expression a suitable and pleasing expression.

a hard drinker a person who frequently drinks large quantities of strong alcohol.

a hard and fast rule one which cannot be altered, a rule without exception.

(See also *Hard* in Chapter 3)

a henpecked husband one who is dominated by his wife.

a herculean task one which requires great effort, which only a *Hercules* could perform.

a high flier a person who is extravagant or very ambitious in his wishes.

a high-flown sentiment an extravagant, exalted sentiment.

an honest penny a small sum of money honestly earned.

a hot line a direct telephone line between heads of government.

a hot potato (informal) an issue that is awkward or embarrassing to deal with.

hot news very recent, important or sensational news.

hot goods (informal) stolen goods which are difficult to sell because they will be recognised by the police.

the hot seat 1 the electric chair for the execution of murderers. 2

an important position from which vital decisions are made, e g as
by a political head of state; a position of great responsibility.

hot water (informal) trouble.

humble pie *to eat humble pie* to humiliate oneself by having to
apologize.

'**hush money** money which is paid as a bribe in order to keep a
matter secret.

a hushed-up affair a matter which is kept from public knowledge
because of its compromising or discreditable nature.

an idle compliment an insincere compliment.

idle talk gossip.

ill-gotten gains money obtained by dishonest methods.

Indian file *(in) Indian file* (of people walking) in a line, one behind
the other.

an Indian summer a period of hot, dry weather in late autumn.

an inside job (informal) a theft committed by someone 'inside' a
building, i e by someone who is employed there, not by a stranger.

an iron hand *to rule with/to have an iron hand* to control like a
tyrant, severely and without mercy.

an iron will a very strong will, determined and inflexible.

an ivory tower a place or state of life that is out of touch with
people and reality.

a 'jail bird (informal) a man who has been in prison more than
once.

a jaundiced eye the prejudice of someone who is intent on finding
fault.

a job lot a miscellaneous collection of goods or articles which are
bought or sold together.

a Job's comforter a person who distresses the person he is sup-
posedly comforting.

kid gloves *to handle someone/something with kid gloves* to treat him/
it with the utmost care, so as not to hurt his feelings, cause trouble
etc. Hence, *kid-glove methods*.

a knotty problem one which is difficult to deal with.

a knowing look a look which suggests that the person knows more
of a matter than has been disclosed.

a 'ladies' man a man who enjoys the company of women.

a lame duck person or enterprise that is not a success and has to be
helped.

a last fling *to have a last fling* to take the last opportunity for
pleasure or amusement before a time of restraint.

the last straw an additional problem or difficulty which makes the
present problem intolerable.

a latchkey child a child who returns from school etc to an empty
house because both parents are working.

'**laughing gas** a gas (nitrous oxide) which causes laughter when inhaled, sometimes given to children by a dentist before taking out teeth.

a leading article a newspaper article which gives editorial comments, opinions etc.

a leading question a question which suggests the answer one desires or hopes for.

a left-hand compliment one of doubtful sincerity or which is ambiguous.

lighting-'up time (GB) the prescribed time when lights in streets and on vehicles must be turned on.

the light-fingered gentry a collective name given to minor thieves, pickpockets etc.

light literature; light reading stories, novels etc written for amusement or entertainment, not for serious contemplation.

a light sleeper a person who does not sleep deeply and who wakes easily.

the 'little people is the name given in Ireland to the fairies and elves.

a 'live wire (informal) a person who is very active and forceful.

the living theatre live theatre performances as opposed to cinema or television performances.

a loaded question one which is intended to trap a person into saying or admitting something which will betray him.

the long last sleep (formal) death.

a 'long shot 1 an attempt to solve a problem which is not expected to be successful, because of certain difficulties, e g lack of facts or evidence. 2 a hopeful guess.

a maiden voyage the first voyage of a new ship.

a maiden speech the first speech in Parliament by a new Member.

the main chance *to have an eye to the main chance* to be on the look-out for making money, advancing one's own interests.

a marked man one who is observed with suspicion or enmity because of some earlier misdeed, scandal etc.

'**marriage lines** (GB) (informal) the certificate of marriage.

the missing link a person or a thing needed in order to clear up a mystery, solve a problem, explain a situation etc.

'**monkey business/tricks** (informal) mischief.

a moonlight flit *to do a moonlight flit* (informal) to move house secretly or overnight in order to avoid having to pay debts; to disappear suddenly in the night.

a moot point an undecided question.

a moral certainty something which seems inevitable, very sure to happen.

mother wit natural common sense, intelligence one is born with.
one's/the 'mother country one's native land.
mountain dew (informal) genuine Scotch whisky, so called because of its former secret distillation in the mountains.
the naked eye the eye unaided by any instrument, eg a microscope.
the naked truth the truth as it is, without disguise.
a narrow escape an escape which nearly failed.
a near thing something which was almost an accident, failure or misfortune.
the new rich people who have become rich only in recent years.
the next world heaven or hell; life after death.
a nine-days' wonder an unexpected happening which at first attracts great interest but is soon forgotten.
the odd man out 1 a person who does not fit in with the others, because he differs in some way, eg he does not share a common interest or ability. **2** a thing (an object, number, idea etc) that cannot be suitably ordered with others of its type.
an old maid (informal) a woman who has not married and who is no longer young.
old hat (informal) out-of-date, no longer fashionable or topical.
an 'old boy/girl a former member of a particular school.
the old school tie (GB) the network of mutual support which is said to prevail among former pupils of the same school.
an old hand (at something) a person with a great deal of practice or experience with it.
an old salt an experienced sailor.
an old 'wives' tale a story or statement about life handed down by tradition, usually foolish and far-removed from modern knowledge, beliefs and practices.
open house *to keep open house* to extend a welcome to all visitors without special invitation.
an open question a matter for discussion which is still without answer or decision.
an open secret one that has become known to all but is still supposed to be secret.
an open verdict a jury's verdict on a death, not specifying it as being accidental, natural, criminal or suicidal, nor specifying a criminal, because of lack of evidence.
an open letter one written for publication in a newspaper or magazine, usually a letter of protest or criticism.
the open season the season for fishing and shooting where there are no legal restrictions.
one's opposite number the person who occupies the same position or has the same function as oneself in another group, department, company etc.

original sin the teaching that it is man's true nature to do bad rather than good.

an outside estimate an estimate which is calculated to be higher than is thought probable.

a `package tour a holiday at a fixed price in which travel and accommodation are all paid for beforehand.

a packed jury a prejudiced jury.

palmy days days of prosperity.

a paper tiger a person who appears to be powerful but who is not.

a parallel passage a passage in a book which strongly resembles another in content and thought or in language.

the parson's nose (informal) is the rump of a cooked chicken.

a parting shot a last effort made before one leaves. *to take a parting shot at someone* to make one last criticism of or attack on him.

a `party line a shared telephone line, i e one which has two or more subscribers.

party spirit devotion to or enthusiasm for one's own political party.

a passing fancy a temporary liking for something or someone.

a `pep talk a friendly talk which tries to give the listener encouragement, enthusiasm and energy.

a pet aversion something or someone greatly disliked.

plain sailing a plan, course of action etc without obstacles or difficulties.

a poison pen a person who writes malicious, slanderous letters anonymously.

a practical joke a trick played upon a person in order to make him look ridiculous.

a `pretty kettle of fish (informal) a total mess, a great mix-up.

the primrose path the pursuit of idle, wasteful pleasure.

the privileged classes the ones who are in a financial position which enables them to enjoy the best educational and social opportunities.

a `put-up job (informal) a pre-arranged matter, planned so as to give someone trouble without his previous knowledge, i e in order to swindle or falsely incriminate him, or to put him at a disadvantage by creating a false impression.

a Pyrrhic victory a victory where the loss is greater than the gain.

qualified praise restricted, modified praise.

a queer customer/fish (informal) a person who is difficult or awkward to deal with, because of his unusual character, nature, attitudes etc.

a quixotic project a project which is considered foolish and extravagantly romantic, totally unrealistic. (In Cervantes's *Don Quixote* the hero is represented as engaging in all sorts of ridiculous and extravagantly romantic feats of gallantry.)

a rainy day a time of financial hardship. *to put away/keep something for a rainy day* to save it for when it is really needed.

a random shot *to take a random shot at something* to make a guess which is not expected to be correct.

a random statement a statement made without much consideration for the actual truth or correctness of a matter.

a raw deal (informal) unjust or harsh treatment.

a ready wit *to have a ready wit* to have a quick mind, which is prompt to answer, make jokes etc.

ready money cash which is immediately available.

a ready pen someone who is able to compose and write easily and quickly.

a red 'letter day a day for celebration, usually of an important or happy event.

red tape excessive official formality.

one's right hand man one's chief helper or agent who is indispensable.

the rising generation the generation of young people who form the next adult generation.

a rolling stone a person who wanders around without staying in any place or in any one job for a long time.

a rough guess an approximate calculation, estimate etc.

a round dozen a full dozen, neither more nor less than twelve.

the royal colours colours displayed on a race-horse owned by a monarch.

a ruling passion a passion or motive which dominates a person's life, eg the love of money, desire for popularity, power etc.

a rum fellow (informal) an odd or unusual person.

a sabbatical year a year of release from regular duties granted eg to some university teachers, for them to pursue further studies, to travel etc.

safe conduct *a letter of safe conduct* an official document which grants the bearer safety to pass through enemy territory in a time of war.

one's 'salad-days the time when one is young and inexperienced.

'sales chat (informal) a talk to a prospective customer by a salesman with the aim of promoting his goods and persuading the customer to buy.

a 'sandwich course (GB) a course of training with a period of practical work in between two full-time periods of study.

a sane policy a sensible, well-reasoned policy.

sanguinary language language which uses many swear-words (eg including frequent use of the swear-word *bloody*).

a 'sausage-dog (GB) (informal) a dachshund.

a saving clause (e g in a contract or any legal document) a reservation or exception which appears in parentheses.

a saving grace a good quality or characteristic which 'saves' or excuses a person who has otherwise only rather bad qualities.

a 'scare headline a newspaper headline in heavy print which creates sensation—or even panic.

a scorched 'earth policy a policy of burning crops and destroying buildings in order to prevent them from being used by enemy forces in a time of war.

sealed orders instructions for action given to a person of authority, only to be opened at a certain time or place or under certain conditions, especially at a time of war.

the 'seamy side of life the disagreeable, unpleasant aspects of life, such as crime and violence, poverty and hunger, disease etc.

the season's greetings greetings at a time of public celebration, expressing good-will, e g *A Happy New Year!*

seasoned food food flavoured with herbs or spices.

seasoned timber wood that has been left to dry thoroughly, so that there is no sap in it.

second fiddle *to play second fiddle (to someone)* to be of only secondary importance (to him).

second nature some acquired habit or talent which seems perfectly natural to someone.

second sight a power or ability to foresee future events or geographically distant events.

second thoughts thoughts after reconsideration; a change of mind, attitude or decision.

a 'security risk a person who represents a risk to a country's security, e g because of his political activities.

a senior citizen a polite way of referring to an old age pensioner.

a settled conviction a fixed, permanent impression or belief, which has been reached after much thought.

settled weather a period of unchanging weather, free from storm and extremes.

the seven deadly sins pride, covetousness, lust, anger, gluttony, envy, sloth.

(the) seventh heaven *to be in (the) seventh heaven* to be extremely happy.

Shanks's mare/pony *to go on Shanks's mare/pony* to use one's own two legs, to walk.

a shadow cabinet the group of members of the Parliamentary Opposition who hope to become the next Government's cabinet.

a sham battle a simulated, pretended battle, arranged for military training purposes.

sharp practice(s) dishonest methods, dealings etc in business.

a sharp tongue *to have a sharp tongue* to use sarcastic, scolding language.

a ˋsheet anchor the last and best hope or refuge for safety when everything else has failed.

a shooting pain a quick, sharp pain, coming suddenly.

the ˋshooting season the restricted time of the year fixed by law when sportsmen may shoot particular game (the shooting season for one kind of game is not always the same as for another).

a shooting star a meteor.

a short cut an easier way or method of doing something, getting somewhere etc.

Siamese twins twins joined together at some part of the body at birth.

ˋsick leave leave granted because of illness.

a ˋside issue a matter which is only indirectly concerned with the question under consideration.

a ˋside-line work done apart from one's main work.

single blessedness a term applied light-heartedly to the unmarried state.

a ˋsinking fund invested money which accumulates and may be used when needed, eg in order to pay off future debts.

a sitting duck (informal) a person or object that is easy to attack, injure etc, a good target.

a sitting tenant the person who is occupying a flat, house etc.

the sitting member (of Parliament) the elected candidate who held the seat before the previous Parliament was dissolved.

the sixth sense the power of intuition.

a ˋslanging match a quarrel consisting of an interchange of insults and rebukes.

a sleeping partner a business partner who provides a share of the capital and therefore owns shares in the business but who does not take an active part in managing it.

ˋsmall arms light weapons which can be carried by one man.

small craft small boats.

ˋsmall fry (informal) insignificant persons or matters.

the ˋsmall hours the hours after midnight up to three or four o'clock.

ˋsmall talk trivial, unimportant conversation. *to make ˋsmall talk* to make polite conversation.

one's social equals the people of the same social standing, the same social class as oneself.

a society journal a magazine which reports on fashionable circles or persons.

a soft spot a liking or fondness for something or someone.

a soft option an alternative which is easy or agreeable.

'**soft soap** (informal) flattery. *to* '*soft-soap* to flatter.

a **sore point** a matter which irritates or hurts when mentioned.

a **sound sleep** a deep, refreshing sleep.

sour grapes a desirable thing which is not obtainable and is therefore despised.

spare time leisure time.

a **special licence** a licence of marriage which permits the marriage to take place under special circumstances, and not only at legally authorised times or places.

the **spitting image (of something/someone)** the exact likeness.

a **splitting headache** (informal) a very severe headache.

a **square deal** a fair bargain or fair treatment (opposite to *a raw deal*).

a **square peg (in a round hole)** a person who is not suited to his position or work, surroundings etc, one who does not fit in.

a **square meal** a meal which offers enough good food to satisfy one.

a **square-toes** a person who is too formal or prim, who does not actively enjoy fun.

a '**stag-party** a party where only men are allowed to be present.

a '**stalking horse** a pretence used to conceal a secret project.

a **standing army** an established, permanent army, as opposed to an army called up only in time of emergency.

standing corn/grain growing corn, not yet harvested.

a **standing joke** a joke which always causes amusement to certain people who know its origin.

a **standing order** (to a bank) an order to pay which the bank carries out automatically (on application of the customer) for payments which occur regularly, e g rent.

standing orders rules and regulations which remain in force until they are cancelled by the authority that made them.

standing water stagnant water, not running or flowing water.

a **stand-up fight** a hard fight either physically or with words.

the **still small voice** one's conscience.

a '**straight play** a serious drama contrasted with light entertainment or variety.

a **straight tip** one that is reliable and can be recommended, e g a tip about promising shares on the Stock Exchange.

strained relations personal relations which are temporarily disturbed by mutual distrust, enmity, irritation etc.

a **straw vote** an unofficial opinion poll which tries to establish public attitudes on matters of current interest.

a '**striking force** a military group which is ready to attack at short notice in an emergency.

strong language angry language consisting of many swear-words.

one's strong point the thing one can do best, knows most about etc.

a stuffed shirt (informal) a pompous, conceited person.

a 'sugar daddy (informal) a rich, elderly man who favours a young woman financially in return for special attentions.

one's Sunday best one's best clothes, in contrast to clothes one works or plays in.

a sweeping statement one which generalises widely, leaving out details, restrictions, exceptions etc.

sworn foes/enemies enemies who do not wish to be reconciled.

sworn friends faithful, close friends even in times of strain.

'take-home wages/pay the amount one receives after tax deduction etc, the sum one can spend.

a tall order a task which is difficult to accomplish or a request which is difficult to grant.

a tall story a statement, narrative etc that is difficult to believe because it seems impossible or unrealistic.

tall talk exaggerated, boastful talk.

'teething troubles the difficulties which arise at the beginning of a new enterprise, expected to become fewer as the enterprise grows.

a thankless task a difficult or unpleasant task for which one will receive no thanks or praise when it is accomplished.

a third party another person in addition to the two already in question.

the three R's the three basic skills of education: reading, writing and arithmetic.

a thumb-nail sketch a small-scale drawing or a brief description.

a ticklish situation (informal) one which must be handled with tact, skill and care.

a tight spot/corner *to be in a (bit of a) tight spot/corner* (informal) to be in a difficult situation.

a tight squeeze (eg in a vehicle) *to be a tight squeeze* to be very crowded, allowing only very little room for each person.

a time-honoured custom a custom which has been maintained for a long time.

a (little) tin god (informal) a person who is mistakenly held in great respect, credited with great powers etc.

a token strike a short strike held as a warning.

(the) top drawer (of) the highest social class.

top dog *to be top dog* (informal) to be the most important person, the chief.

top people the people who have reached the top of their profession and who are in the highest positions.

total abstinence complete abstinence from alcoholic drink.

total war war in which all forces and resources of a country are mobilised or involved, including industrial power.

a tough customer (informal) a person who is difficult to manage or persuade.

tough luck (informal) bad luck.

a towering passion a violent rage, a fit of anger.

our transatlantic cousins Americans.

the treble chance a method of filling in football pools by predicting drawn matches, wins for matches played away and at home. *to do the treble chance* to do this.

a Turkish bath a steam bath followed by a shower and massage.

Turkish delight a sweet pink or white jelly covered with powdered sugar.

the twelfth man a reserve player in a game of cricket.

a twice-told tale a well-known story which everybody has heard.

a universal rule one which can be applied without exceptions.

an untimely end premature death.

an unwritten law one which has become law by tradition or use, but is not precisely stated in print.

an uphill task a difficult task.

(the) upper crust (of) the highest social class.

the upper storey (informal) one's brain.

a Utopian scheme a praiseworthy, desirable scheme which is, however, impossible to accomplish.

a vested interest a connection with some enterprise that involves personal gain.

a vexed question a question which causes much discussion or dispute but which remains unresolved.

a vicious circle a state of affairs which cannot be cleared up or altered because the cause of the problem and the effect of the problem are interdependent and self-perpetuating.

virgin soil soil which has never been cultivated or built on.

a vulgar fraction a fraction written thus: $\frac{3}{4}$ (in contrast to *a decimal fraction*, written thus: 0.75).

the 'weaker sex women.

the wee (small) hours (US) the hours after midnight.

Welsh rabbit/rarebit hot buttered toast covered by hot melted cheese.

a wet blanket (informal) a person who spoils a jolly atmosphere, or who does not join the fun of others, thereby reducing it. (See *white* in Chapter 12)

a wild 'goose chase a search for something which has no chance of being successful.

wishful thinking the state of imagining something to be true because one wishes it to be true.

a working lunch/dinner a meal at which the participants discuss business.

a would-be author/philosopher etc is a person who aspires to being an author etc, but who is not really one, whose success has not been established.

the yellow press the term given to newspapers which concentrate on printing sensational stories.

a young hopeful a young man or woman who shows promise and who seems likely to succeed.

'**zero hour** the important or decisive time when something is planned to start, e g a military operation, the launching of a rocket.

F   Noun phrases

an apple of discord (formal) the subject of envy or quarrel.

the apple of one's eye something or (more usually) someone who is very dear to one; an object of delight.

a bag of bones (informal) a very thin person.

the whole bag of tricks everything; the whole lot without exception.

bags under the eyes soft, dark skin under the eyes.

a baker's dozen thirteen.

a bed of roses an easy, pleasant situation.

a bed of thorns a difficult, unpleasant situation.

the bill of fare (formal) the menu.

a clean bill of health a certificate or announcement stating that someone/something is healthy, acceptable etc.

a bird of passage a person who roams from one place to the other, not staying in any one place for very long.

birds of a feather people who have the same interests, the same kind of character or disposition and who therefore tend to associate closely (the phrase is often uncomplimentary).

a bolt from the blue a surprise or shock.

a bone of contention a subject of argument or disagreement.

a bull in a 'china shop an awkward, tactless or clumsy person.

a case in point an illustrative case connected to the subject of discussion.

a cast in the eye a slight squint.

castles in the air plans which cannot be realised.

the cock of the walk the most dominating person in a group.

a cog in the machine an unimportant person in or a small part of a large complex, enterprise, organisation etc.

a cuckoo in the nest a child whose parentage is doubtful and may therefore not belong by blood to the family.

contraband of war goods which are not allowed to be sold by a neutral country to a country at war.

the crack of dawn the time when it first begins to get light.

the crack of doom the end of the world; the loud noise announcing it.

the ʻcrux of the matter/question the central or decisive point of an issue.

crumbs from a rich man's table a small comfort or compensation given to the poor or unfortunate by the rich or more fortunate.

days of grace the time allowed for payment of a bill beyond the fixed date for payment. *to give someone two/three etc days' grace* to allow him two/three etc extra days.

a diamond of the first water a reliable thing which is perfect of its kind.

a drug on the market goods on the market for which there is no demand.

the fall of man the first sins of Adam and Eve; the first step of man from innocence to sin.

a feather in one's cap an accomplishment of which one can be proud.

feet of clay *to have feet of clay* to be weak or cowardly.

a fish out of water a person who feels uncomfortable in his present surroundings.

a flash in the pan something which lasts only a short time; an effort or partial success which soon turns to failure; a short-lived outburst of enthusiasm for something.

a fly in the ointment something which prevents a state of perfect pleasure; a circumstance which spoils the total situation.

a friend at court a person well disposed towards one, who can use his influence to help.

the gift of the gab *to have the gift of the gab* (informal) to be a good, persuasive speaker.

the ins and outs (informal) *to know the ins and outs (of something)* to be fully experienced (in something); to know the full details (of something).

a Jack of ʻall trades a person who is capable of doing many different kinds of jobs, but who is not really expert at any of them; (hence the phrase *Jack of ʻall trades, (but) master of ʻnone*).

the land of the living the ordinary world of people and events; reality; consciousness.

the land of nod a children's expression for sleep.

a leap in the dark a risky attempt to do something, because one cannot foresee the likely results; an act of pure faith.

the life and soul (of the party) the person who is the centre of attraction because he is the most amusing or lively and provides fun for the others.

a limb of the law a lawyer, policeman etc.

the lion's share the greater part.

a man/woman about town one well used to life in fashionable city circles.

a man/woman in a thousand one of unusual qualities or talents.

a man/woman of letters a writer and scholar.

a man/woman of spirit a courageous one.

a man/woman of straw a cowardly, weak one, who can be manipulated.

a man/woman of the world one who has a broad cosmopolitan outlook, who has much experience of life, and has travelled widely.

a mare's nest a discovery which looks valuable or promising but which turns out to be worthless.

the milk of human kindness a feeling of sympathy for other people.

money for jam (informal) money earned without any effort.

(a) pie in the sky (informal) promises or hopes which are unrealistic, and thus useless.

a pig in a poke an article which was bought without previous inspection and which turns out to be worthless or worth much less than one paid.

a pillar/the pillars of society a person/the people considered to uphold society's moral and conservative values most reliably (because of social standing and profession, eg teachers, doctors, judges).

any port in a storm any place or person is good enough to go to for help when there is urgent need or great difficulty.

the pros and cons the arguments for and against a matter.

the Queen's speech (GB) the speech delivered each year at the opening of Parliament.

the rank and file soldiers who are not officers; ordinary people without any special position; the masses.

a rogue's gallery a collection of photographs of (known) criminals.

the root of all evil money (which is thought to corrupt people).

a rope of sand a bond or promise which is easily broken.

a rule of thumb a practical rule which has proved useful through experience.

the salt of the earth that person/those people who make the world a better place.

the seeds of time (formal) the passage of time.

a shot in the dark a wild guess.

a sight for sore eyes (informal) something welcome which one enjoys seeing.

the sinews of war the money required to carry on war or any difficult undertaking.

a skeleton in the cupboard a past event which is kept secret by a family; something embarrassing or shameful.

the skin of one's teeth *to escape by the skin of one's teeth* to only just manage to escape.

a slap in the face (informal) a nasty rebuff or a snub by someone.

a slip of the tongue an unintentional mistake in speaking.

a smack in the eye (informal) a great disappointment or set-back.

a snake in the grass a person who pretends to be a friend but who at the same time is secretly damaging one.

a soldier of fortune a military adventurer who will fight for any side for money; a mercenary.

a 'spoke in someone's wheel *to put a 'spoke in someone's wheel* (informal) to cause a hindrance or stumbling-block to his plans.

a 'stone's throw a short distance.

a storm in a tea-cup a lot of excitement and discussion about a trivial matter.

the talk of the town (informal) a person or event which excites much attention.

the thin end of the wedge a small matter which is likely to lead to bigger matters, demands, changes etc.

a tower of strength a person who can be relied upon for help, comfort etc in a time of trouble or grief.

the tricks of the trade the most successful ways and methods of attracting customers, doing good business etc.

the ups and downs (of something) the times of prosperity and adversity, the happy and the sad times.

the 'villain of the piece the person in some matter, who was wicked or caused trouble.

a word in season advice or warning given at the right time.

the worm of conscience remorse.

the writing on the wall an event or indication which points to impending dangers, misfortune or difficulties.

G   Proper names (adjective + noun)

This list groups together proper names which are in the form *adjective + noun*, and which always appear in print with capital letters. The list does not include eg purely geographical names but special names for concepts, objects, places etc, which have a special meaning or association in English and which cannot be guessed by the learner.

the Big Four the four major banks in Britain: Barclays, Lloyds, Midland, and National Westminster.

the 'Black Country (GB) the highly industrialised area of Central England, especially in the counties of Warwickshire and Staffordshire, so called because of the smoky air and blackened buildings from the heavy industry.

the Black Death the outbreak of bubonic plague in different parts of Europe in the 14th Century, which killed a very great number of people.

Black Power the name of a movement to promote the interests of black people everywhere.

Bombay Duck a small, dried fish of South Asia.

'Boxing Day the day after Christmas Day, 26th December.

the Celtic Fringe those people of the British Isles who are descended from Celtic-speaking forefathers; also the regions which they inhabit, ie Scotland, Ireland, Wales, Cornwall and the Isle of Man.

'Civvy Street (GB informal) civilian life (as opposed to military life).

the 'Dark Ages refers to Europe of the Fifth to the Tenth Centuries when intellectual and moral life was at a low level.

the Deep South the south-eastern states of the United States, especially South Carolina, Georgia, Alabama, Mississippi and Louisiana.

the Emerald Isle Ireland.

the Eternal City Rome.

Father Christmas a (mythical) old man, dressed in red, who brings presents to children while they are asleep on the night before Christmas.

the Four Freedoms the basic human freedoms: freedom of speech, freedom of religion, freedom from fear, freedom from want.

the Free Churches the nonconformist Protestant churches.

the Golden Age the period in a country's history which was characterised by increased prosperity and cultural activity.

Good Friday the Friday before Easter Sunday.

the Great Crash the time (1929) when the New York Stock Exchange 'collapsed', denoting the end of the boom period of prosperity in the twenties.

the Great Lakes the five lakes on the border between the United States and Canada: Superior, Michigan, Huron, Erie, Ontario.

the 'Home Counties (GB) the counties around London: Middlesex, Surrey, Kent, Essex, Hertfordshire, Buckinghamshire.

the Iron Curtain the political frontier between Eastern and Western Europe.

the 'Ivy League (US) a group of eight long-established universities in the eastern part of the United States, denoting scholastic and social prestige (so called because of the ivy-covered buildings of some of the old colleges).

Jack Frost a (mythical) old man who brings frost during a winter night.

John Bull the English nation, the typical Englishman, English character etc.

the Jolly Roger the black flag bearing *the skull and crossbones*, flown by pirate ships.

the 'Lake Poets the three poets who lived in the Lake District of England at the beginning of the 19th century: Southey, Coleridge and Wordsworth.

Madison Avenue the advertising industry of the United States.

the 'Melting Pot the United States, being a country in which immigrants of many nations and races are united together in citizenship.

the 'New World North and South America.

the Old Bailey the criminal court in London where important trials are held.

the Promised Land Canaan, the land promised in the Bible by God to the Israelites, because of its fertility; any promised state of future happiness and prosperity.

Santa Claus (= St Nicholas) see *Father Christmas* above.

the Star-Spangled Banner the flag of the United States of America.

the Third World developing countries which are not politically aligned to either the East or the West.

Tin-Pan Alley (US and GB) the popular music industry.

Uncle Sam the United States, the typical American, American character etc.

'Wall Street the centre of American finance.

the West End the fashionable, central part of London with its shops, theatres, restaurants etc.

the 'White House the residence of the President of the United States; the Presidency itself; the United States.

the Yellow Pages (GB) a telephone directory with numbers listed according to trades and occupations, printed on yellow paper.

5 Idioms with verbs and nouns that are used together

general note

The English language has many turns of expression which the learner can only learn to use if he is brought into direct contact with them. A student may know a large number of verbs and nouns, but may not know exactly how they can be put together to form typical English expressions. We shall try in this chapter to give the learner useful lists for reference and for learning typical *verb-noun* and *noun-verb* collocations, i e words which go together.

List A gives nouns (the grammatical object) which follow certain verbs. List B gives verbs which follow certain nouns. List C gives the names of animals' cries. If the lists are referred to frequently, the collocations should become part of the learner's active vocabulary.

A Verb + noun collocations

Certain verbs are followed automatically by certain nouns (the grammatical objects of the verbs). The verb may have different meanings in different collocations. For example, *to bear fruit* means 'to produce fruit', and *to bear cold* means 'to endure cold'. The following list gives verbs which commonly take certain nouns after them or which naturally go together with certain nouns. This will help the learner to know which nouns he can use together with which verbs. Explanations are provided for these collocations that are true idioms, i e whose meanings cannot be derived from the meanings of the individual words alone. In Chapter 10, major verbs are fully dealt with. There, not only nouns that are the grammatical object but also other idiomatic constructions can be found. Prepositions after verbs are dealt with in Chapter 8.

to abandon *ship; all hope, a plan; one's wife and child.*

to achieve *an aim, a purpose; success, distinction in public life.*

to acknowledge *receipt of a letter; defeat, one's mistake; kindness.*

to acquire *knowledge, a taste (for something); an accent.*

to adopt *a child; a plan, an idea, a custom, new measures.*

to air *the bed(s), a room; one's views/opinion(s)/knowledge.*

to alleviate *suffering, pain.*

to apprehend *danger, difficulty; a criminal.*

to ask *a question, permission, the way, the time, the price of something, a favour of someone.*

to attend *a meeting, a lecture; school, church.*

to bandy words (with someone) to exchange quick remarks (with him) in a quarrel.

to bear *a burden, arms; responsibility, punishment, (the) cold/heat; resemblance to someone/something; witness (to something), false witness (against someone); a grudge (against someone), ill will/malice (towards someone); the expenses/charges/costs (of something).* **to bear fruit, children** to produce them. **to bear sway** to exercise authority. **to bear (someone) a hand** to help him. **to bear the brunt of something** to endure the worst part or main strain of something.

to bind *a book, the edge of a carpet; a prisoner, someone's hands and feet.*

to break *a promise, a resolution, one's word, a contract; the law, the peace; the silence; one's leg, arm etc; a seal, a link; contact with someone.* (See also Chapter 10.)

to bring *an action/an accusation against someone; someone to justice; a letter/lecture etc to a close.* (See also Chapter 10.)

to build *a house, a ship; hopes.* **to build castles in the air** to talk or think about things in the future which most probably will not come true.

to burn *a cake (in the oven), toast etc; wood, oil; a hole in something; bricks/lime/charcoal; one's fingers etc.* **to burn one's fingers** to suffer because you have interfered or meddled in someone else's affairs.

to bury *a bone* (dogs). **to bury oneself in one's books/studies** to spend a lot of time reading/studying. **to bury the hatchet** to become friends again after a quarrel or fight.

to call *a doctor, a taxi; a meeting, a strike; (someone's) attention to something; someone (on the phone).* **to call someone names** to describe him in abusing or insulting terms. **to call a halt (to something)** to say that it is time to stop something, to forbid it. **to call the banns** to announce a forthcoming marriage publicly in church. **to call someone's bluff** to invite him to carry out his threat because you do not believe that he will. **to call someone/**

a meeting to order to ask for orderly behaviour because some-one/a meeting was too loud, undisciplined etc. **to call a spade a spade** to speak frankly, plainly.

to cancel *an order (for goods etc); a meeting.* **to cancel a (postage) stamp** to mark (or *frank*) it with the name of its place of origin.

to carry *a burden; arms/a weapon; news, a message; a resolution, a motion.* **to carry weight** to be influential, important. **to carry the day** to be victorious. **to carry everything be'fore one** to be completely successful. **to carry something too far** to con-tinue it (eg a joke, a risk) beyond what is reasonable or safe.

to cast *a vote, lots; anchor; a glance at something; a gloom/shadow on/over something.* **to cast an 'eye over something** to examine it briefly. **to cast a new 'light on something** to make it (eg a situation, a problem) easier to understand. Moulting birds **cast feathers** ie shed them.

to catch *(a) fish; a ball; a thief; a train/bus; a cold, an infection; the spirit of an occasion; a glimpse/glance of something, sight of some-thing/someone; hold of something/someone.* **to catch fire** to begin to burn. **to 'catch it** (informal) to get a scolding or punishment from someone for doing something wrong. **to catch someone's eye** to attract his attention when he looks in your direction. **to catch a Tartar** to encounter an adversary who is too strong for you.

to change *one's clothes; trains; money.* **to change one's mind** to decide to do something different. **to change one's tune** to change to a different viewpoint, attitude etc.

to clear *the table (after a meal); a jump/hurdle.* **to clear the decks (for action)** to get ready to do something. **to clear the air** to get rid of suspicion or doubts by telling the true facts. **to clear one's name (of suspicion etc)** to remove all suspicion etc from one. **to 'clear oneself (of a charge)** to prove one's inno-cence.

to close *a meeting/discussion; a shop; a school; a bank account; a road.* **to close a deal/bargain** to agree on terms and complete the deal/bargain.

to collect *stamps, coins etc; rents, taxes; statistics, data, news, in-formation; votes.* **to collect one's thoughts/ideas** to think care-fully about one's thoughts/ideas before voicing them.

to compare *prices, offers; ideas, findings.* **to compare notes (with someone)** to exchange opinions, thoughts (with him).

to cook *food.* **to cook the books** to falsify a firm's accounts or re-cords to one's own advantage. **to cook someone's goose** to stop him from doing mischief, to put an end to his plans.

to cross *a road/river/the sea etc; a cheque.* **to cross a person's path** to meet him unexpectedly. **to cross someone's palm with**

silver to give silver money to a fortune-teller to have one's fortune told. **to cross swords (with someone)** to argue (with him).

to **cultivate** *the land; an acquaintance, someone's friendship; an accent; the mind.*

to **cut** *oneself, one's finger etc; flowers; corn; bread, cake etc.* **to cut a corner/corners** to take a short-cut. **to cut a disc/record** to make a gramophone record. **to 'cut a person ('dead)** to ignore someone when passing him. **to cut a tooth** to have a new tooth coming through the gum. **to cut the Gordian knot** to solve a problem by force. **to cut a dash** to show brilliant appearance and behaviour to draw attention. **to cut capers** to play tricks, pranks.

to **desert** *a friend, one's wife, one's country, one's colours, a cause.*

to **deserve** *praise, credit, a reward, thanks; punishment.*

to **dig** *a hole, a grave, a well, a trench, a foundation; the garden, the ground.*

to **direct** *a remark at someone; one's attention to something; an orchestra, a play; the traffic; one's energies towards (doing) something.*

to **draw** *a cart; a gun; a tooth; a/the curtain; a picture; blood; breath; water; money from the bank/one's account; a conclusion, an inference; a distinction/a parallel/an analogy (between two things).* **to draw the line (at something)** to fix a limit.

to **drink** *water etc; poison; the health of someone/someone's health/to someone/to someone's health.*

to **drive** *a car etc; cattle; a bargain.* **to drive a hard bargain** to be hard in a business deal, not to give in easily to another person. **to drive someone mad** to behave in such a way as to irritate or anger him.

to **drop** *anchor; one's voice.* **to drop a word in someone's ear** to inform him confidentially of something. **to drop a line to someone** to write to him. **to drop someone a hint** to give him a hint. **to drop someone** to stop being his friend. **to drop Maths/History etc** (at school etc) to stop learning that subject. **to drop the subject** (in conversation) to stop talking about it. **to drop a stitch** (in knitting) to let a stich slip off the needle. **to drop a brick/clanger** (informal) to do or say something which is very tactless or indiscreet.

to **eat** *food, one's dinner etc.* **to eat one's heart out** to suffer in silence because of worry, fear, anxiety. **to eat one's words** to admit that what one said was wrong. **to eat humble pie** to apologise, to humble oneself.

to **enter** *a trade/profession; the army; the Church; a school; a convent.*

to exercise *a horse, troops; discipline, control, authority; caution, patience; one's talents; one's limbs.*

to feed *a baby, animals; an engine (eg with water, petrol); a furnace (with coal); information to someone.*

to fill *a glass, bottle etc; an office; a post, a vacancy; a tank with petrol.* **to fill the bill** (informal) to meet the need or requirement.

to find *something that was lost; courage; a solution; time; a cure for something; oil, gold.* **to find favour (with someone)** to be acceptable (to him). **to find fault (with something/someone)** to criticise (it/him) negatively. **to find one's voice/tongue** to be able to speak after a period of silence because of shyness or nervousness. **to find one's feet** to gather confidence, to act independently.

to follow *an example/someone's example, a principle, an ideal; a leader, a guide; the road; the fashion; a trade.* **to follow suit** to do the same as someone else.

to form *an opinion, a resolution, an alliance, a plan; an attachment to someone/something; judgements, conclusions; a line, a company (eg soldiers); good habits, bad habits; someone's mind/character (eg a child's); (a) part of something.*

to formulate *ideas, thoughts, a doctrine.*

to gain *time; knowledge; power; a victory over something/someone, an advantage over someone; strength, importance; weight.* **to gain ground** to make progress. **to gain the day** to be victorious. **to gain the upper hand** to win an advantage over one's enemy, rival, competitor etc.

to give *evidence (at court), offence, praise, thanks; chase, help, a (helping) hand; a ride/lift; trouble, cause for complaint; (a) warning, advice, notice; a shout, a scolding, a shock; an/the impression; permission/authority (to do something); the alarm.* (See also Chapter 10.)

to grant *a favour, a request, permission.*

to grow *flowers, vegetables; a beard.*

to hang *a person for murder.* **to hang wallpaper** to fix it on a wall. **to hang fire** (of a gun) to be slow in going off, (of a person) to be slow in developing.

to have *a house, a farm etc; abilities, talents, authority; room (for something); possession (of something); an appointment (with someone); influence; patience; a taste for something, an interest in something/someone; (an) effect; dealings with someone; a quick eye; a (good) understanding of something; a cold, a fever.* (See also Chapter 10.)

to hear *a noise, a voice, a shout etc; a report, a rumour, the news; evidence, a witness.* **you could hear a `pin drop** (informal) it was very still and quiet.

to hold *an/the opinion/view; a post/appointment/position; an examination; a meeting/session; a council/parliament; a party/reception; one's breath; an audience.* **to hold the fort** to be in charge during someone's absence. **(not) to hold water** (not) to be logical, valid (eg an argument, hypothesis). **to hold the line** (when speaking on the telephone) to keep the connection and wait. (See also Chapter 10.)

to keep *a secret, a vow, a promise; faith; silence; the peace; guard, watch; a fast, a festival* (ie observe)*; a horse, sheep; company with someone/someone's company; a shop; a diary, accounts/books.* **to keep house** to direct a household. (See also Chapter 10.)

to lay *a foundation; a plan, a trap, an ambush; the table; a wire, a pipe; bricks; a tax on imports, a duty on wines; a wager; a charge against someone; siege to something; something to someone's charge. A hen* **lays eggs.** (See also Chapter 10.)

to lead *an army, a gang; the way (to somewhere); a busy/easy life; the fashion; the choir/singing; a (political) party.* **to lead someone astray** to cause him to do wrong. **to lead someone by the nose** to make him do anything you wish him to do. **to lead a woman to the altar** to marry her. **to lead someone 'on** (informal) means to persuade or entice him to do something that he does not really wish to do.

to leave *the room, home, school; (someone) a legacy.*

to lend *a book, money; assistance, a (helping) hand; one's name/support to a project.* **to lend one's ear to something** to listen attentively.

to light *a cigarette, a lamp, a fire.*

to load *a cart, a ship, a donkey; a gun; one's stomach (with too much food).* **to load the dice (against someone)** to do something which will give one an unfair advantage (over him).

to lose *one's life, one's reputation, one's job/position, one's way, one's memory, one's bearings, one's case (in a court of law), one's (eye-) sight; favour (with someone); men (in a war); money; patience (with something); interest (in something).* **to lose one's temper** to become angry. **to lose one's head** to lose the ability to think clearly and logically, to panic. **to lose one's reason/senses** to become wild with emotion or excitement. **to lose the thread of something** to fail to follow or remember the main line or thoughts of an argument, story etc. **to lose heart** to become discouraged. **to lose one's tongue** to say nothing because of shyness or nervousness. **to lose track of someone/something** to lose contact with him/it.

to love *a person, a pet animal; one's country; music, painting etc; comfort, good food etc.*

to make *a speech, a suggestion/proposal, a promise; arrangements (for* *someone/something) ; an assertion, a statement ; a fuss, a row, a noise, a disturbance ; a will ; a record (of something), a copy (of something), a sketch/outline (of something) ; a complaint (to someone about something) ; a charge (against someone) ; an effort ; an experiment ; an appointment/arrangement (with someone) ; a road, a railway, a canal ; a journey/voyage ; a bargain, an offer ; the beds ; a cake, a dress, a meal ; music ; friends ; progress ; terms, peace (with someone, a nation etc), war (on a nation) ; an application (to someone) (for something) ; a guess (at something) ; allowances (for someone/something) ; an impression (on someone) ; a remark (to someone) (about something) ; a request (to someone) (for something) ; an allusion (to something) ; a law ; a profit/loss ; one's escape ; one's living (as/at/by/from).* **to make a pile/packet** (informal) to earn lots of money. (See also Chapter 10.)

to open *a door ; a shop ; a debate, a discussion ; negotiations (with someone) ; the bowels ; a canal, a new road ; fire (on/at someone/ something) ; a bank account ; the bidding (at an auction) ; Parliament.*

to pass *an examination ; a law ; sentence (at court) ; the time, the evening ; a remark (about something) ; an opinion/judgement (on something/someone) ; the butter etc ; the Customs ; forged money.*

to pay *a bill, debts, tax(es) ; money to someone/someone money (for something) ; attention (to someone/something) ; someone compliments ; someone one's respects ; someone a visit ; tribute (to someone) ; regard/heed to someone/something.* **to pay one's way** not to get into debt. **to pay someone back in his own coin** to retaliate, treat him in the same way as one was treated by that person.

to place *a bet ; an order (with someone for something).*

to play *a musical instrument, a tune ; a game ; tricks, pranks ; a part/ role (in a play).* **to play the fool** to act like a fool. **to play a dirty/mean trick (on someone)** to say something or to act in such a way which will injure him or put him at a disadvantage. **to play truant** to stay away from school etc without good reason. (See also Chapter 10.)

to put *any object anywhere ; a price/value on something ; a question to someone.* **to put pen to paper** to start writing. **to put one's case** to set one's case forward for consideration by others. **to put the blame on someone** to make him responsible for the mistake. **to put pressure on someone (to do something)** to press someone hard to persuade him to do something. **to put an end/ a stop to something** to end it completely. **to put the brake(s) on (something)** (informal) to slow something down (in speed of progress, development etc). **to put life into something** to make it lively, eg a party, a meeting, a show. (See also Chapter 10.)

to **raise** *a question, an objection, a difficulty; a shout; a rebellion; a standard (ie a flag): an army; taxes, money; the price of a thing; the alarm; one's voice; one's hopes; one's hat (to someone); the temperature.* **to raise a smile/a laugh** to make someone smile/laugh. **to raise someone to the peerage** to make him a peer. **to raise a/the dust** to cause a disturbance by something one does or says. **to raise one's glass to someone** to drink his health. **to raise an embargo** to remove it. **to raise a siege/a blockade** to end it. **to raise someone from the dead** to restore him to life. **to raise one's hand to someone** to make a move as if to hit him with one's hand. **to raise hell/Cain/the devil/the roof** (informal) to cause a great uproar or disturbance. **to raise the wind** (informal) to get money as quickly as possible by any means.

to **read** *a book; a will; someone's handwriting; music, figures, signals, road signs; a dream/riddle (ie solve); someone's thoughts; a subject at university (ie study).* **to read someone's hand/palm** to interpret his past and future from the lines on his palm. **to read between the lines** to look for or discover the underlying and actual meaning of someone's words or actions. **to read the writing on the wall** to understand or interpret signs or actions which are a warning about future events.

to **receive** *a letter, money, wages; information, news (of something), warning (of something); a good education; a warm welcome; guests; notification (of something); stolen goods; support (for something); a radio/TV programme.*

to **remove** *an obstruction; an error; doubts, fears.*

to **resist** *temptation; an attack, the enemy; authority; (of material, eg glass) heat.*

to **restore** *law and order, the peace; an old building; a custom; stolen property.*

to **run** *a risk/the risks (of doing something); risks; a race; errands/messages (for someone); the chance/danger of something; a business, a company, a car, a house; a car into a tree etc; a mile/kilometer etc.* **to run riot** to behave wildly, lawlessly. **to run a temperature** to have a high body temperature because of illness. **to run the show** (informal) to be the boss of an undertaking, to be in charge. (of children) **to run the streets** to spend time in the streets without supervision, usually because the parents are not at home.

to **say the word** to say 'yes' to something to express agreement, so that another person can act accordingly. **to say one's piece/say** (informal) to state what one has to say about a matter.

to **see** *a ghost; an error/mistake (ie perceive); land; a doctor/lawyer (ie visit).* **to see the sights** to see all that is famous or interesting to see, eg on a tour. **to see stars** (informal) to see unclearly after a blow on the head. **to be 'seeing things** to see things which are not there, to have hallucinations. (See also Chapter 10.)

to seek *advice (from someone); shelter (from a storm etc).* **to seek one's fortune** to try to make money (in a new place).

to seize *a/the chance/opportunity (of doing something).*

to serve *a customer; a meal; a prison sentence (ie endure); a ball (in tennis); one's time/apprenticeship; a person, one's country.* **to serve time** to undergo a period of imprisonment. **to serve one's needs/purpose(s)** to meet one's requirements. **to serve two masters** to divide one's time, interest, loyalty between two opposing principles, people, situations etc.

to set *a table; a trap, a snare; a broken limb; an example; a clock; the fashion; one's hair.* **to set sail (to/from/for somewhere)** to start a journey. **to set a price (on something)** to declare what it will be sold for. **to set the scene** to describe the situation, people, activities (in a play, novel, sporting event etc). (See also Chapter 10.)

to show *(someone) a picture, photograph; (someone) the way; courage, fear, signs of fatigue/stress etc; flowers, a dog etc (ie exhibit).* **to show fight** to show readiness to fight, to be competitive. **to show one's teeth** to show anger or aggression. **to show one's hand/cards** to show or say what one's plans or intentions are. **to show a leg** (informal) to get out of bed, to make an appearance to start doing something (usually used in the imperative form). **to show one's mettle** to show one's true capabilities, qualities, courage etc. **to show the white feather** to show signs of cowardice.

to sign *one's name; a document, a contract, a cheque.*

to sow *seed; a field, land; discord, the seeds of rebellion.* **to sow one's wild oats** to lead a wild life in one's youth.

to spend *money (on something); time (on/in doing something); all one's energies (on/in doing something).*

to spin *cotton, wool; (of a spider) a web; a top (ie a child's toy).* **to spin a yarn** to tell a tale which is probably untrue or exaggerated.

to spread *butter (on bread etc); (of a bird) its wings; the table; a lie/ rumour; (a) disease/infection.*

to spring *a mine, a trap (ie bring into action).* **to spring a leak** to begin to leak.

to strike *(someone) a blow; a man, a dog etc; a match; (of a clock) one/two etc, half-past six, the hours; gold, oil (ie discover); a chord (on a musical instrument); a bargain (with someone); fear/terror/ alarm (into someone); a balance (between two things); a note of warning etc.* **to strike one's flag** to lower it as a sign of surrender. **to strike tents/camp** to pack up the tents, to get ready to leave the camp. (of a plant) **to strike roots** to make roots.

to support *a political party; a claim; a theory; a football team; one's wife and children, a family etc.*

to take *a seat; a walk, a drive; a photograph (of someone/something); steps/precautions/measures (not) to do something; revenge (on someone); control (of something); refuge, shelter; poison, medicine; a course (of action); offence; advice (from someone); one's leave (of someone); aim (at something); flight; (someone) captive; a fancy (to something), a liking (for something); exception to something; credit for something; pleasure/delight in something; charge (of something); care (of someone/something); the direction of (somewhere) (ie go in that direction); hold of something; account of something; advantage of someone/something; the liberty of doing something; possession of something; an interest in someone/something; pride in (doing) something.* **to take part (in something)** to join it. **to take place** to occur, happen. **to take the place of someone/something** to do what he/it was to do. **to take a stand (on something)** to be prepared to defend, argue about it. **to take (one's) time (about doing something)** to be slow in doing it. (See also Chapter 10.)

to teach *a person, a pupil, a class (how) (to do something); a subject; (someone) manners, obedience.*

to tell *a story, a tale, the truth, a lie; (someone) the time.* **to tell someone his fortune** to predict his future. **to tell the world** to tell everybody. **to tell the tale** (informal) to tell a sad story about oneself in order to get sympathy from others. **to tell tales (about/on someone)** to tell his secrets or private affairs to others in a malicious way.

to throw *a ball, a stone etc; dice; an opponent (in wrestling); light on/upon something; doubt on/upon something.* **to throw a party** (informal) to give/hold a party. **to throw a fit** to have a fit. **to throw one's weight about** to behave in a commanding, important manner. **to throw dust in someone's eyes** to mislead someone, to prevent him from seeing the true situation. **to throw cold water on something** to discourage enthusiasm for it (eg a plan, an idea).

to turn *a wheel, a handle; one's head; one's attention (to something); a corner; a somersault; one language into another (ie translate); one's mind/thoughts to something.* **to turn something to (one's) advantage** to make it useful to one. (See also Chapter 10.)

to use *any instrument (to do/for doing something); force, persuasion; someone's name (eg as a reference).* **to use one's head** (informal) to think intelligently. **to use one's fists** to hit someone.

to wear *a coat etc; a crown; a sword; a smile; a flower (in one's buttonhole).* **to wear a hole in one's shoe/trousers/sock etc** to cause one to appear.

to **weave** *cloth; flowers (into a garland); a plot, a story (i e compose); one's way (eg through the traffic, the woods).* **to weave a web of lies/illusions/deceit etc** to create a complex structure of them.

to **win** *a prize, a scholarship, money, a game, a race, a battle; a stake (in something); honour, admiration, success.* **to win the day** to be victorious. **To win one's spurs** to win honour, a good reputation.

to **withdraw** *troops (from somewhere); money (from a bank, a company etc); an application; a statement; one's labour.*

to **work** *a machine; a 40-hour week; shifts.* **to work one's passage** to earn a sea-passage by working during the journey, not by paying money for it.

B   Noun + verb collocations

We now look at some nouns (mostly abstract nouns), which are typically followed by certain verbs or verbal phrases.

an **accident** *happens, occurs, takes place*

aggression *mounts, builds up, abates*

anger *flares up, mounts, abates*

an **argument** *develops, takes place, flares up, is settled, is resolved, peters out*

an **attempt** *fails, succeeds, peters out*

attention *wanders, is fixed (on)*

an **audience** *gathers, assembles, disperses*

a **battle** *rages*

beauty *fades*

a **bomb** *explodes, goes off, drops, is defused*

business *flourishes, prospers, picks up, slackens (off), booms*

colour *changes, fades*

complications *set in, arise*

conscience *pricks, troubles, stirs*

a **contract** *is drawn up, is signed, comes into force, expires*

crime *increases, breeds, decrasese, abates, falls off*

a **crisis** *arises, develops, dies down*

a **crowd** *forms, scatters, breaks up*

danger *threatens*

darkness *falls*

difficulties *arise*

disease *spreads*

doubt *sets in, spreads, overcomes*

duty *calls*

efforts *succeed, fail, increase*

an **epidemic** *breaks out, spreads*

an **event** *takes place*

excitement *mounts, dies down*

an **experiment** *succeeds, fails*

a **fire** *glows, burns, flickers, crackles, dies down, dies out, breaks out, spreads*

friendship *develops, grows, strengthens, cools down/off*

frustration *mounts, grows, increases*

a **habit** *forms, grows, catches*

hardship *is borne, is suffered*

health *improves, picks up, deteriorates*

history *is made, repeats itself*
hope *builds up, dies, is stifled*
hysteria *breaks out, spreads, dies down*
an idea *occurs to someone, is conceived, develops, matures*
an incident *occurs*
interest *(in something) grows, develops, wanes, dies, is taken, is aroused, is lost*
knowledge *is imparted, spreads*
laughter *is stifled, breaks out*
a meeting *starts, finishes, ends, breaks up, is postponed, is cancelled*
memories *fade*
the memory *improves, deteriorates, fails*
a need *arises*
an occasion *arises*
an opportunity *presents itself, arises*
a plan *materialises, succeeds, is realised, backfires, miscarries, fails*

a problem *arises, presents itself, crops up*
a promise *holds good, is kept, is broken*
a quarrel *develops, takes place*
a rule *applies, is kept, is broken*
a rumour *spreads, goes about*
a secret *leaks out, is kept*
a storm *brews up, comes up, dies down*
a strike *is called, is broken, is called off, spreads*
the temperature *rises, goes up, soars, fluctuates, drops, falls*
tension *mounts, dies down*
time *flies, passes, drags, hangs heavy, stands still*
trouble *starts, brews up, threatens, sets in, dies down, subsides*
violence *increases, breeds, threatens, breaks out, flares up*
war *breaks out, is declared, is waged*
wealth *accumulates, is acquired*

C   Animals' cries

apes *gibber*
asses *bray*
bears *growl*
bees *hum, buzz*
beetles *drone*
birds *sing, twitter*
bulls *bellow*
camels *grunt*
cats *mew, purr*
cattle *low*
cocks *crow*
cows *low*
crickets *chirp*
crows *caw*
dogs *yelp, bark, whine, growl, howl*

donkeys *bray*
doves *coo*
ducks *quack*
eagles *scream*
elephants *trumpet*
flies *buzz*
foxes *yelp, bark*
frogs *croak*
geese *cackle, hiss*
goats *bleat*
hawks *scream*
hens *cluck, cackle*
horses *neigh, snort, whinny*
hounds *bay*
hyenas *laugh*

jackals *howl*
kittens *mew*
lambs *bleat*
larks *sing, warble*
lions *growl, roar*
magpies *chatter*
mice *squeak*
monkeys *chatter, gibber*
nightingales *sing, warble*
owls *hoot, screech, scream*
oxen *low, bellow*
peacocks/peahens *scream*

pigeons *coo*
pigs *grunt, squeal*
puppies *yelp*
rabbits *squeak*
ravens *croak*
rooks *caw*

seagulls *scream*
sheep *bleat*
small birds *chirp*
  twitter, pipe
snakes *hiss*
swans *cry*

thrushes *whistle,*
  sing
tigers *growl, roar*
turkeys *gobble*
vultures *scream*
wolves *howl*

6   Idioms with prepositions and adverbs

general note

What we consider in this chapter is a) phrases which begin with a preposition and b) phrases which consist of two adverbs. In the first section, we show typical uses of the main prepositions when they are followed by nouns or noun phrases. Verbs which typically go together with the prepositional phrase are indicated, e g *to know someone by sight, to jump/leap out of the frying-pan into the fire.* Prepositional phrases which are used with any typical, suitable verb and not only with particular verbs are preceded by *to do something . . .*, e g *to do something out of kindness.* 'To do something' can represent any number of typical, suitable verbs, such as *to act/ help/ask/give/show/lend etc out of kindness.* Idiomatic prepositional phrases which can only follow the verb *to be* are treated fully in Chapter 10. In the second section, useful Phrase Prepositions are listed for reference, of the type *by virtue of, in connection with* etc. Similar pairs of Phrase Prepositions, e g *in view of/with a view to* are listed, together with an explanation of the difference in meaning and examples of use. A short section then considers difficulties with certain prepositions which are often encountered by learners. The final section groups together useful phrases composed of two adverbs.

Prepositional Phrases

A   Prepositions with nouns or noun phrases

about

about six o'clock (ie approximately); *a discussion about something* (ie concerning, on the theme of); *to be about to do something*, to be on the point of doing it.

above

to do something above board without deception or secrecy; *to be a`bove oneself* to be in high spirits; *to get a`bove oneself* (informal) to be conceited; *to be above asking* to be too proud to ask; *to be above suspicion* too worthy, honest etc to be suspected; *to marry above one's station* to marry someone of a higher social standing; *to be above all/any meanness/pettiness/harshness etc* not to possess any of these bad qualities.

across

across the road; across the ocean; across the room; a bridge across a river.

after

after lunch/dinner etc; after dark; time after time repeatedly; *after consultation with someone; a painting after Reynolds* one in the style of him; *to make something after a model* to base it on a model; *to do something after a fashion* to do it in an unsatisfactory manner; *a man/woman after one's own heart* one of one's liking, who thinks and feels in the same way as oneself.

against

against the rule(s); against the law; to go against orders; to vote against a motion; to swim against the current; to work against time; to lean against a wall; to act against someone's advice/will/wish(es); to act against one's conscience; to sail against the tide; to take precautions against fire/theft etc; to be/go against the grain to be/go contrary to one's wishes, to displease one.

along

along the beach/road etc; to pass along the bus to move up to the other end to make more room for other passengers; *along here* in this direction; *along there* in that direction.

amid, amidst

amid danger; to do something amidst many difficulties/interruptions etc to do it in the middle of, in the presence of difficulties.

among, amongst

to be among(st) friends; one among(st) many (eg persons, reasons, problems); *to hide among(st) the trees etc.*

around

to travel around the country from one part to the other; *around 6 o'clock* a little before or after 6 o'clock.

at

As an expression of time: *at Christmas*; *at 6 o'clock*; *at breakfast*.

As an expression of place: *at the corner*; *at the bank*; *at school*; *at the theatre*.

to be at an advantage/disadvantage, to put someone at an advantage/disadvantage; *to be/lie at anchor* (ie a ship); *to hold/keep someone at bay* to keep him at a distance, under control (eg the enemy, a fierce dog); *to be/keep something at the boil* (eg water, soup) at boiling point; *to do something at choice* to choose to do it; *to have something at one's command*; *to do something at all costs* to do it at any price, disregarding difficulties; *to be at someone's disposal/to put something at someone's disposal*; *at a distance*; *to do something at the drop of a hat* (informal) to do it immediately and readily at the slightest suggestion or encouragement; *to be/feel at ease/to put someone at (his) ease*; *to do something at someone's expense*; *at fault*; *at a glance*; *at first hand* directly; *to be at the head of something* to be in charge of something; *to be sick at heart*; *to lend money at interest*; *the question at issue*; *to be at leisure*; *to be at liberty (to do something)*; *to sell something at a loss/profit*; *to be at someone's mercy/to have someone at one's mercy*; *to do something at short notice* to do it without much warning; *to buy/sell shares etc at par/to be at par*; *to be at peace/at war (with a country)*; *to run at full pelt* (informal) to run at full speed; *at a pinch* (informal) if absolutely necessary: *I can have the work finished at a pinch by 4 o'clock this afternoon*; *at play*; *at the point of death* (formal); *at close quarters* very near; *to do something at random* to do it haphazardly, without a particular intention; *at this rate* if things continue like this; *at that rate* if that is so; *to do something at one's own risk*; *to be at someone's service*; *at first sight* immediately: *I recognised at first sight that he wasn't telling the truth*; *to travel at a speed of 50 mph*; *to be at a standstill* not moving or progressing; *at a stretch* without pausing; *to be at variance (with someone)* in disagreement; *to do something at will* whenever one wishes; *at work*.

before

As an expression of time: *before breakfast*; *before Christmas*; *to come before time* to come before the arranged or fixed time.

As an expression of order: *A comes before B*; *ladies before gentlemen*.

As an expression of place, *before* is formal, *in front of* is preferred. But: *to appear before a magistrate/judge etc* in the presence of the judge.

behind

As an expression of place: *behind the house*; *behind a cloud*.

behind the scenes privately, not in the public eye; *to do something behind someone's back* to do it secretively, without his knowledge; *to be behind schedule/time* to be late; *to be behind the times* to be old-fashioned.

below

below average; *below par* (eg shares); *below the rank of captain/ director/minister etc*; *below freezing-point (ie temperature)*; *to marry below one's station* to marry someone who is of a lower social class; *to hit/strike below the belt* to fight unfairly.

beneath

beneath notice too unimportant to be worthy of notice; *beneath one's dignity*; *beneath contempt*.

beside

beside the chair etc at the side of; *beside the point/question/mark* irrelevant, having nothing to do with the subject under discussion; *to be be`side oneself (with grief, joy etc)* to be at the end of one's self-control because of grief, joy etc.

besides

besides all this in addition to all this; *three children besides John* as well as, in addition to John.

between

As an expression of time or place: *between 6 and 7 o'clock*; *between the two world wars*; *between sunrise and sunset*; *between London and Liverpool*.

war between two countries; *between you and me/between ourselves* in confidence; *between you, me and the gatepost* (informal) in strict confidence; *there's nothing to choose be`tween them* they are alike, there's no difference; *to divide something between persons* (when there are only two persons), *to divide something among persons* (when there are more than two persons); *to read between the lines* to understand the implied meaning.

beyond

As an expression of place or distance: *beyond the village*; *beyond the trees*; *beyond the limits*.

beyond belief incredible; *beyond description* not possible to describe; *beyond dispute* without reason for dispute; *beyond doubt* there is no doubt; *beyond expectation* more than one could expect; *beyond hope* there is no hope; *beyond measure* very much; *beyond question* nobody needs to question it: *His honesty is beyond question*; *beyond reach* out of reach; *beyond recall* too long ago to be remembered; *beyond repair* too badly damaged to be repaired; *beyond one's scope* not within one's capabilities or knowledge; *that's (going) beyond a joke!* that is too serious to joke at, it is beyond the limits of a reasonable joke; *it's be`yond me/you/him etc* it is more than I/you etc can understand.

by

As an expression of place: *by the bridge*; *by the side of the road.*

to go by the board (of plans, actions etc) to be abandoned, to fail; *to go by the book* to be guided by what is usual or accepted; *to pay by cheque*; *by chance* accidentally; *to play music by ear* without using written music; *to do something by fits and starts* spasmodically, not systematically; *by force*; *by force of circumstance(s)* compelled by one's circumstances; *by good fortune*; *to learn/know something by heart* to remember it perfectly; *to do something by hook or by crook* by any means at all (expressing determination); *to travel by land/sea/air etc*; *to do something by leaps and bounds* to make rapid progress; *by a `long chalk* by far; *not by a `long chalk* not nearly; *by the `look of it* as things appear, judging by the appearance of things; *related by marriage*; *by `all means* certainly (showing consent or agreement); *by `any means* in any way possible; *by `no means* not at all, certainly not; *to do something by mistake/accident*; *to know someone by name/by sight/by reputation*; *by nature* as made by nature: *Jim is by nature very lazy*; *by post/ phone/telegram*; *a lawyer etc by profession*; *to communicate by radio*; *to do something by the skin of one's teeth* to just manage to do it; *to do something by snatches* to do it only for short periods at one time; *to do something by stages* to do it systematically by gradual steps; *to be taken by surprise*; *a carpenter etc by trade*; *to do something by turns* by sharing the action among the people involved; *to sell something by weight* (by the pound, the yard etc); *it's 7 o'clock by my watch*; *a room twenty feet by fifteen*; *too long by two yards*; *greater by half*; *older by five years*; *to grab/catch etc someone by the arm/hand etc*; *to sit by oneself* alone; *to do something by oneself* to do it without help; *by itself* without apparent external cause: *The clock stopped by itself.*

down

to walk down the road/hill etc; *tears ran down her face*; *to be/look down in the mouth* to look miserable or depressed; *to throw money down the drain* (informal) to waste or throw away money; *to suit someone down to the ground* to suit him in every respect, completely; *down under* (informal) Australia and New Zealand: *visitors from down under*; *to get down to work/business* to start work seriously; *to come 'down in the world* to fall into a lower social class or position, eg through loss of money, a lower-paid job etc; *down the ages* through the ages from the past to recent times.

during

during the war; *during the holidays*; *during the space of a year*; *during the reign of Henry VIII*; *during their visit*.

except

all countries except England; *every day except Saturday*; *I've read all his books except two*.

for

for the asking if one asks for something: *It's yours for the asking*; *to turn out/happen for the best*; *to change for the better*; *to know (something) for certain/sure* to be certain about a fact; *to do something for a change* as an alternative; *to go (along) (with someone) for company* in order to be a friendly companion only; *to do something for a consideration* (formal) for a small reward, a little money; *for dear life* as if one's life depended on something: *he heard the shot and ran for dear life*; *to be taken/left for dead* believed to be dead; *for ever and a day* for a very long time. *to do something for fun/amusement/pleasure*; *for good* permanently; *For goodness sake!* (informal) (an exclamation of alarm or surprise); *for hire/sale*; *to jump/shout etc for joy*; *for keeps* (informal) permanently; *for life* for the whole of one's life; *to do something for love/money*; *to go for lunch*; *for no rhyme or reason* without a reason; *for nothing* 1 for no money 2 in vain; *for now* for the present time; *for this once* only for this one time; *for 'my/'your etc part* as far as I etc am concerned; *for the 'most part* mostly; *to buy/sell something for a song* very cheaply; *for a spell* for a short time; *for 'that matter* so far as that matter is concerned; *for 'one thing* for one reason; *to do something for two pins* (informal) to feel so annoyed or impatient as to act in a certain way: *For two pins I could have slapped him in the face!*; *for words* to describe: *too silly for words*; *(not) to do something for the world* on no account/on any account: *It's a secret that I wouldn't tell anyone for the world*; *for all one is worth* with the greatest possible effort: *he ran for all he was worth*; *to take someone for someone else* to wrongly recognise him: *I took you for your brother*; *to set out/leave for somewhere*; *to be blind/lame etc for life*; *to flee/run for one's life* as fast as one can to save one's life; *for all I etc know* as far as I etc know.

from

to judge from appearances to judge from the way someone/something looks; *to know something from A to Z* to know something very thoroughly; *to go from bad to worse*; *from a child* from the age of being a child; *from the cradle to the grave*; *to go from door to door*; *to know/tell from experience*; *from the first* from the beginning; *to separate the good from the bad*; *to live from hand to mouth*; *to release someone from a promise/vow*; *to do something from gratitude/fear/the kindness of one's heart*; *safe from danger*; *free from care*; *to rescue someone from death/the enemy etc*; *away from home*; *a long way from London*; *a young man from the country*; *to go from pillar to post* to be forced to go from one place to another.

in

in abeyance (of a plan, problem etc) awaiting decision; *in the abstract* put into theoretical terms; *in advance*; *in authority*; *in black and white* printed, in writing; *in bondage*; *ten feet in breadth*; *in one breath* without stopping for breath; (of plants) *in bud/flower/blossom*; *in bulk* in large quantities; *in `most cases* generally; *to keep something/someone in check* under control; *in class*; *in code*; *in colour*; *in one's true colours* as one really is; *to live in comfort/wealth/luxury/poverty/misery*; *to have something in common (with someone)* to share the same interests etc; *in conclusion*; *to tell something to someone in confidence* as a secret; *in due course* eventually, as time passes; *in danger*; *in a daze*; *in debt*; *in demand*; *in detail*; *in difficulties*; *in disgrace*; *in disguise*; *in distress*; (of ships) *in dock*; *in doubt*; *in `evening dress*; *in `fancy dress*; *in the end* finally; *to do something in good faith* to do it without intent to deceive; *in fashion*; *in fear*; *in flames* burning; *in a flash* very quickly; *in the flesh* alive, in physical form: *I saw the Prime Minister in the flesh last year*; (of birds) *in flight*; (of the enemy) *in flight* running away; (of a photograph) *in focus* clear, sharp; *in form* in good physical condition; *to run away in fright*; *to write/tell/explain/describe something in full* in detail; *to cut something in half*; *to sing in harmony*; *in haste*; *to speak in heat* angrily; *in hiding*; *to do something in someone's honour* to honour him; *to be in a good/bad humour* good/bad tempered; *in a hurry*; *to write in ink/pencil*; *in an instant* very soon; *to speak in jest* not seriously; *in a jiffy* (informal) very soon: *I'll be back in a jiffy*; *in the kitty* (informal) in joint financial reserve; *in labour* in the process of giving birth to a child; *to be in love (with someone)*; *to give one's daughter in marriage to someone*; *in some measure* partly; *in a minute* very soon; *in moderation*; *in a moment* very soon; *in motion*; *in mourning*; *to do something in someone's name* on someone's behalf, for someone; *in need*; *to answer in the negative* to say no; *in the news*; *in ˋno time* very quickly; *in a nutshell* concisely; *in office* in (the specified) position of authority; *to be in the offing* (informal) to be likely to happen: *there's a good job in the offing*; *in the open* either outside or publicly; *in ˋmy/ˋyour etc opinion*; *in order*; *in the original*; *in pain*; *in part* partially; *to take a joke in good part* without offence; *in pieces* broken; *in play* during play; *in position*; *in power*; *in practice* 1 actually. 2 having had sufficient practice; *in preparation*; *in principle* according to the principles; *in print*; *in prison*; *in private*; *in all probability* very likely; *in proportion*; *in someone's protection/care/charge*; *in public*; *in reality*; *in good/bad repair*; *in reserve*; *in ˋevery/ˋno respect*; *in ˋall/ˋsome respects*; (of the enemy) *in retreat*; *to give something (to someone) in return (for something)*; *in revolt*; *to speak in riddles* to express oneself in a strange or unclear manner; *to be in the right/wrong*; *in rough* in an unfinished form: *an essay written in rough*; *in ruins*; *in theˋlong run* ultimately: *studying costs a lot of money, but in the long run it's worth it*; *in a rush*; *in safety*; *in season*; *in a sense* partially; *in all seriousness* very seriously; (of clothing) *in shreds* badly torn; *in silence*; *in spirit* in one's thoughts, inwardly; *in step (with someone/something)* 1 at the same pace 2 conforming; *in stock*; *in store* expected: *trouble in store*; *to take something (all) in one's stride* to do something easily when the time comes; *in succession* one after another: *to read three books in succession*; *in suspense* expectantly; *to be in full swing* to be fully working, happening etc (eg a celebration, a discussion); *in good/bad taste*; *to get/be in a temper* annoyed; *in theory* according to the theory; *in the thick of something* in the middle of a happening; *a man etc in a thousand*; *in good time* early; *in transit* travelling through; *in trim* in good form or condition; *to do something in a trice* very quickly; *in triumph*; *to sing in tune* to sing the proper notes; *to do something in a twinkling* very quickly; *to sing in unison* together, not in parts; *in unison* in agreement, harmony; *in use*; *in vain* to no purpose, for nothing; *in vogue* in fashion; (of clothing) *to be in the wash* (informal) being washed; *in a way* partially; *to speak in a whisper*; *in a word* briefly; *to say something in so many words* to give a clear and unmistakable hint about something; *to go in at one ear and out of the other* (informal) to be heard but not understood: *I don't understand the professor's explanations —they go in at one ear and out of the other*.

into

Used to indicate motion or direction: *to go into a room; to fall into the river.*

Used to indicate a change, especially after *to turn, to change*: *to turn water into steam; to change from winter into spring; to translate Spanish into English.*

Used to indicate changing emotional states: *to burst into tears; to fly into a rage; to frighten someone into fits.*

to get into trouble/difficulties; to let someone into a secret; to force someone into submission/compliance etc; into the bargain in addition: *He lost all his money and his good name into the bargain.*

near

to sit near someone; to stand near the door; a shop near the church; to be near death.

of

Used to indicate the cause of something: *to die of hunger/starvation/exposure; to happen of itself* to happen without apparent external cause: *The fire must have broken out of itself.*

Used to indicate personal characteristics: *a man of courage/distinction/many talents etc; a man of influence; a man of means* wealthy.

Used meaning 'made of': *a table of solid wood; a crown of gold.*

Used to indicate the amount or measure of something: *a pound of apples; an acre of land; a box of matches; a book of stamps.*

Used meaning 'belonging to': *the capital of Spain; the city of London; a native of Tonga; the inhabitants of Rome.*

to do something of one's own accord freely; *of no account* not important; *to be of no avail* to be no help/use; *of consequence* important; *of no consequence* unimportant; *to be of help to someone; of interest* interesting; *to be of a kind* of a similar kind or type; *to be of a/one mind* to be in agreement; *of note* noteworthy, distinguished: *an author of note; of old* in the past: *in days of old* (i e a long time ago); *to be of the opinion that . . .; to be of a size* to be of similar size, almost the same size; *of a sort* of an inferior kind or quality: *I've just bought a car—well, a car of a sort!; to come of good/bad stock* to be of good/bad breeding, to come from a high-quality/defective family background; *to be of (some/little/great/no) value (to someone)*; *of the first water* (informal) of the best quality; *to do something of one's own free will*; *in days of yore* (formal, old use), in former times.

off

Used meaning 'some distance away from': *an island off the China coast*; *a building off the main road*; (of a ship) *to anchor off the coast*.

to do something off one's own bat (informal) using one's own initiative, without outside help; *to get something off one's chest* (informal) reveal something that has been troubling one; *to do something off the cuff* (informal) to do it without preparation or previous thought; *to catch someone off his guard* unprepared; *to fly off the handle* (informal) to become suddenly angry; *to get something off one's hands* to get it out of one's charge, to get rid of the responsibility for it; *to get off the mark* to start; *to be quick/slow off the mark* to make a fast or slow start, to be quick or slow to do something; *to buy one's clothes off the peg* ready-made; *to wander/get off the point* to talk about something which is irrelevant to the theme of discussion; *to be/go off the rails* (informal) to be/become unreasonable or mentally unbalanced; *off the reel* continuously, without pausing: *to quote Shakespeare off the reel*; *to put someone off the scent* to deliberately prevent someone from finding the right result, solution etc by giving wrong information etc; *to go/fly off at a tangent* to suddenly change one's ideas, thoughts or actions and go in another direction; *to go off the top* (informal) to become angry; *to speak off the top of one's head* to express an opinion without long thought; *to get off the track* (informal) to speak irrelevantly, to lose the relevant theme of discussion; *off the trail* off the right track eg when pursuing something or someone.

on

to take money on account as a part payment; *on no account* on no condition; *on someone's account* for him; *to act on someone's advice*; *on the alert* on the look-out, prepared; *to take goods on appro* (abbreviation for 'approval') (informal) to take them with the right to give them back to the shop if they do not satisfy; *to do something on someone's authority*; *on (an/the) average*; *on balance* considering everything; *to be on board (ship)*; *to be on someone's books* to be a regular customer; *to have something on the brain* to be continually enthusiastic about something, always talking or thinking about it; *to go on business* to go because of business; *to stand on ceremony* to be unrelaxed, too formal; *to buy/do something on the cheap* as

cheaply as possible; *on any/no condition* in/under any/no circumstances; on one condition, i e only if one thing happens/is done;
to have something on one's conscience to have feelings of guilt about
something; *on the contrary*; *to buy goods on credit*; (of a ship) *to be/
go on deck*; *to pay on demand*; *to be/go on a diet*; *on the dot* punctually; *what/how/when etc on earth ...!* (exclamation) what/how/
when ever ...! *to set someone's teeth on edge* to make someone
nervous by producing an unpleasant sound (eg a scraping or
scratching noise); *on end* continuously: *three days on end*; *on fire*
in flames; *to go on foot*; *to go on all fours* on hands and knees; *to
have something on hand* to have it nearby; *on hire*; *to promise something on one's honour*; *to go on horseback*; *on the hour* exactly on the
full hour, eg at three o'clock; *on the house* free (eg drinks and
refreshments); *to act on impulse* to act without thoughtful preparation; *on inquiry*; *on land*; (of property, land) *on lease*; *on the
level* (informal) honest; *on these/those lines* in this/that way; *on the
loose* (informal) in a casual, unsettled style of life; *on the move*
active, moving from place to place; *to pay on the nail* (informal)
promptly; *to get on one's nerves* to irritate one; *to do something on the `off-chance* although the chance is remote: *to call to
see someone on the `off-chance* (in case he is there); *on the `one
hand ... on the `other hand*; (of goods) *be on order* be ordered; *on
one's own* alone; *to have a lot/plenty/enough on one's plate* to have
a lot of duties, tasks, work, responsibility, worry etc; *to go on a
picnic*; *to do something on principle* because of one's moral attitude;
to put something on a proper footing to make it sound, organised,
reliable; *to do something on the q.t.* (informal) secretly; *on the radio*; *on
reflection* after thinking; *on the rocks* (informal) greatly disordered;
whisky etc on the rocks pure with ice; (of goods) *on sale*; *on a large/
small scale*; *to arrive/depart etc on schedule* punctually, as planned;
on second thoughts after reconsidering; *to do/have something on the
side* in addition, as an extra; *to do something on the sly* secretly; *to
do something on spec* (abbreviation for 'speculation') (informal)
without having planned or organised; *to go (out) on a spree* to seek
enjoyment (usually in town); *to go on a `spending/`buying spree* to
spend a lot of money, buy many things for enjoyment; *to do something on the spur of the moment* without hesitation, without considering; *to have something on the stocks* to have it in preparation
or definitely planned for the future (eg an order or commission
from someone); *to do something on the supposition that ...*; *on
television*; *to stand/walk on tiptoe*; *to buy/take goods on tick* (informal) on credit; *to have something on the tip of one's tongue* to
have a word, phrase etc on the point of being uttered; (of work,
circumstances etc) *get on top of one* prove to be too much, too
difficult etc for one, causing nervousness, aggravation etc; *to take*

something on trust to believe that it is so; *on the up* (informal) improving; (of a bird) *on the wing* in flight.

out of

Used to indicate a cause, reason or motive: *to do something out of pity/fear/kindness/gratitude/anger/revenge/curiosity.*

to come out of the blue unexpectedly, as a surprise; *out of breath*; *out of character* not typical; *to get out of someone's clutches* to escape from his power, influence; *to be/feel left out in the cold* to feel ignored socially by others; *out of condition* not fit; *out of crop* not being cultivated; *out of danger*; *out of date* old-fashioned; *out of debt* no longer in debt; *to be/feel out of one's depth* in a situation that one cannot cope with; *out of doors*; *to be/feel out of one's element* uncomfortable, in disagreeable, unfamiliar surroundings; *out of fashion* unfashionable; *out of favour* not specially liked; *out of focus* not sharp in outline (e g a photograph); *to jump/leap out of the frying-pan into the fire* from a bad situation into a worse one; (of a car) *out of gear*; *out of one's grasp* not available; *out of hand* not under control; *out of one's head* of one's own invention; *out of hearing* too far away to hear; *out of humour* bad-tempered; *out of a job* unemployed; (of a limb) *out of joint*; *out of luck* having no luck; *(from/since) time out of mind* (since) long ago; *out of one's mind* (informal) not reasonable, mad; *out of the mouths (of babes and sucklings)* young and innocent children may speak sense and wisdom; *out of office* no longer holding a position of authority; *out of order* not functioning properly; *out of the ordinary* unusual, different; *out of place* not suitable, not appropriate; *out of pocket* (informal) financially worse; *out of position* not in the right position; *out of practice* not having practised for a long time; *out of print* (of a book) not available; *out of proportion* exaggerated; *out of the question* not to be considered; *out of reach*; *out of all reason* completely unreasonable; *out of season*; *out of one's (right) senses* not reasonable, mad; *out of sight* too far away to see; *out of step (with someone/something)* 1 not at the same pace. 2 not conforming; *to be/feel/look out of sorts* unwell; *out of temper* in a bad temper; *out of town*; *out of trim* not in good physical condition; *to sing out of tune* not to sing the proper notes; *out of use* not used; *out of work* unemployed.

over

over age more than the required age; *to do something/go over someone's head* without previously asking for his permission or approval; *to show someone over a house/building etc*; *to travel over land* by train or car etc in contrast to plane or boat; *to stay over night/over the weekend*; *to talk over the phone*; *to look over one's shoulder*; *to have an advantage/power/influence/a hold over someone*; *to jump over a wall etc.*

past

past comprehension too difficult to understand or comprehend; *past control* not able to be controlled; *past cure* too ill to be cured; *past endurance* not able to be endured; *past hope* ie there is no hope; *past recall* too long ago to be remembered; *past recovery* too ill to recover; *past 6 o'clock*; *a woman past fifty*; *to be past caring* to have become too indifferent to care.

round

to be/go round the bend (informal) to be/become mad; *to work/sleep round the clock* for 24 hours; *to walk round the garden/town etc*; *to travel round the world*; *to get round someone* to persuade someone, win someone's favour or approval.

through

Used to express direction: *to walk through the town*; *to jump through the window.*

through the ages for many centuries; *to go through fire and water for someome* to do anything for him out of love, admiration etc in spite of all difficulties; *through life* during the whole of life; *to go through thick and thin* to go through all difficulties and hardships, great or small, as they arise.

to

Used to express direction or movement: *to drive to work*; *to go to the baker's*; *ten miles to London*; *to turn to the right*; *to go to bed/prison/church/school/university.*

to do something to advantage in the best way, to ensure the most favourable results; *to all appearances* seemingly; *to boot* in addition; (of cooking) *to be done to a cinder* to be burnt; *to bring something to a close* to end it; *to one's cost* involving a loss for one; *to a/the day/minute etc* exactly; *to this day* up to the present time; *to fight/a fight to the death*; *to no end* in vain, with no effect; *to do something to excess* too much; *to fall to the ground*; *to a great extent* mostly; *to some extent* partly; *to someone's face* directly: *She told him to his face that she didn't like him*; *to a fault* too much; *to the full* in every way, fully; *to hand* prepared, within reach; *to bring to heal* to make controlled; *to fight/argue etc to the last* until the end; *to the letter* in exact detail; *to one's liking/taste* liked by one: *The bright red colour of the curtains is not to my liking/taste*; *to a man* everyone; *to `my/your etc mind* in my etc opinion; *to the point* relevant; *to `no/`little purpose* with no/little result; *it stands to reason that . . .* it is reasonable that . . .; *to run to time* to take the expected length of time; (of cooking) *to be done to a turn* exactly right.

under

under age less than the required age; *under arms* equipped with weapons; *under arrest* arrested; *to say something under one's breath* very softly; *under the circumstances*; *to act under compulsion/force/pressure*; (of a plan etc) *under consideration*; *under control*; *under cover* in hiding; *under discussion*; *under duress* force being applied; *under fire* exposed to the enemy's gun fire; *under a handicap*; *under the impression that . . .*; *under the influence* (informal) drunk: *He was fined heavily for driving under the influence*; *under lock and key* safely locked away; *under the name of . . .* using this name; *to do something under someone's nose* immediately in front of someone; *to be under an obligation to do something/to do something under obligation*; *to act under orders*; *under someone's protection*; *under repair* in the state of being repaired; (of a ship) *under sail* moving; *under sentence/threat/fear of death etc*; *to work under someone* to be directed by him; *under a spell*; *to do something under one's own steam* to do it oneself, without help; *nothing under the sun* nothing anywhere; *under suspicion*; *under treatment (from the doctor)*; *under a vow* (eg of celibacy); *under water* flooded; *to be under way* begun, started; *to inherit money under someone's will*.

with

to do something with care, with difficulty, with pleasure; *to do something with (a) bad/good grace* to do it unwillingly/willingly; *to do something with a will* to do it eagerly, enthusiastically; *to walk with haste*; *to pass an examination with credit* to do well in it; *with effect from a certain date* to apply from that date onwards; *to do something with the intention/purpose/aim/hope of doing something*.

within

within call near enough to hear when called; *within easy distance (of somewhere)* not far away; *to keep within doors* not to go outside; *within hearing* near enough to hear; *to live within one's income/means* not to spend more than one's income; *within limits*; *within one's power*; *within range*; *within reach*; *within reason* reasonable; *within a week/an hour etc,*

without

without ceremony without formalities, roughly; *without delay*; *without (a) doubt*; *without end*; *without exception*; *without fail*; *to dismiss someone (from work) without notice*; *without recourse (to certain actions)* without having to perform certain actions; *without result*; *without rhyme or reason* without reason.

B Phrase prepositions *preposition + (a/the) + noun + preposition*

English has many phrases which are made up of *preposition + noun + preposition,* for example *to the satisfaction of, in response to.* While most of these do not cause difficulty and do not require explanation, others must be noted and distinguished carefully, as they are similar in form but different in meaning, for example *with respect to, in respect of; in the face of, on the face of.* List (i) gives commonly used phrase prepositions, most of which do not require explanation. List (ii) explains and exemplifies pairs that are similar in form but different in meaning.

(i) *Phrase prepositions*

in accordance with	in the event of
on account of	with the exception of
in addition to	in exchange for
in agreement with	at the expense of
in aid of	with an eye to (= with the
in answer to	intention of)
in anticipation of	by force of
on the basis of	in the form of
on behalf of	for the good of
for the benefit of	in the habit of
on the chance of	at the head of
in charge of	by/with the help of
in combination with	in honour of
in compliance with	in/with the hope of
in conflict with	with the intention of
in conjunction with	to the joy of
in connection with	for lack of
in consideration of	in lieu of (= instead of)
in contrast to/with	for (the) love of
in the course of	in the matter of
in the custody of	by means of
in defence of	in memory of
by dint of (= by means of)	in mistake for

in need of   in remembrance of
in obedience to   in response to
on the occasion of   in return for
in opposition to   on/to the right/left of
by order of   at the risk of
on the part of   for the sake of
at peace with   to the satisfaction of
in **peril of** (= in danger of)   in search of
in place of   by the side of
on/under the pretence of   in **sight of** (= able to see)
in proportion to   in spite of
for the purpose of   on the strength of
in pursuit of   (= relying upon)
at the rate of   in support of
by reason of   to the surprise of
in recognition of   in **token of** (= as a sign of)
with **recourse to** (= using)   by **virtue of** (= because of)
with/in reference to   in **the wake of** (= behind,
in relation to   following)

(ii) *Similar pairs of phrase prepositions, explained and exemplified*

in case of—in the case of

in case of when there is; in the event of. *In case of emergency, dial 999!*

in the case of considering; regarding. *The teacher said the essays were mostly very good, but in the case of Jane's and Tom's, there was still much room for improvement.*

in (the) face of—on the face of (it)

in (the) face of in the presence of. *He can't possibly win in the face of such difficulties. John was very brave in face of great danger.*

on the face of (it) from appearances; judging from the way things look. *On the face of the results, the examination was too difficult. On the face of it, he seems to be telling the truth.*

in favour of—in favour with

in favour of supporting; on the side of. *Over half the members voted in favour of the suggestion.*

in favour with having the approval of; liked by. *You can't expect to be in favour with Sue if you're always criticising her.*

for fear of—in fear of

for fear of because of being afraid of, out of anxiety about. *I never carry a large sum of money with me for fear of losing it.*

in fear of anxious for the safety of. *He ran in fear of his life when he heard the shots.*

by the name of—in the name of

by the name of named, with the name. *A man by the name of Johnson rang this morning.*

in the name of 1 in the cause of, for the love of. *In the course of history, many cruel deeds have been committed in the name of religion.* 2 on the authority of. *Stop in the name of the law!*

at the point of—on the point of

at the point of approaching (a state). *The old man is at the point of death.*

on the point of on the verge of (*doing* something). *I was on the point of going to bed when the telephone rang.*

in possession of—in the possession of

in possession of having in one's possession. *I'm not in possession of all the details, so I can't give my valid opinion of the matter.*

in the possession of possessed by, belonging to. *The documents have been in the possession of the British Museum for fifty years.*

in/with regard to—out of regard for

in/with regard to regarding, concerning. *With regard to the safety of the operation, I have the following measures to propose.*

out of regard for because of respect for, out of consideration for. *Out of regard for your work, I'm recommending you for promotion.*

in respect of—with respect to

in respect of with regard to, as regards, as far as something is concerned. *In respect of social improvement the Government's policy is sound, but it disregards the grave need for economic improvement.*

with respect to with reference to. *With respect to your request for a salary rise, a final decision will be taken by the management next week.*

at the sight of—in the sight of

at the sight of when seeing. *She burst out laughing at the sight of his new hair-cut.*

in the sight of from the point of view of. *From a moral point of view, his conduct is understandable and even excusable, but in the sight of the law he is guilty of slander.*

at the time of—in time of

at the time of at the particular point of time of. *I was in India at the time of my mother's death.*

in time of at a general time of, during. *In time of need one is thankful for small comforts.*

in view of—with a view to

in view of considering. *In view of his recent successes, Jones has been asked to stand for the next election.*

with a view to with the intention or purpose of. *He's bought the old house with a view to renovating it and selling it at a profit.*

for/from want of—in want of

for/from want of because of the lack of. *Many crops and trees have already died from want of rain.*

in want of in need of, needing. *I'm badly in want of a pair of new shoes, but I've no time at the moment to go out and buy them!*

C   Particular difficulties with certain prepositions

in—into

(In modern usage the difference between *in* and *into* is becoming less clear, as *in* is often used where *into* was used in the past.)

1 *Into* is used where motion or direction is expressed: *The cat ran into the kitchen. I looked into his bedroom but John wasn't there. Bill's gone into the garden. Into* is often used after the verb *to go.*

2 *Into* also expresses a change of condition: *He translated the sentence into Spanish. If you let the milk stand, it will turn into curds. I wish I could change water into wine. He sorted the sticks into bundles.*

3 *In* expresses the place where something is or can be found: *The cat is in the kitchen. John isn't in his bedroom.*

4 *Into* cannot be used to express place, position or state if there is no movement involved.

5 Some phrases are fixed and should be learnt by heart (see Chapter 8):

to fall in love	**to bring/put into force**
to put in touch	**to burst into tears/laughter**
to set in motion	**to fall into decay/disuse/dispute**
to take in hand	**to take into consideration**

in—within

> *In* and *within* as *expressions of time* are often confused. *In an hour* means 'after an hour': *Mr Wilson will be back in an hour*. To express 'during the course of an hour', ie before the hour has passed, the preposition *within* must be used: *Mr Wilson will be back within an hour*.

at the same time—in the same time

> *We reached London at the same time*, ie at the same hour of the day.
> *We reached London in the same time*, ie each person taking the same amount of time to reach London.

in time—on time

> *In time* means 'early enough to do something': *Am I in time for tea? I was in time to wave John goodbye at the station.*
> *On time* means 'punctually': *The London train always leaves on time. Jane is hardly ever on time when she arranges to meet someone.*

Adverbial Phrases

Idiomatic phrases formed from two adverbs

> The phrases in this group are composed of two adverbs. It is important to note that the order of the two adverbs is fixed by usage and cannot be changed.

again and again repeatedly.
back and forth ⎫ from A to B, then back to A again
backwards and forwards ⎭ (once or many times).
by and by (old-fashioned) after a while; later. *By and by, the son began to realise the wisdom of his father's advice.*
by the by (informal) 'by the way'; (it always stands at the beginning of a sentence to introduce a new theme casually). *By the by, did Mary tell you about her latest adventure?*
by and large 'on the whole'; considering all things. *By and large, the results are quite encouraging.*
down and down far down. *Down and down to the bottom of the ocean.*
far and near ⎫ everywhere.
far and wide ⎭
first and foremost firstly; in the first place. *First and foremost, we have to consider the morality of the enterprise.*

here and there in various places. *There were wild daffodils growing here and there all over the field.*

here, there and everywhere everywhere; in all possible places. *Where have you been? I've been looking for you here, there and everywhere all morning!*

neither here nor there unimportant; irrelevant. *Your essay is very good. There's one slight inaccuracy, but don't worry about it, it's neither here nor there.*

in and out coming and going continually. *There's no hope for Jim. He's been in and out of prison for ten years solid now.*

more or less approximately; almost. *He more or less told me that I had got the job.*

now and again/then occasionally; sometimes. *Now and then the thought crosses my mind that I should go and live alone on an island.*

off and on ⎱ (informal) irregularly. *It's been raining on and off all*
on and off ⎰   *morning.*

on and on without stopping; continually. *Mary's inclined to chatter on and on for hours and hours.*

once or twice a few times; occasionally. *He's only been here once or twice.*

once and for all finally; for the last time. *I'm telling you once and for all that I don't want to marry you!*

out and out completely; thoroughly; (more often used as an adjective. *The first performance of the play last night was an out and out disaster—everything went wrong.*

over and over (again) (informal) repeatedly; very often. *I've told you over and over that . . .*

round and round (with a verb of movement) repeatedly or continually round. *to spin/run/fly round and round.*

through and through (informal) entirely, completely; (used at the end of the clause). *I was caught in the rain and now I'm wet through and through. I'm a democrat through and through.*

to and fro from A to B, then back to A again, many times.

up and about on one's feet again and able to walk about after an illness.

up and down 1 (of repeated motion along, or upward-downward) *Up and down the street. Up and down the stairs.* 2 in varying mood, health etc. *I've been up and down a lot lately—I think I need a holiday.*

(on the) up and up (informal) improving; succeeding. *My health's been on the up and up ever since I moved to live in the country.*

7 Adjectives with prepositions

general note

Prepositions are a constant cause of difficulty to the learner, because there are no rules to govern their usage. They are especially difficult after adjectives and participles, as there is no way of knowing which preposition follows unless the student has met the phrase before and has remembered it. Here, we give a list of adjectives and participles with the appropriate prepositions. Each adjective phrase is followed by an example which will help the learner to fix the correct preposition in his mind. It is stressed that the only profitable method of learning the appropriate prepositions is constant practice and use of them in context. This chapter also provides a useful list for quick reference.

abhorrent to *Slavery is abhorrent to a humane man.*

abounding in/with *English is a language abounding with idiomatic expressions.*

abreast of *It is important to keep abreast of the progress of technology.*

absorbed in *She was absorbed in an exciting novel.*

acceptable to *Is this arrangement acceptable to you?*

accessory to (legal) *This man was accessory to the crime.*

accompanied by *Lady Armstrong was accompanied by her son.*

according to *The house was built according to the owner's plan.*

accountable to someone for something *It is not pleasant to be accountable to one's boss for everything one says and does.*

accruing to (formal) *The profits accruing to him from the business will be greatly reduced this year.*

accurate in *John is never accurate in his calculations!*

accused of something by someone *He was accused of theft by his own brother!*

accustomed to *Mary is accustomed to making long journeys abroad alone.*

acquainted with *We are not well acquainted with our neighbours yet. Are you acquainted with the works of Thornton Wilder?*

acquitted of *He was acquitted of murder after a trial lasting four months.*

adapted for/to *The book has been adapted to the needs of foreign students. The book has been well adapted for its present purpose.*

addicted to *Never become addicted to alcohol!*

adequate to *The supply of material is not adequate to the needs of the industry.*

adjacent to *The two houses stand adjacent to each other.*

adorned with *The drawing-room was adorned with old masterpieces.*

affixed to *The syllable -en affixed to an adjective often forms a verb : eg broad, to broaden.*

afflicted by/with *He was greatly afflicted by the sad news. George has been afflicted with rheumatism for as long as I can remember.*

afraid of *Peter is not afraid of ghosts.*

aghast at *We were aghast at the terrible sight.*

agreeable to *Bill is always agreeable to our plans.*

akin to *His uncle treats him in a manner akin to hostility.*

alarmed at/by *We were alarmed at the sight of the accident. The country was alarmed by rumours of war.*

alive to *He is not yet alive to the danger he is in.*

allotted to *He enjoys the task allotted to him.*

ambitious for *Jack is very ambitious for his children.*

amenable to *Joan won't mind—she's always amenable to our suggestions.*

angry at something *The teacher was angry at the pupil's conduct.*

angry with someone *The teacher was angry with the pupils for talking in class.*

animated by *He was animated by the beauty of the countryside.*

annoyed at something *I was annoyed at my mistake.*

annoyed with someone *He was annoyed with you for being impertinent.*

anxious about *John is anxious about his exam results.*

anxious for *Most fathers are anxious for their children's advancement.*

apart from *He sat apart from the other men.*

applicable to *Your criticisms are not applicable to the subject.*

apprehensive of *He is very apprehensive of the future.*

appropriate to *He gave a speech appropriate to the occasion.*

ashamed of *He looked quite ashamed of his shabby appearance.*

associated with *I do not wish to have my name associated with his!*

astonished at *I was quite astonished at his quick reaction.*

attentive to *Now please be attentive to what I have to say.*

averse from/to *He's averse to all manner of work.*

awake to *Bill is not awake to his opportunities.*

aware of *I was not aware of your intention.*

away from *Don't stay away from home too long.*

bare of *Some parts of the country are almost bare of vegetation.*

based (up)on *The play is based upon a novel by Graham Greene.*

belonging to *He stole a horse belonging to the farmer.*

beloved of/by *He was greatly beloved of his fellow countrymen.*

bent on *The two boys were bent on mischief.*

beneficial to (formal) *Regular exercise is beneficial to health.*

bereaved of (formal) *During the war she was bereaved of her husband and all her children.*

bereft of (formal) *He is a lonely man, bereft of all comforts.*

beset with *It's an undertaking beset with difficulties.*

blended with *The colour is green, blended with grey.*

blessed with *My grandfather has been blessed with good health all his life.*

blind in *Jim has gone blind in his right eye.*

blind to *Most of us are blind to our own faults.*

boastful about/of *Jack has always been boastful of his own accomplishments.*

born of *Mary was born of intelligent parents.*

born in (a condition) *A child born in poverty will always be disadvantaged.*

bound for *The ship is bound for the Far East.*

burdened with *He is burdened with a bed-ridden wife.*

busy at/with *They're all busy at work. John is busy with his boat.*

capable of *Jack is capable of violence when he's angry.*

careful of *It is wise to be careful of one's health.*

careless about/of *Sally is careless about the risks she runs in her business. Jack has taken on too much responsibility, but he is quite careless of the consequences.*

cautious of *Be cautious of giving offence.*

celebrated for *Racine is celebrated for his contribution to the drama.*

certain of *He felt quite certain of success.*

characteristic of *It is characteristic of Molly to want to have the last word!*

clear of *He is now clear of all business difficulties.*

close to *His house is close to mine.*

clothed in *The widow was clothed in black.*

clumsy at *She's rather clumsy at needlework.*

cognisant of (formal) *For a time he was not cognisant of my presence.*

commensurate with (formal) *You will receive a salary commensurate with your abilities.*

common to *Love of freedom is common to man and beast.*

comparable to/with *From the point of view of health, the town* is not comparable with the country. The caste system in Hindu society is in some ways comparable to the class system of European society.

compatible with It would not be compatible with the public interest to reduce the strength of the police force.

complained of The goods complained of were immediately exchanged by the manager.

composed of Water is composed of oxygen and hydrogen.

concerned about We are very concerned about our father's illness.

concerned for He is greatly concerned for the safety of his family.

concerned in These two men were also concerned in the affair.

conducive to (formal) Long walks in the fresh air are conducive to good health.

confident of Tom is confident of good exam results.

congenial to His new surroundings proved congenial to his composing music.

conscious of He was conscious of being watched.

consecrated to We visited a monument consecrated to the memory of the dead.

consistent with His conduct in the affair was not consistent with his usual politeness and gentleness.

conspicuous for General Peel was conspicuous for his bravery.

content with Are you content with the quality of the teaching?

contiguous to (formal) Iran is contiguous to Afghanistan.

contrary to This has turned out contrary to my expectations. His opinions are always contrary to mine.

convenient to/for It's not convenient to me to receive visitors tomorrow. The bus-stop on the corner is very convenient for us.

conversant with (formal) He is conversant with all the modern authors. Geology is a science I'm not conversant with.

convulsed with Jack was convulsed with laughter when I told him what you'd said.

corresponding to Your exam results are not corresponding to your true abilities.

covered with Next morning the ground was covered with snow.

covetous of (formal) You should not be covetous of other people's possessions.

cross with (informal) You know I always get cross with you when you criticise my family.

crowned with His efforts have been crowned with success.

crushed by superior force.

crushed to death, pulp.

crushed with grief.

cured of John has been cured of his bad habits.

deaf to Susan is deaf to advice, to reason, and to all entreaty.

deficient in *This diet cannot be recommended as it is deficient in vitamins.*

delighted with *Uncle Jim was delighted with his Christmas present.*

dependent on *I am not dependent on my parents for money.*

deprived of *The prisoner was deprived of the right to defend himself.*

derogatory to (formal) *It is derogatory to my reputation to call me a tyrant.*

descriptive of *The book was accurately descriptive of life in village communities.*

deserted by *Jim was more or less deserted by his friends after the war.*

deserving of *praise, merit,*

desirous of (formal) *He is desirous of obtaining a position in the management.*

destitute of (formal) *He found himself destitute of all means of subsistence.*

detrimental to (formal) *His criticism could prove detrimental to your success.*

devoid of *He is a man devoid of all fine feeling.*

different from *His views are not very different from my own.*

diligent in (formal) *He has always been very diligent in business.*

disagreeable to *The news of your failure was disagreeable to him.*

disappointed with *James was disappointed with his exam results.*

disappointed in *We were disappointed in our expectations.*

disgusted with *We became disgusted with the bribery and corruption.*

disgusted at *We were disgusted at the sight of the dirty, disorderly rooms.*

displeased with *Bob's boss is becoming more and more displeased with his laziness.*

displeasing to *His vulgar manner was most displeasing to us.*

distasteful to *Travelling in public has become distasteful to the old man.*

distinct from *The two sorts of whisky are clearly distinct from one another.*

due to *What would you say inflation is mainly due to?*

dull of *hearing, comprehension.*

eager for *fame, praise.*

eligible for *Are you eligible for free medical treatment?*

endowed with *Jane is endowed with many talents.*

enraged at/by something *The teacher was enraged at the boy's impudence.*

enraged with someone *The teacher became so enraged with the boy that he beat him.*

envious of *John is envious of Tom's success.*

equal to *This angle is equal to that. Are you equal to the occasion/task?*

essential to *Hard work and perseverance are essential to success.*

exclusive of *The book costs two pounds, exclusive of postage.*

exempt from *Old age pensioners should be exempt from taxation.*

exhausted with *Bill's health is bad—he's exhausted with hard work and worry.*

expert at something *Bill is expert at accounts.*

expert in doing something *Tom is expert in writing up reports.*

exposed to *danger, wind, ridicule.*

expressive of *His look was expressive of gratitude.*

faithful to *Jim is always faithful to his promise.*

false to *He has proved false to his professed principles.*

familiar to *The name is familiar to me.*

familiar with *I'm not familiar with the works of Thorton Wilder.*

famous for *Thailand is famous for its handwoven silk.*

fatal to *The wound proved fatal to him. The battle was fatal to the outcome of the war.*

favourable to *He is favourable to our plan.*

fearful of *He is fearful of the consequences of his rash behaviour.*

fit for *His old car is really not fit for sale. I'm so tired I feel fit for a month in a convalescent home.*

foiled in *The enemy were foiled in their attempt to destroy the harbour.*

fond of *Most children are fond of sweets.*

forgetful of *Mary is sometimes forgetful of her promises.*

fraught with *The enterprise was fraught with danger/difficulty/complexity.*

free from *Jack is happy now that he's free from debt.*

friendly with someone *James and Peter have been friendly with each other for years.*

friendly to something *Bill is friendly to our cause but won't support it actively.*

full of *Life is full of surprises. The vase is full of flowers. My glass is full of wine.*

gifted with *Mary is gifted with great musical talent.*

given to doing something *Dick is much given to exaggerating his adventures.*

glad of *I'm glad of the opportunity to repay you for your kindness.*

good at *Tom is good at languages.*

good for *All those trousers are good for now is gardening in. That medicine is good for coughs.*

grateful to *I'm most grateful to you for looking after the children.*

grown over with *Our garden is grown over with weeds.*

guilty of *He was found guilty of manslaughter.*

hard of *hearing.*

heedless of *He continued with his plans, heedless of the consequences.*

hidden by *The house is hidden by the trees.*

hidden from *The house is hidden from view by the trees.*

hopeful of *He's still hopeful of success, although he's had many disappointments.*

hostile to *He is hostile to my plans.*

hurtful to *If this news becomes public, it could be hurtful to your good name.*

ignorant of *I was completely ignorant of his intentions.*

ill with *Jack is ill with flu at the moment.*

illustrative of *This case is illustrative of the way he conducts all his affairs.*

imbued with *The manager is imbued with a sense of his own importance.*

impatient at *We were impatient at the unexpected delay.*

impatient for *I was impatient for the arrival of my friend.*

impatient with *The teacher is often impatient with the children.*

important to *This document is important to our case for the defence.*

impressed on *His final words are strongly impressed on my memory.*

incapable of *He is incapable of committing such a crime.*

incident to (formal) *Bear in mind the risks incident to the profession of a racing driver!*

inclusive of *The sum covers the cost inclusive of postage.*

inconsistent with *Your story is inconsistent with the policeman's report.*

incumbent (up)on someone (to do something) (formal) *It is incumbent on all citizens to obey the law.*

indebted to someone for something *I am greatly indebted to you for your help.*

independent of *It is very pleasant to be independent of public transport in winter.*

indifferent to/towards *He seems to be totally indifferent to my advice.*

indignant at something *He was indignant at my suggestion.*

indignant with someone *He was indignant with me for making the suggestion.*

indispensable to *My secretary is indispensable to me.*

inferior to *This material is inferior in quality to that.*

infested with *The cellar is infested with rats!*

informed of *Please keep me informed of your movements.*

inhabited by *This part of the country is inhabited by only very few people.*

injurious to (formal) *Large quantities of alcohol are injurious to health.*

innocent of *He is innocent of the crime.*

intent on (doing something) *He was so intent on his book that he* *didn't hear me come in. Keith has become intent on writing a novel.*

interested in *Jim is very interested in antiques.*

intimate with (formal) *Are you intimate with the Forsythes?*

inundated with *The department has been inundated with applications for the new post.*

inured to *These men are well inured to hardships.*

involved in something *How did you come to be involved in this lawsuit?*

involved with someone *Who else was involved with you in the crime?*

irrespective of *John does just as he pleases, quite irrespective of my wishes.*

irritated by something *He was irritated by the unexpected change of plan.*

irritated with someone *I was irritated with him for taking such a long time over the job.*

jealous of *Jim was jealous of Peter's success.*

kind to *I tried to be kind to them, but got only hostility in return.*

lame in *a leg.*

lavish of something *He is never lavish of praise.*

lavish in doing something *We've decided to be lavish in decorating our house.*

level with *the ground, floor, shelf, roof etc.*

liable for *I am not liable for my son's debts.*

liable to something *He is liable to imprisonment for a month.*

lost to *He is lost to all sense of shame.*

loyal to *He has remained loyal to his principles.*

mad with *rage, disappointment, desire etc.*

made from *coal etc* (ie coal is the basic substance from which the end product was produced). *Most people don't realise that toilet soap is made from coal and its by-products.*

made of *wood etc* (ie the end product is wood). *This table is made of good, solid oak.*

married to *an English girl, my brother, an Indian etc.*

mindful of *Always be mindful of your promises!*

moist with *The air was still moist with the morning dew.*

moved by *an entreaty, her tears, the incident etc.*

moved to *tears, action, anger etc.*

moved with *pity, sympathy, sorrow etc.*

natural to someone *Crying for attention is natural to babies.*

neglectful of *duty, one's promise, one's family etc.*

negligent in *work, speech, writing etc.*

notorious for *He is notorious for coming late!*

obedient to *A well-trained dog is always obedient to its master.*

obnoxious to *The sight of purposeful cruelty is obnoxious to me.*

observant of (formal) *He's always careful to be observant of the rules.*
occupied with something *He is occupied with the latest report at the moment.*
occupied in doing something *Yesterday he was occupied in translating last week's report.*
odious to *The sight of those ugly men is odious to me.*
opposite to *Whose house is opposite to yours? What you're doing is quite opposite to what I suggested.*
overcome by someone *The soldiers were finally overcome by the enemy.*
overcome with something *He was overcome with fatigue.*
overrun with *The garden is overrun with weeds.*
overwhelmed by someone *He was overwhelmed by two thieves.*
overwhelmed with something *She was overwhelmed with grief at the sad news.*
painful to *The news was very painful to me.*
pale with *fear, hunger, anger, weakness etc.*
parallel to *This line is parallel to the other.*
partial to *Jack has always been partial to a good wine.*
peculiar to *This style of architecture is peculiar to the Moors.*
pernicious to *The competitive ethic is pernicious to one's moral development.*
pertinent to *These remarks are not pertinent to the subject.*
pleasant to *Soft rhythmic music is pleasant to the ear.*
popular with *Astrology has become popular with teenagers lately.*
possessed by *guilt, ambition, an idea etc.*
possessed of (formal) *He is possessed of great wealth.*
praised for *Alexander Pope is praised for the subtlety of his wit.*
precious to *These memories are precious to me.*
preferable to *A week's holiday is preferable to a week's work!*
prefixed to *The syllable 'un-' prefixed to a word often reverses the meaning of that word.*
prejudicial to *Their decision may turn out to be prejudicial to our interests.*
preparatory to (formal) *He attended night-school preparatory to entering college.*
previous to (formal) *He left previous to your arrival.*
prior to (formal) *This happened prior to my receiving your letter.*
productive of (formal) *Is self-denial productive of happiness?*
proficient in (formal) *A good secretary must be proficient in shorthand and book-keeping.*
profitable to *The new partnership should be profitable to business.*
prompt in *Peter is always prompt in paying bills.*
prone to *I'm prone to falling asleep after a big meal in the middle of the day.*

proper to (formal) *Are those the books proper to the course of study?*
proportionate to *Rewards should be proportionate to merit.*
proud of *Paul is proud of his accomplishments.*
quick at *arithmetic/understanding arithmetic.*
radiant with *The two young men looked radiant with happiness.*
ready for *action, duty.*
reduced by/from/to *His salary has been reduced by £1000, from £5000 to £4000.*
regardless of *Tom is strong-willed and regardless of the consequences of his actions.*
regretted by *Your departure will be regretted by us all.*
relative to *Relative to wages in the United States, my salary is miserably small.*
relevant to *One's state of mind is very relevant to one's state of health.*
remarkable for *This boy is remarkable for his skill at chess.*
renowned for *He was renowned for his knowledge of Greek philosophy.*
replete with *His speech was replete with humour and amusing quotations.*
reposed in (formal) *He betrayed the confidence reposed in him.*
repugnant to *The idea of marrying Tom is repugnant to Jane.*
responsible for something to someone *I am not responsible to my wife for everything I say and do!*
rid of *I am glad to be rid of the responsibility.*
sacred to *This temple is sacred to the Greek goddess Artemis.*
satisfied with *We are quite satisfied with the results of the survey so far.*
secure against something (eg *attack, burglary, insult, harm*).
secure from someone *Put the medicine in a place secure from the children.*
seized with *The man was seized with panic at the sight of the gun.*
sensible of (formal) *He is sensible of his privileged position.*
short of *money, time, food etc; a destination, a target, an objective etc.*
short on (informal) *patience, sympathy, humour, moral sensitivity etc.*
sick of (informal) *I'm sick of waiting in the rain.*
significant of (formal) *The company one keeps is usually significant of the sort of person one is.*
similar to *I'm very similar in character to my brother.*
skilful in *Jack is skilful in arguing and debating.*
sorry for *I feel sorry for Jim's wife and children.*
startled at *She was startled at the sudden crash in the room next door.*

starved to *death.*

starved with *hunger.*

strange to *The customs of the English are very strange to me.*

struck with *fear, alarm etc; the appearance of something.*

studded with *The belt was studded with jewels.*

subject to *The plan is subject to approval from the management.*

subsequent to (formal) *This event occurred subsequent to the king's death.*

successful in *The millionaire had been successful in all his business dealings.*

sufficient for *This money should be sufficient for the purpose.*

suitable for doing something *Is the material suitable for wearing in the tropics?*

suitable for/to *Her dress was not suitable to the occasion.*

suited for/to *He is not suited to the post. John is not suited for office work.*

superior to *James's new job is superior to Paul's. Mary is superior to flattery.*

sure of *He felt sure of being elected to Parliament.*

surprised at *We were very surprised at the news of Jane's engagement.*

surrounded by *He is surrounded by faithful supporters.*

susceptible of (ie *capable of*) (formal) *He is susceptible of deep feeling.*

susceptible to (ie *sensitive to*) *He is susceptible to pain.*

suspicious of *Men in high positions are often suspicious of one another.*

sympathetic towards/to *He was very sympathetic to the old lady when she told him her troubles.*

thankful to *I am very thankful to you for telling me what really happened.*

tired of *I'm so tired of your constant grumbling.*

tired to *death.*

troublesome to *The foxes are troublesome to the farmers.*

true to *Always be true to yourself when dealing with others.*

uncared for *Children who are left uncared for will become troublesome when they grow older.*

unfit for *This meat is unfit for human consumption.*

unheard of *Explorers in South America have discovered tribes which were unheard of before now.*

unknown to *The language of the Etruscans is unknown to modern man.*

useful to *This little book will prove very useful to you.*

versed in *Jack is well versed in the working of a motor-car engine.*

vexed with *I'm vexed with her for ringing me up when I was asleep.*

void of *Sometimes he seems to be void of all feeling.*

weary of *The old man was weary of wandering and his donkey was weary of its burden.*

worthy of *Her courage is worthy of the highest praise.*

zealous for *In past centuries most young soldiers were zealous for fame and honour.*

8   Verbs with prepositions and adverbial particles

general note

    A particular difficulty experienced by learners is the handling of expressions consisting of verbs in combination with prepositions or adverbial particles, e g *take off, sit in on, leave out*. Many learners with a good command of other aspects of English prefer to avoid these constructions if possible. But this is not the answer, as such verb combinations are a typical and frequent occurrence in all types of English, but most especially in every-day spoken English.

    Sometimes, the combination of verb + preposition or particle results in a separate unit of meaning, which may be highly idiomatic, i e the total meaning of the combination may bear little or no relationship to the meaning of the individual words of the combination. This can be illustrated. The verb *pack something in* presents no difficulty in the sentence:

She opened her suitcase and packed all the clothes in.

However, in the sentence:

He decided to pack his job in.

the individual meanings of *pack* and *in* do not at all convey the meaning 'abandon, renounce'.

    Here is another example. *Take someone off* may mean 'take away to another place' as in the sentence:

As soon as John arrived, Harry insisted on taking him off.

Conversely, it may mean something quite different which cannot be guessed from the individual meanings of *take* and *off*. It may also mean 'imitate humorously'.

Verb combinations with prepositions and particles are not necessarily idiomatic; of the idiomatic ones, some are more idiomatic than others. It is these 'more idiomatic' combinations which are presented in this chapter.

Any one combination may have several idiomatic meanings, depending on the words which precede and follow it, ie its 'collocations'. *Take off* provides a good example of this. Here are some of its possible collocations and meanings:

1 *The aircraft/plane/helicopter/pilot/passenger took off*,
  ie left the ground.
2 *The thief/boy/dog* (persons or animals) *took off*,
  ie ran away, moved off in a hurry.
3 *The sales/product/article/economy took off*,
  ie began to make definite improvement or profit.

The collocations of *take something off* are also numerous and provide several different meanings. Here are some of them:

1 *take weight/pounds/inches/surplus fat off*,
  ie get rid of, lose.
2 *take a bus/train/flight off*,
  ie withdraw from service.
3 *take tax/surcharge/duty/a sum of money off*,
  ie remove.

However, perhaps the main source of difficulty is not so much knowing the meanings of the combinations, but knowing how the combinations are used correctly in sentences. One important point should be mentioned here.

Possibilities of word order in the combinations may give trouble. This is a matter of determining whether the verb is followed by a preposition or a particle. This is, in many cases, a decision which is difficult to make. Consider the following sentences:

A 1 *I read the letter through.*
  2 *I read through the letter.*
B 1 *I saw the plan through.*
  2 *I saw through the plan.*

The differences in meaning and use may not be immediately apparent to the learner. In set A, *through* is a particle in both sentences, although it looks confusingly like a preposition in A2. Because it is a particle in both, there is no difference in meaning. In set B, *through* is a particle in 1 and a preposition in 2. There is a difference of meaning in the two sentences. B1 means: 'I persevered until the plan was satisfactorily completed', and B2 means: 'I recognised the deception of the plan'. It therefore becomes clear that differences between the constructions can be quite important.

In order to solve these difficulties for the student, and to make the question of word order simple, the combinations treated in this chapter indicate exactly where the Direct Object and particle or preposition stand. This is indicated by using *someone* or *something* to stand for the object in its proper place, e g *see something through, see through something.*

This chapter is based on the scheme of verb patterns presented by A. P. Cowie and R. Mackin in their *Oxford Dictionary of Current Idiomatic English*, Volume One. Six basic verb patterns are presented, three for transitive verbs (i e with a direct object) and three for intransitive verbs (i e without a direct object). The three patterns for each set are:

Verb + Particle
Verb + Preposition
Verb + Particle + Preposition

This gives six patterns:

1 Intransitive + Particle
  e g *slow down; get on; take off*
2 Intransitive + Preposition
  e g *go off someone/something*
     run through something
3 Intransitive + Particle + Preposition
  e g *come up against someone/something*
     put up with someone/something
4 Transitive + Particle
  e g *pack something in; pack in something*
     take someone off; take off someone
5 Transitive + Preposition
  e g *put someone off something*
     get someone through something
6 Transitive + Particle + Preposition
  e g *put someone up to something*
     take someone up on something

Pattern 4, *pack something in*, should receive extra attention. In this pattern, it is possible to say

He decided to pack his job in.
He decided to pack in his job.

The Object can either precede the particle or follow it without a change in meaning. However, when the Object is a pronoun, (*me, you, him, her, it, us, them*), it can only precede the particle, as in:

He decided to pack it in.

Here are more examples:

I rang up my brother/I rang him up.
He cleaned the room out/He cleaned it out.
He brought the children up/He brought them up.

The use of *someone* and *something* in the entries does not only indicate where the Direct Object stands; it also indicates differences of meaning within the constructions. The meaning of the verb may be different, according to whether the object is a *person* or a *thing*. If this is so, separate entries are made, as for example, *work on someone* and *work on something*. If there is no difference in meaning, the entry indicates this by the use of the slant /, as in *walk out on someone/something*, and *shake someone/something off*.

A few verbs of the pattern *Transitive + Particle* do not allow the Object to precede the particle without changing the meaning. For example, *take in someone* and *take someone in*:

Mrs Robinson takes in students/lodgers/paying-guests.

means 'she provides accommodation for payment'. On the other hand, *take someone in* means 'deceive, cheat someone'. In order to avoid confusion on the part of the learner, the few expressions of this sort are entered separately, clearly showing the position of the object. The rule for Objects that are pronouns still applies, of course. The learner should therefore note the following example carefully:

Mrs Robinson takes in students.
She takes them in.

The examples given with the entries serve a two-fold purpose. They indicate typical collocations of the verb, ie nouns which typically precede and follow the verb, eg in *answer for something*: 'If you drive that car without a licence, you'll have to *answer for the consequences.*' Secondly, the examples indicate how the verb is typically used. Often an example in the Passive form is given. This indicates that the verb is commonly used in the Passive:

I've been laid up with rheumatism for a week.
His opinion is looked down on by his fellow students.
There are no problems that cannot be ironed out.

Sometimes, the example gives a nominalised form, i e a noun which is formed from the verb + particle/preposition, e g *a breakthrough a let-down, a slip-up, a write-off*. There is a tendency for present-day British English to absorb such new noun forms from American English. However, several of these are slang, e g *a rip-off*, meaning 'a robbery, a cheat', and for this reason must only be used very carefully by the learner. The noun forms which are included in the examples of this chapter are informal or neutral in style; they can, therefore, with care become part of the learner's active vocabulary. The more common nominalisations have been given in the examples. They are listed here for easy reference:

blow-up	**hold-up**
break-down	**let-down**
break-in	**let-out**
break-out/outbreak	**lie-in**
breakthrough	**looking-over**
break-up	**put-down**
brushing-down	**put-on**
build-up	**sell-out**
carry-on	**set-back**
catching-up	**set-up**
check-out	**show-off**
clean-up	**slip-up**
come-down	**take-off**
dressing-down	**take-over**
drop-out	**turn-out**
give-away	**walk-out**
goings-on	**write-up**
grown-up	**write-off**

For a full list of nominalised forms, readers are referred to the *Oxford Dictionary of Current Idiomatic English*, Volume One.

This chapter presents only a selection of verbs with particles and prepositions; the list is by no means complete. However, it give the most *common* verb combinations, the most *idiomatic* and the most *useful*. Not all possible meanings of verb combinations have been given in all cases, but care has been taken to include the meanings which the learner will encounter and wish to use most widely in everyday situations.

act up (informal) cause annoyance through awkward behaviour. *The children always start acting up when it's time to go to bed. The car's been acting up again this week; I've been late to work every day.*

add up (informal) make sense, be logical. *When the police found the murder weapon, the facts of the case suddenly began to add up.*

add up to something (informal) amount to; signify. *The new information adds up to very little, I'm afraid.*

agree with someone suit someone's health, digestion etc. *The fish didn't agree with me; I feel ill. The Brighton air must agree with Tom; he looks very well.*

allow for something take into consideration; make concession for. *The dress I made is too short. When I cut it out, I forgot to allow for the hem. We'll set off an hour earlier to allow for delay or stops on the way.*

angle for something (informal) try to get a response or information indirectly by hinting. *Mary's always angling for compliments, but she never seems to get any. Bob managed to get the information he'd been angling for.*

answer (someone) back return a rebuke in a rude manner. *Johnny got a surprise when he answered his teacher back. Don't answer back when I'm talking to you!*

answer for something take the blame or responsibility for. *If you drive that car without a licence, you'll have to answer for the consequences!*

argue someone down bring to silence through strong argument. *Jack delights in arguing his opposers down. John can't be argued down very easily.*

argue something out argue until a result is reached. *They've been arguing the matter out since it was brought up at the meeting this morning. Can't the problem be argued out tomorrow evening?*

ask after someone inquire about someone's well-being. *I saw George yesterday; he asked after you and the children. Was Aunt Sarah asked after, too?*

ask someone out invite someone to go out for a meal, entertainment etc. *Jane's been asked out to dinner by her boss. Jim has asked Sally out several times, but she never accepts.*

attend to someone/something look after, manage. *A good salesman is always polite when attending to customers. I can't attend to everything at the same time—please come and help!*

back out (of something) withdraw (from); take back one's promise. *You can't back out of a contract once you've signed it. If you've paid your money, it's not advisable to back out.*

back someone/something up support. *Bill is expecting us to back him up at the meeting tomorrow. Will you back up my story to the police?*

bank on someone/something (informal) rely on; expect. *Bill is banking on Bob to lend him the money he needs. Don't bank on fine weather for the weekend—it's going to rain!*

bargain for something (informal) expect; be prepared for. *When Mary offered to look after her neighbour's four children, she got more than she bargained for!*

be after something (informal) aim at getting; want. *John's after a promotion to head of department. Jim visits his old uncle every week; he's after the old man's money!*

be at someone (informal) nag at; complain about; blame. *Jill's always at her husband to stop smoking. The tax office will be at you again when they find out you haven't paid your income tax.*

be down for something have one's name registered for or listed as. *The Smiths have been down for a new council house for over a year, but there's a long waiting list. I'm down for captain in the new team!*

be down on someone/something (informal) be critical of; be unfavourable towards. *The critics are very down on Stevenson's new book, but I like it. Susan's been down on Jane ever since that affair with James.*

be in for something (informal) be due for; be likely to get. *Bill's in for a nasty surprise—he's about to lose his job. He'll be in for trouble if he doesn't work harder!*

be in on something (informal) be informed about; be fully participating in; be involved with. *Bob wasn't in on the plan, so we can't expect him to know. Who else is in on the scheme besides ourselves?*

be in with someone (informal) be on favourable terms with. *Jim always makes sure he's in with the most influential people.*

be on to someone/something (informal) be approaching knowledge of; be on the track of. *The police are on to the thief who did the supermarket robberies. The reporter thinks he's on to a good story.*

be out for something (informal) be determined to get; aim at getting. *He's out for all he can get, whether it's money or favours.*

be up against someone/something be confronted with (something difficult). *Jim will be up against tough competitors in his new job. David's up against a tricky problem at the moment.*

bear down on someone approach threateningly. *The professor bore down on the poor student, who looked terrified.*

bear something out support; confirm as true. *I hope you'll bear my story out when I tell it to the police. I'm afraid that my suspicions are borne out by the facts.*

bear up manage to carry on in spite of difficulties, hardships etc. *How is she bearing up after the death of her husband?*

blow over (informal) cease to arouse interest and be forgotten. *The whole affair has caused a lot of trouble, but after it's blown over, no one will talk about it any more.*

blow up 1 (informal) suddenly become angry. *I'm sorry—I didn't mean to blow up at you in that way.* 2 arise and develop to a crisis. *Some trouble has blown up at the factory—the workers are very dissatisfied.*

blow someone up (informal) reprimand angrily. *The boss blew Mary up for being late without a good excuse.*

blow something up 1 (informal) exaggerate in importance. *The incident has been blown up in the press for publicity's sake.* 2 enlarge photographs etc. *These prints would look very good blown up. I'd like to put a blow-up of this snapshot on my wall.* 3 cause to explode. *Another bridge has been blown up by enemy troops.*

boil something down (informal) reduce in length; summarise. *He didn't give his proposals in full but just had time to boil them down to the essentials.*

boil down to something be summarised as; be reduced to. *The whole issue boils down to the same old problem: how do we fight inflation without lowering our standards of living?*

bowl someone over (informal) greatly astonish; overwhelm. *John completely bowled me over with his good news. We were bowled over by the unexpected beauty of the landscape.*

break down 1 stop functioning through mechanical defect. *Fred's car's broken down again, so he's come on his bicycle. The local train had a breakdown this morning, so I missed my connection to Birmingham by twenty minutes.* 2 come to nothing; fail; be discontinued. *Negotiations over the pay dispute have broken down again. The political unrest and rioting have led to a breakdown in diplomatic relations between the two countries.* 3 lose emotional control because of grief. *Mrs Roberts broke down completely when she heard the news of her husband's death.* 4 collapse due to bad health. *Mr Brown had been overworked for some time before he finally broke down in his office and had to be rushed into hospital. His wife is heading for a nervous breakdown, too.*

break something down 1 overcome; beat. *Some people experience shyness as a barrier to communication, but this can be broken down gradually. The breaking-down of the union's resistance to the new scheme will prove a difficult task for the management.* 2 analyse; reduce to details. *The boss wants us to break these figures down still further. Can you submit a breakdown of your expenses by tomorrow?*

break in 1 interrupt to speak. *At meetings, Joe always breaks in with some trivial matter and holds up the proceedings.* 2 enter illegally by force. *Burglars broke in last night and stole two hundred pounds. There have been two more break-ins this week at the supermarket.*

break someone in (informal) help to adjust to a new situation. *I'll give you some easy task to do first, so as to break you in gradually* *to this new kind of work. The sergeant major doesn't believe in breaking army recruits in slowly. They are broken in by long periods of physical exercise.*

break off 1 stop speaking. *Mr Jackson broke off in the middle of his speech because of shouts of protest from the audience.* 2 stop one's work for a break. *Shall we break off for lunch and continue this afternoon?*

break something off discontinue; bring to an abrupt end. *Jim and Sally have broken their engagement off. Unfortunately, the negotiations have been broken off and are not expected to be resumed.*

break out 1 escape; become free. *Three prisoners have broken out again this week and are on the run. There have been several break-outs recently. Build the fence as strong as possible or the horse will break out.* 2 appear and spread rapidly. (Note: the noun form for this meaning is *outbreak*.) *Fighting has broken out on the border and is expected to continue until a settlement is reached. There's been a second serious outbreak of food-poisoning.*

break through make a major discovery or advance. *Nuclear physicists claim to have broken through in several new aspects of the nature of the atom. Another major breakthrough isn't to be expected for several years until research has been completed.*

break up 1 come to an end; disintegrate. *The partnership is expected to break up. I was sorry to hear of the break-up of Susan's marriage.* 2 disperse for holidays. *When does school break up for the Christmas vacation? Several firms break up for a month in summer rather than staggering the employees' holidays.* 3 end. *People started to leave at 11 o'clock and the party finally broke up at midnight. What time is the meeting expected to break up?*

break something up stop (often by force). *A fight started in the High Street last night, so the police were called in to break it up. The meeting was broken up by the chairman when the discussion got out of hand.*

bring something about cause to happen; initiate. *The new government is expected to bring a large number of improvements about. This failure has been brought about by your own negligence.*

bring someone down 1 cause to be defeated. *This scandal may well bring the Government down at the next election.* 2 cause or persuade to reduce in price. *After much argument, I managed to bring the dealer down to a price of £300.*

bring something down lower; reduce. *Supermarkets are bringing the price of sugar down. Government expenditure has been brought down radically by large cuts in grants to local authorities.*

bring someone in 1 arrest; detain for questioning at the police-station. *Constable Jenkins has just brought a man in for disorderly conduct. The man's been brought in before for the same thing.*

2 cause to be involved. *Why did the management bring a financial advisor in? Our firm is capable of solving its own problems.*

bring something in 1 introduce. *A new Bill has been brought in to regulate strike measures.* 2 produce. *More overtime would bring the workers higher wages in.* 3 harvest. *If this good weather continues, the farmers will be able to bring the crops in as planned.*

bring something off (informal) complete successfully. *Jim has had plenty of practice in bringing business deals off. You can rely on Janet to bring it off with her usual skill and charm.*

bring something on cause; lead to. *It's the eye-strain from reading that brings these severe headaches on. There's a lot of trouble between the two brothers, but I don't know what brought it on. Mary's hay fever was brought on by the coming of spring.*

bring someone out 1 cause to strike. *The union leader is threatening to bring his miners out.* 2 help to become less shy. *Jane was very shy before she met John; he brought her out a lot.*

bring something out 1 publish; put on the market. *This publisher is bringing a new series of cheap paperbacks out next month. A new line in household equipment has just been brought out.* 2 reveal. *It's difficult to bring out the exact meaning of some words when you translate them into a foreign language. All the finer points of the poem were brought out by our teacher.* 3 show to advantage. *The sunlight brings the colours of the trees out beautifully.* 4 develop. *A good teacher should try to bring out the individual talents of his pupils. In times of hardship, one's true character is brought out most clearly.*

bring someone round 1 restore to consciousness. *Joan fainted, but the fresh air soon brought her round.* 2 persuade. *Michael didn't agree with the suggestion at first, but we soon brought him round to our way of thinking.*

bring someone up 1 educate, rear. *It's difficult to bring children up well in a large family. Molly was brought up by her grandmother.* 2 bring to trial at court. *Williams was brought up for disturbing the peace.*

bring something up 1 introduce for discussion, mention. *Who brought this matter up? The question of higher membership fees was brought up at the last meeting.* 2 (informal) vomit. *The mother told the doctor that the child was still bringing up his food.*

brush something aside disregard, reject as being unimportant. *I didn't expect him to brush my idea aside in such a rude way.*

brush someone down (informal) reprimand. *The boss is always brushing his secretary down for making careless mistakes. The teacher will give you a good brushing-down for forgetting your homework again.*

brush up something (informal) improve by revision. *It's time you* *brushed up your French, if you want to go to France on holiday. Peter wants to brush up his knowledge of statistics so that he can apply for a new job.*

build up develop, increase in intensity. *Tension is building up among the workers of the chemical industry.*

build someone up 1 develop the physical strength of. *The doctor says David is much better but now he needs building up with vitamins and fresh air.* 2 (informal) increase someone's fame by praise. *He's only an average performer, but the critics have built him up to a star of television. Before the director retired, he gave his successor a marvellous build-up.*

build something up develop, increase or extend gradually. *Mr. Green built up his business from nothing. His fortune has been built up over the years by careful investment.*

burst in enter suddenly. *Jeremy burst in and interrupted our discussion.*

burst out exclaim suddenly. *When Aunt Sarah made her usual remarks, Janet burst out that she was tired of hearing her complaints.*

buy someone off (informal) pay money in order to gain or protect one's interests. *It would be cheaper to buy the competitors off, rather than run the risk of losing all our business. The blackmailer will have to be bought off, or he'll ruin your good name.*

buy someone out obtain financial control of. *There's a rumour that Jackson & Co are buying Clarke & Co out. Large companies can easily buy out the shareholders of small companies.*

buy something up buy as much as is available. *Speculators have bought up the entire building land in this area. All supplies of this material have been bought up by the chemical industry—there's none available to private householders.*

call by make a short visit. *Don't go out, Uncle Harry's calling by this evening.*

call for someone/something 1 collect. *I'll call for you on my way to work. You can call for the tickets on the way home.* 2 demand; require. *This position calls for a man of absolute integrity. This new situation calls for immediate action. Congratulations! This news calls for a celebration!*

call in stop somewhere on the way to somewhere else. *I'll call in at the butcher's on the way to the post office.*

call someone in summon. *We'd better call in a doctor if the temperature doesn't go down.*

call something in demand the return of. *The banks have begun to call all the old coins in. I must take this book back to the library; it's been called in.*

call someone off (informal) order to stop. *The commander called his men off when he realised that the search was hopeless. Call the dogs off! They'll kill him!*

call something off cancel. *If it rains, we may have to call the cricket match off. The meeting was called off due to lack of attendance.*

call someone out 1 summon. *Never call the ambulance or a doctor out unless it's absolutely necessary.* 2 order to strike. *The dockers have been called out to support another wage-claim.*

call someone up 1 telephone. *I'll call you up in your office.* 2 summon for military service. *Jack wasn't called up until the war was nearly over.* 3 bring in to help. *The commander called reinforcements up.*

call something up recall to the memory. *The sight of the children playing called up scenes of early childhood.*

call upon someone 1 request. *The chairman called upon Mr Black to deliver his speech.* 2 urge; appeal to. *The prisoner called upon the jury to show understanding for his situation.*

carry someone away fill with emotion or enthusiasm. *He's a brilliant speaker, who can carry his audience away. I was carried away with enthusiasm and completely forgot the time.*

carry off something obtain; win. *John was an excellent pupil. He carried off all the prizes at school. All the trophies were carried off by the team from Edinburgh.*

carry something off (informal) make a success of. *Sally's a good actress—she always carries her role off well. I'm not looking forward to giving the party—I don't feel that I shall carry it off as well as usual.*

carry on 1 continue. *Carry on telling me the story—sorry I interrupted.* 2 (informal) argue; make a fuss. *Mrs. Jones was carrying on to the butcher about the cost of his sausages. There was such a carry-on when Mr Green was elected mayor and not Mr Grey.* 3 (informal, disapproving) have a sexual relationship. *The boss had been carrying on with his secretary, but that soon stopped when his wife found out.* 4 (informal) behave badly or noisily. *The children always carry on when we have visitors.*

carry on something maintain. *Mr White carries on a small grocery. He expects his son to carry on the business when he retires.*

carry out something 1 perform. *Many experiments have been carried out in this field. I don't think Jack will have the courage to carry out his plan.* 2 fulfil. *I expect you to carry out your duties and obligations without complaints.*

catch on 1 (informal) understand; grasp the situation. *Jimmy's a bright boy. He catches on very quickly.* 2 (informal) become popular. *The singer has a good opera voice, but I don't think he'll catch on with young people.*

catch someone out trap; discover; outsmart. *Billy was copying his homework under the desk, but the teacher caught him out. It's difficult to catch Tommy out. He knows all the answers.*

catch (something) up (informal) perform so as to make up for (lost time). *I missed a lot of work through illness, so I've a lot of catching-up to do. I must catch all that reading up.*

catch (someone) up (informal) run after so as to reach. *You can run on ahead and I'll catch (you) up later.*

catch up on someone (informal) overtake; get the upper hand of. *Old age is catching up on him now.*

catch up on something perform so as to make up for (something lost). *I've a lot of sleep to catch up on this week. I'll have to catch up on my homework before I watch TV.*

change down (driving) put in a lower gear. *I often brake before I change down.*

change up (driving) put in a higher gear. *Change up, you're going too fast for the second gear.*

charge something (up) (to someone) put on someone's account. *Don't bring me a bill—just charge it up. Charge the visitors' hotel bills to the company's account. Have the goods charged up to me.*

chase someone/something up (informal) search for in order to get information. *I've been chasing the manager up for a week, but he's never in. Have you chased up the title of that book yet?*

check in (at) register one's arrival. *When you arrive at the airport, check in immediately. Have you checked in at your hotel yet?*

check something off mark off as correct on a list. *Will you check these names off as I read them out, please?*

check on someone/something investigate; test the truth of. *Have you checked on Robins? Has he got the necessary qualifications? We'd better check on his story before we use him as a witness.*

check out (of) register one's departure. *Mr Ramsey checked out early this morning, but he's left a forwarding address for mail. Can you tell me where the check-out desk is, please?*

check something out investigate; test the truth of. *Could you check this information out with the computer, please?*

check up (on someone/something) investigate; test the truth of. *I'm not sure what time the plane leaves. Could you check up? We ought to check up on the figures; perhaps they are invalid.*

clean (something) up 1 make tidy or clean. *It was a lovely party, but it took me hours to clean up after it.* 2 reform; improve. *The town council is going to clean the slum area up. It's time the town was given a good clean-up.*

clear off (informal) go away. *I told the children to take their football and clear off. Clear off and leave me alone!*

clear something off 1 complete the payment of; settle. *Next year at this time I shall have cleared off all my debts.* 2 dispose of; sell out. *The shop on the corner is clearing off old stock. There are some good bargains.*

clear out (of) (informal) leave and not return; leave quickly. *Jim's cleared out. He was fed up with the conditions at home. You'd better clear out of here before the boss comes in and catches you!*

clear someone out (of) remove; send away. *The council has cleared the people out of the slums.*

clear something out make tidy. *I'm going to clear the kitchen cupboards out today.*

clear up 1 make tidy by removing mess. *I always make the children clear up before they go to bed.* 2 (of weather) improve. *It rained all the morning, but then it cleared up quite unexpectedly.*

clear something up 1 make tidy. *I hope you're going to clear up that mess yourself!* 2 explain; solve by removing doubt. *Can we clear the matter up ourselves, or shall we call in the police? Has the mystery of the missing key been cleared up yet?*

come across be understood clearly. *His speech was carefully prepared, but it didn't come across very well. Listen to this description and tell me if the meaning comes across.*

come across someone/something meet or find by chance *I came across old Mr Hill in the High Street the other day. Where did you come across these old documents?*

come across with something (informal) provide; hand over. *He came across with £20 just when I was in need of it.*

come along 1 hurry. *Come along, we haven't much time!* 2 arrive; turn up; be present. *If the chance comes along, take it!* 3 accompany someone. *We're going to a show. Why don't you come along?* 4 develop; make progress. *How's your work coming along? Bob broke his leg, but it's coming along much better now. He'll be skiing again next month!*

come back 1 become fashionable again. *Grey-flannel trousers are coming back.* 2 return to one's memory. *I think I've forgotten all I've learnt. I hope it all comes back in the exam!*

come back at someone reply angrily. *When I told him my opinion, he came back at me angrily.*

come by something obtain. *A job with such good prospects is not easy to come by. How did you come by this beautiful Chinese vase?*

come down 1 fall; be reduced. *The price of milk is coming down next week. He's had to resign from the board of directors and take a job in a fish-and-chip shop—what an embarrassing come-down!* 2 be demolished. *This whole row of old houses is due to come down.* 3 be passed on by family tradition. *The estate has come down through six generations.*

come down on someone 1 (informal) criticize; punish. *The new traffic laws come down heavily on drunken drivers. The boss will come down on you like a ton of bricks when he finds out what you've* *done.* 2 claim money. *They've come down on us for increased membership fees this year.*

come in 1 become fashionable. *Pleated skirts are coming in this season.* 2 be elected; gain political power. *It's time the liberals came in again!* 3 take a place in a competition. *Jack came in third in the last race.* 4 play a part. *The plan's good, but where do we come in?* 5 **come in useful/handy** (informal) prove to be useful. *Don't throw that old box away. It might come in useful one day.*

come off 1 (informal) take place. *There was a lot of talk about the takeover, but it never came off.* 2 (informal) succeed. *Do you think his plans will come off?* 3 fall from. *Jim came off his motor-bike and hurt his leg.*

come on 1 begin. *I've got a headache coming on. When the rain came on, the players left the field.* 2 appear; make an entrance. *When the star of the show came on, everybody applauded.* 3 progress; develop. *My cabbages and spring onions are coming on nicely.* 4 be shown (on a cinema or TV screen). *My favourite programme comes on at 8 o'clock on Tuesdays.* 5 follow later. *Julie's arriving today and David is coming on with the luggage tomorrow.*

come out 1 appear. *The sun's coming out.* 2 strike. *The miners are coming out again next week.* 3 be published; be available on the market. *David's book came out last month.* 4 blossom. *Have your roses come out yet?* 5 result, turn out. *The photographs of the wedding came out very well.* 6 take a place in an examination etc. *Michael came out bottom in history and top in maths!* 7 be revealed; be made known; become public. *When is the news of the engagement coming out? It was meant to be a secret, but it came out.*

come out with something (informal) say or reveal something which may surprise. *You never know what children are going to come out with next! When I asked him where he'd been, he came out with a very confused story, which was obviously untrue.*

come round 1 regain consciousness. *'Jill's fainted!' 'Get her into the fresh air; she'll soon come round.'* 2 (informal) pay an informal visit. *I shall be at home tomorrow evening. Would you like to come round?* 3 (informal) become friendly again after a bad mood. *Sue didn't speak to me for a week after our quarrel, but then she gradually came round.* 4 be persuaded; change one's attitude. *Bob refused to take on the work at first, but he soon came round when he heard how much money he would get for it. Can't you influence David to come round to our way of thinking?*

come to regain consciousness. *When he came to, he found himself in a hospital bed.*

come to something 1 amount to. *How much did the bill for the car repairs come to? What it all comes to, is that he won't give us any further support.* 2 be a question of. *Mary's very good at painting*

*and playing the violin, but when it comes to baking a cake and sewing
she's hopeless!*

come up 1 present itself. *I've been looking for a new job for ages,
but nothing suitable has come up yet.* 2 be mentioned or discussed.
The matter of housing came up at the council meeting last week.

come up with something (informal) produce. *Bill usually comes
up with some good ideas. Janet always manages to come up with the
right answer!*

cook something up (informal) invent; fabricate. *If you don't want
to get into trouble, you'll have to cook up a good excuse for not attending the meeting.*

cork something up (informal) repress. *Tell Jane that you're angry
with her. It's better than corking up your feelings and pretending that
everything is fine.*

count someone/something in (informal) include. *Shall we count
you in on the deal? The country will soon have 30 universities, counting in the three which are under construction.*

count on someone/something rely on. *You can always count on
John to come punctually. We had been counting on completion of the
project by Christmas.*

count someone/something out (informal) exclude; not consider.
*You'd better count me out, if the costs will be so high. I've still got ten
bills to pay—and that's counting out the one for the car repairs!*

cry someone/something down (informal) criticize; belittle; present as unimportant. *In an election campaign, it's natural for one
party to cry down the achievements of another.*

cry off (informal) withdraw. *Sally promised to come and now she's
cried off at the last moment!*

cut back (on) something reduce (production). *On account of the
decrease in trade, it will be necessary to cut back production. If we
don't cut back on expenditure, the company will be faced with serious
difficulties.*

cut down (on) something reduce (consumption). *Jim has cut
down his daily intake of calories by half! We saved up for the holiday
by cutting down on luxuries.*

cut in 1 (informal) interrupt. *I wish Jack wouldn't keep cutting in
when other people are talking.* 2 (informal) drive in front of another car sharply after overtaking it. *I wish big lorries wouldn't cut
in like that.*

cut off turn. *The policeman saw the thief cut off down a back street.*

cut someone off 1 break a telephone connection. *I got through to
the right number but we were cut off.* 2 isolate. *The floods cut the
villagers off from the town for over two weeks.* 3 disinherit. *Lord
Quincey has threatened to cut his son off without a penny if he
marries that girl from the village.*

cut something off 1 interrupt the supply of. *If you don't pay the bill, they'll cut your gas off! The water supply was cut off this morning for an hour.* 2 isolate. *Several villages on the moors have been cut off by snow.*

cut out stop functioning. *I'm having trouble with the engine. It keeps cutting out.*

cut someone out (informal) eliminate. *The firm's policy has been to cut out competitors by fair or unfair means.*

cut something out 1 (informal) stop; refrain from. *Cut out bread and potatoes and you'll soon lose weight. Cut out all that silly chatter!* 2 exclude. *If you cut out paragraphs four and seven, the essay will read much more clearly. Let's cut out the preliminaries and get down to the important business.*

cut someone up 1 (informal) upset. *The bad news naturally cut him up. He was terribly cut up about his father's death.* 2 (informal) injure; damage. *The car crash cut him up a bit, but he's fully recovered now.*

dash something off produce hurriedly. *I'll just dash off a few letters before lunch. Although this sketch was just dashed off in five minutes, it's still an excellent likeness.*

deal in something trade in; do business in. *The new shop will deal in electrical applicances. Does Mr Robinson still deal in hardware or has he changed over to paints and wallpaper?*

deal with someone 1 trade with; give one's custom to. *I've been dealing with Mr Lee for six years. His firm has always given me satisfaction.* 2 punish; take action against. *Don't deal too harshly with him—remember what you were like at that age.*

deal with something 1 treat; be concerned with; discuss. *The book deals with the topic very well on pages 30–38. It's time we dealt with the matter of new salary scales. Our employees are expecting the rises before Christmas.* 2 handle; tackle; solve. *My job is mainly to deal with customer complaints and inquiries. Inflation is one of the most difficult issues for any government to deal with.*

die down decrease; lose intensity. *The trouble at the factory seems to be dying down now; most of the men have come to work this morning. Bill was furious over the affair, but his anger soon died down when he realised that he couldn't alter things.*

die for something (informal) (continuous tenses only) long for; want very much. *I'm dying for a cup of tea and a cigarette!*

do for someone 1 (informal) keep house; clean, cook etc. *My grandparents have done for themselves for years, but now they're getting too old to run their own house.* 2 defeat; ruin. *The bank has gone bankrupt—we're done for!*

do for something 1 (informal) serve for or as. *Don't throw those old clothes away. They'll do for the children to play with, or they can* *even do for cleaning rags.* 2 (informal) do to succeed in getting. *I don't know what people do for groceries when they live miles away from a town.*

do something out/over (informal) clean or redecorate thoroughly. *I'm going to do out the kitchen this afternoon. It's time the spare bedroom had a good doing-over, as well.* 2 (informal) paint or wallpaper a room. *Fred said he'd do the living-room over while he's on holiday.*

do someone out of something (informal) cheat of; prevent from getting. *I still think it was Williams who did me out of that promotion. The tax office have done me out of £500!*

do something up 1 renovate; improve the condition or appearance of. *Mrs MacDonald is having the old cottage done up.* 2 fasten. *Can you do my dress up at the back, please?* 3 parcel; wrap up. *Have you done up the children's toys for the Christmas party? Do the washing up so that I can take it to the laundry.*

do with something 1 (informal) (used with *can/could*) want; need; benefit from. *I could do with a nice hot cup of tea at the moment! John's car can do with a good wash and polish!* 2 (informal) (used with *can not*) tolerate. *I can't do with noise and disturbances when I'm concentrating.* 3 (used with *have to*) be concerned with; be relating to. *Robert's work has to do with computers, I think.*

do without someone/something manage without; forgo. *You'll have to do without your neighbour when she moves house! Can you do without the car tomorrow? I need it.* 2 (informal) (used with *can/could*) dispense with; not require. *I can do without your troubles, I've got enough of my own! I could do without Mary coming tomorrow. I really haven't got time to see her.*

draw in 1 (of hours of daylight) get shorter; (of hours of darkness) get longer. *The autumn evenings are drawing in; it will soon be winter.* 2 (of a train) arrive. *The Edinburgh express drew in ten minutes late.* 3 (of a vehicle) stop at the side of the road. *The lorry drew in and the driver got out.*

draw someone in attract. *The advertising campaign has drawn in hundreds of Christmas shoppers. The crowds have been drawn in by the special offers in wines and spirits.*

draw on come nearer. *The night was drawing on and her husband still hadn't returned.*

draw out 1 (of hours of daylight) get longer. *As soon as January is over, the days begin to draw out noticeably.* 2 (of a train) leave. *When I arrived at platform 6 the Manchester train was just drawing out.* 3 (of a vehicle) move into traffic. *The lorry drew out unexpectedly and almost caused an accident.*

draw someone out (informal) encourage to be less shy. *Susan was* *always very quiet at school, but when she started work the office girls soon drew her out. Tony's a nice boy, but he's too shy; he needs drawing out a bit.*

draw something out 1 obtain from one's bank etc account. *I've drawn out all my savings for my holidays.* 2 (informal) make longer; prolong. *My speech only lasts ten minutes. I'll have to draw it out to make it last a quarter of an hour. The meeting last night was drawn out until 10 o'clock.*

draw up (of a vehicle) come to a stop. *The ambulance drew up in front of the house.*

draw something up 1 place or pull near. *Draw the armchair up to the fire!* 2 set out; compile; formulate. *Has the agreement been drawn up by the lawyer yet? It's a carefully drawn-up report, accurate and clear.*

dress someone down (informal) reprimand. *The boss summoned Jackson to his office and dressed him down for being rude to some visitors. The student teacher was given a good dressing-down by the headmaster for being too casual with his pupils.*

dress up 1 put on one's best or formal clothes. *Is the reception quite informal or do we need to dress up? Poor old Fred felt quite uncomfortable in the dinner jacket. He'd been dressed up for the occasion by his wife.* 2 wear a disguise or fancy-dress costume. *What are you dressing up as at the New Year Eve's Ball?*

dress someone up disguise. *They dressed her up as a witch for the school play.*

dress something up (informal) improve; make to appear or sound better. *Your proposal is fine. Dress it up a bit and then send it to the committee.*

drink something in 1 (informal) listen eagerly. *Whenever there's any gossip in the neighbourhood, Mrs Green drinks it all in and spreads it as fast as she can!* 2 absorb enthusiastically. *We stood on top of the hill, drinking in the beautiful view.*

drink something off finish drinking in one action. *He drank the bottle off in thirty seconds!*

drink something up drink until finished. *The children drank up their hot milk and went to bed. Drink up, lads, and I'll order another round!*

drive at something (informal) aim at; try to say; mean. *David doesn't explain very well, but I think I know what he's driving at.*

drive something in (informal) explain repeatedly; get into one's head. *They drove it in to me at school that mathematics was vitally important.*

drop across/by/in (on)/over (informal) pay someone a casual visit. *Mrs Barton lives on the other side of the road. She often drops across to have coffee with us. Do drop by when next you're in the area.*

I'll drop in on Aunt Gertrude for a chat after work. Drop over any time for a game of cards.

drop something across/by/in (on)/over bring or take. *I'll drop the book across to you this evening. I've still got your electric drill; I'll drop it by on my way home tomorrow. Could you drop the hammer in?—I've a small job to do. 'Where did the typewriter come from?' 'Jill dropped it over for you this afternoon.'*

drop off 1 (informal) fall asleep. *I was just dropping off when the telephone rang.* 2 (informal) decrease. *Sales are dropping off alarmingly. There's too much competition. Harry doesn't talk about Jean much now. His interest must have dropped off.* 3 get off (a vehicle). *Where did you drop off? At the bus stop just round the corner.*

drop someone off (informal) allow to get off (a vehicle). *Tom dropped me off at the post-office and I've walked the rest of the way. Ask the bus-driver to drop you off at the Odeon Cinema.*

drop something off (informal) deliver. *I can drop the laundry off on my way to work.*

drop out cease to attend, belong or participate. *Norah sang in the choir for over three years, then she suddenly dropped out for no apparent reason. There are only twelve students on the diploma course now. Three have dropped out. Francis is living the life of a drop-out from society in a commune in Wales.*

drop out of something withdraw from; abandon. *When Peter saw that he hadn't a chance, he dropped out of the race. Janet's dropped out of amateur dramatics altogether. She's been too busy since she got married.*

dry up 1 (informal) dry the dishes. *Henry always dries up for me after Sunday lunch. Whose turn is it to do the drying-up?* 2 (informal) be unable to speak further. *Poor old Arthur kept drying up in the middle of his speech, so he had to get out his paper! The play was good, but one of the actors was nervous and dried up twice in the second act.* 3 (informal) stop talking. *I wish old Joe would dry up. He's been talking about his years at sea for over an hour!*

dwell on something spend too much time, discussion or thought on. *I wish Grandfather wouldn't dwell on the past so much. It makes me feel that he's not happy. The speech was too long. Robinson dwelt too much on the achievements of the firm.*

ease off (informal) decrease tension, pressure or speed. *I've advised Jim to ease off a bit. He's been working too hard. The tension eased off slowly when the two sides began negotiations.*

ease up (informal) become less urgent; slacken off. *I'll be glad when the pressure of work has eased up a little. I'm far too busy at the moment.*

eat into something dissolve; consume; use up. *Rust has eaten into the car's bumpers. The holiday in Canada will eat into our savings.*

eat someone up worry; make nervous. *What's been eating Jill up lately?*

eat something up 1 (of food) finish. *Make sure the children eat their vegetables up!* 2 use up; consume. *Bob's new sports car just eats up petrol.*

egg someone on encourage; urge. *Stop egging him on to drink more! You can see he's had enough!*

end up (informal) end. *If you don't slow down, you'll end up in hospital! I ended up by telling Mary the whole story, although that wasn't my intention.*

face up to something (of problems or difficulties) accept; confront. *He just can't face up to the fact that he's too old to work any more. It's time Peter learnt to face up to his parents.*

fall back on someone/something go back to for help; use as a reserve. *We can always fall back on Bill if we can't get anyone else. Thank goodness we've got your savings to fall back on!*

fall for someone (informal) be romantically infatuated with. *Paula's fallen for her new professor.*

fall for something 1 (informal) like very much; want to have. *Anne always falls for the most expensive dresses in the shop!* 2 (informal) be tricked into believing. *You didn't fall for his sad story about his sick wife and children, did you? He tells that to everyone just to get sympathy! I wish my wife wouldn't fall for all this sales talk. She's just bought another vacuum cleaner!*

fall in with someone get to know by chance; begin to associate with. *We fell in with some French tourists from the same hotel. When Ted worked in Soho, he fell in with some people of dubious character.*

fall in with something accept; agree to; comply with. *I'll fall in with your plan after all. George will fall in with any suggestion that involves eating and drinking.*

fall off 1 decrease. *Sales tend to fall off just after Christmas. Attendance at lectures fell off towards the end of the course.* 2 become worse; deteriorate. *Janet's cooking is falling off. I didn't enjoy the last meal we had there at all! The service in this restaurant has been falling off for a long time. It's time they employed better waiters.*

fall out 1 (informal) happen. *Don't worry! Things will fall out all right in the end.* 2 (informal) quarrel. *She's always falling out with her neighbour. Don't get angry! I don't want us to fall out on your birthday!* 3 withdraw. *Five people were working on the project, but two had to fall out because of illness.*

fall through (informal) fail; not develop or take place. *I hope the plan doesn't fall through a second time. We're going on a picnic tomorrow, unless it falls through because of the weather.*

feel up to something (informal) feel capable of. *Shall we continue with the work? Do you feel up to it today? After three weeks in hospital, I don't feel up to decorating the house any more. Let's get a decorator to do it.*

fight someone/something off repel; defeat. *The police had a difficult job fighting off the reporters. The fans had to be fought off before the filmstar could safely get into the car. Did your husband manage to fight off his cold?*

fill in (informal) do a job temporarily for someone else. *'Have you got a new secretary?' 'No, she's just filling in until Miss Brown gets back from her holidays.'*

fill someone in (on something) (informal) give details (about). *Can you fill me in on James? What's his qualification for the job? I've just been filled in by Peter on the latest changes in policy.*

fill something in/out/up complete by giving information. *Please fill in all your particulars on this form. I haven't filled the football pools out yet. Is this application form correctly filled up?*

finish something off end; complete; use up. *Finish the letter off and I'll post it for you. Has the last of the French brandy been finished off yet?*

finish off/up with something end with. *Let's finish up with a chorus of 'Old Lang Syne'!*

finish with someone 1 (informal) end a friendship or connection with. *Jane's finished with her new boyfriend already. I've finished with our butcher! He's overcharged me three times!*

finish with something finish using; not need any more. *When you've finished with the book, will you pass it on to me?*

fit in go into the space provided. *The shelf is too small. The big books won't fit in.*

fit in (with) match; harmonize (with). *That picture doesn't fit in here. It's too modern for the rest of the furnishings. George doesn't really fit in with the rest of his group. He's too unconventional.*

fit someone/something in find time or space for. *I hope the hairdresser can fit me in today. There are still three patients to be fitted in this afternoon. Can you manage to fit this small table in somewhere? The doctor can't fit in any more visits this week.*

fit something on put on; fix on. *We can see if the dress needs alteration after we've fitted it on. The joiner's coming to fit the new door on next week.*

fit someone up (with something) equip (with); supply (with). *Jack needs some new car tyres. The garage across the road could fit him up. Old Mr Watson needs fitting up with a new hearing-aid.*

fit something up (with something) fix; equip (with). *Can we fit an extra cupboard up in the kitchen? The place has just been fitted up with new equipment.*

fix on something (informal) decide on; choose. *Have you fixed on a date for the party yet?*

fix something on fasten; attach. *If you don't fix the top on properly, the milk will spill out.*

fix up (informal) arrange. *Have you fixed up to go on holiday yet?*

fix someone up (with something) (informal) supply (with). *Can you fix me up with a part-time job? He rang up the hotel for a room and was fixed up immediately.*

fix something up 1 (informal) arrange. *Let's fix up a time that suits everybody. I've fixed an appointment up for tomorrow.* 2 install. *Jim has fixed up a work-bench in his garden shed.*

follow something through continue to the end. *Richard is determined to follow his plan through. Follow the argument through to its logical conclusion.*

follow something up 1 investigate; pursue further. *The editor thinks this story is worth following up. I think we should follow up his suggestion; it sounds reasonable.* 2 follow; reinforce. *The series is to be followed up by another programme of a similar theme.*

get about 1 travel. *John gets about all over Europe, even though he hasn't got a car.* 2 walk. *Old people can't get about very well in the winter weather.* 3 spread. *The news got about that the firm was closing down.*

get across communicate one's ideas. *The advertisement's basic message gets across very well.*

get something across (to someone) communicate (to); make one's meaning or ideas clear (to). *Jim's a good speaker. He always gets his ideas across to his audience without the slightest effort. She managed to get the feeling across that she wasn't content with the way things were managed there.*

get along 1 (informal) leave; depart. *We must be getting along now or we'll be late for the cinema.* 2 make progress; manage; succeed. *How are the builders getting along with your new house? My work's getting along much better now. How's Alec getting along in Canada?* 3 pay one's way; manage to do something under difficulties. *The Robinsons only have a small pension, but they seem to get along all right. How are you getting along without your wife? When does she get back from Scotland?* 4 have a good relationship. *The two brothers don't get along at all. They are very different in character.*

get at someone 1 (informal) criticize. *She's always getting at her husband for not helping with the housework. No names were mentioned, but we all knew who was being got at.* 2 (informal) bribe; influence. *Someone appears to have been trying to get at the jury.*

get at something 1 reach. *Put the papers somewhere where the* *children can't get at them.* 2 learn; get to know. *The truth is very difficult to get at. I've been trying to get at some information on the subject.* 3 mean; try to say; hint at. *I'm afraid I don't know what you're getting at. If I correctly understood what she was getting at, it seemed to be a good idea.* 4 start work on. *If the rain stopped, I could get at the garden. There's so much work to be done.*

get away with something (informal) escape reprimand or punishment for. *The child ought to be punished. You shouldn't let him get away with telling lies!*

get back at someone (informal) get revenge on. *She'll get back at him for telling everybody her secret! Just you wait and see!*

get by manage. *If you want to learn a language well, you can't get by without mastering its idioms.*

get someone down (informal) depress. *This miserable weather really gets me down.*

get something down 1 (manage to) write (in a hurry, with difficulty etc). *Did you get the last sentence down, or was I dictating too quickly?* 2 swallow. *The medicine is so bitter that it's an effort to get it down.*

get down to something (informal) start serious work on; tackle. *It's time you got down to some reading or the other students will leave you behind! The task isn't as difficult as it seems when you really get down to it.*

get in 1 enter. *The rain can get in through this window.* 2 arrive. *What time does your train get in?* 3 be elected. *Do you think the Conservatives will get in?* 4 be admitted. *We've registered our daughter at the new school, but as there's a long waiting-list I don't think she'll get in this year.* 5 (informal) act to gain an advantage. *The supermarket got in first with cut-price cigarettes, so everyone buys them there now.*

get someone in (informal) summon. *I think we should get the electrician in to fix this loose wiring. Her temperature's gone down. I don't think it's necessary to get the doctor in.*

get something in 1 collect; bring in. *If the good weather continues, the farmers will be able to get the harvest in. Have you got the washing in? It's starting to rain!*

get in with someone (informal) get on good terms with in order to gain an advantage. *James always tries to get in with the most influential people, that's why he's joined the riding club.*

get off 1 (informal) depart; start a journey. *We got off early and arrived before lunch. Did the plane get off on time or was it delayed because of fog?* 2 escape punishment, reprimand, injury etc. *The judge was very lenient. Dick got off with a warning and a small fine. Alex was lucky. He crashed his car but got off with only a few scratches.*

get off something 1 dismount; alight from. *She asked the conductor where to get off the bus.* 2 stop talking about. *Let's get off the subject of work! Let's talk about something pleasant!*

get someone off save from punishment. *The lawyer got Smith off, but he wouldn't have got him off so easily if it hadn't been a first offence.*

get something off 1 take off; remove. *I can't get my boots off. They're too tight. I couldn't get the coffee stains off your shirt.* 2 send off; dispatch. *Please get these letters off by the 12 o'clock post. They're important.* 3 (informal) learn. *It's the school play next week and Norah hasn't got her lines off properly yet!*

get off with someone (informal) spend time intimately and romantically with. *Michael got off with his best friend's girl at the party last night.*

get on 1 make progress. *How's the broken leg getting on? Johnny isn't getting on very well in French or History.* 2 manage, succeed. *How's Tom getting on in France? Did Jean get on all right in the exam? How would you get on without me?* 3 become late; grow older. *It's getting on; we'd better go home. Mr Williams is getting on now, he must be nearly seventy.* 4 (informal) have a good relationship. *They get on well at work but not privately.*

get on to someone 1 trace; detect. *The police have got on to the murderer at last.* 2 get into contact with. *I complained to the shop about the faulty washing-machine, and they said they'd get on to the manufacturers.*

get on to something 1 proceed to. *If you don't know the answer, leave the first question and get on to the second.* 2 become aware of; realise. *I'm surprised that he didn't get on to the truth of the matter long ago!*

get out 1 (informal) go outside; go out to enjoy oneself. *Old Mrs Ward doesn't get out much these days. You work too hard! You should get out a bit more!* 2 leave; escape. *When the fighting broke out, George thought it better to get out before it was too late, so he came back to England* 3 become known, leak out. *The news has got out about the takeover, although it wasn't to become public until next month. Don't let it get out that I knew about it!*

get someone out rescue. *The house burnt down but the fire-brigade managed to get all the occupants out.*

get something out 1 remove. *Can you help me with this wine bottle? I can't get the cork out. Did you get the ink stain out of your skirt?* 2 make an utterance. *Paul sometimes stutters. He can't get his words out. Mr Clarke managed to get out an apology, but he was obviously under great pressure to do.* 3 (informal) publish; put onto the market. *The publishers hope to get a third edition out before Christmas.* 4 borrow from a library. *I haven't got any books out at* *the moment.* 5 solve. *I've been trying to get this sum out for half an hour, but I'll have to ask the teacher how to do it.*

get out of something (informal) avoid having to do something. *Fred always gets out of doing the washing-up by saying he's busy working in the garden.*

get over someone (informal) stop being emotionally involved with. *Barbara has got a new boyfriend now, but she never really got over Peter.*

get over something 1 overcome; surmount. *Has Walter got over his financial difficulties yet? She got over her disappointment quite quickly.* 2 recover from (an illness, shock, surprise etc). *Grandfather has just got over an attack of asthma. I thought Robert would never get over the shock of losing all his money, but he's starting up in business again. I can't get over Jack leaving for Australia without telling us!*

get something over 1 manage to communicate one's ideas etc. *Professor Wright knows his subject, but he's not very good at getting his ideas over to his students.* 2 (informal) complete; perform. *As soon as Brian gets his exam over, he's going on holiday. As soon as the formalities had been got over, the consulate was quick to issue the work permit.*

get round someone (informal) coax; persuade. *Tom's trying to get round his father to buy him a car. Don't let him get round you! He doesn't deserve your help.*

get round something avoid; evade. *It's no use trying to get round paying the income tax! I'm sure the regulations could be got round, if we studied them closely enough.*

get someone round 1 (informal) summon. *'My lawnmower's broken.' 'Get Tom round. He'll mend it for you.'* 2 revive; bring back to consciousness. *Polly's fainted. Jane's trying to get her round.*

get something round send. *I'll get the book round to you by tonight.*

get round to someone/something (informal) find time for. *Tell Mrs Walker I can't get round to her this afternoon, so she can go home and come back tomorrow at ten. I haven't been able to get round to looking at your essay yet, but I'll read it this evening.*

get through 1 manage to pass through. *There's a hole. That's why the water gets through* 2 succeed; pass (a test). *It was a difficult examination. Not all candidates got through.* 3 get a telephone connection. *All the lines were engaged. I couldn't get through.*

get through something 1 finish; complete successfully. *I got through the book in one evening.* 2 use up; exhaust. *I've usually got through my salary by the middle of the month. Jimmy got through a big plate of meat and vegetables and then asked for a second helping!*

get through to someone succeed in establishing an understanding with; communicate with. *Charles is so shy and nervous that no one can get through to him.*

get someone through 1 help to pass an examination. *The teacher got all his pupils through without difficulty.* 2 help to contact; connect (by telephone). *The operator finally got me through to Mr Blake's extension number.*

get something through 1 cause to be approved or accepted (by). *It was the personnel manager who helped to get my promotion through. The Bill was finally got through Parliament and made law.* 2 cause to pass through (and arrive). *The villagers were cut off by an avalanche, but the army managed to get supplies through to them. Jack always manages to get a double allowance of spirits through the Customs.*

get up 1 get out of bed. *I'm not used to getting up early.* 2 (of wind etc) rise; increase. *There's a storm getting up.*

get someone up 1 call from bed; awaken. *Can you get me up at six tomorrow?* 2 dress; put in fancy-dress costume. *The children were got up in their best clothes for the occasion. We got Grandfather up as Father Christmas.*

get something up 1 arrange; organise. *We're getting up an evening of folk singing. The students have got up another petition against the building of nuclear power stations.* 2 study; memorise. *Bill is getting up his history dates for the test tomorrow.*

get up to something 1 reach the standard or level of. *I hope to get up to the required speed for the shorthand exam within the next two months.* 2 be involved in; be busy with (usually something undesirable). *What mischief have the children been getting up to now? I wonder what he'll get up to next!*

give someone away 1 betray. *Nobody knows I've done this, so please don't give me away!* 2 lead the bride to the groom at a marriage ceremony. *The bride was given away by her uncle, as her father was in hospital at the time of the wedding.*

give something away 1 present or distribute free. *John gave all his possessions away and became a monk.* 2 betray. *Please don't give my secret away! The guilty look on his face was a real give-away.*

give in surrender; yield. *You can't win the game, so you may as well give in. The rioters were at last forced to give in to the police.*

give something in submit. *The soldiers gave their guns in to their enemy. Don't forget to give in your names if you wish to be considered for membership.*

give out 1 come to an end; be used up. *We had just reached home when the petrol gave out. His strength had almost given out when the rescuers found him.* 2 stop functioning. *We were ten miles from the next town when the engine gave out.*

give something out 1 distribute. *The president's wife gave out flowers to the soldiers.* 2 announce. *The list of names was given out over the microphone. It was given out that the Prime Minister had died suddenly.*

give up (informal) lose interest and admit defeat. *Oh, I give up! I'm tired of trying to guess the answer!*

give someone up 1 surrender; betray. *They knew he was a spy and a sense of duty forced them to give him up to the police.* 2 no longer expect to come. *I had already given John up, when suddenly he walked in!* 3 no longer expect to recover after illness. *The doctors had given the patient up, but he made a remarkable recovery.*

give something up 1 surrender; relinquish. *He refused to give the documents up, even under pressure. I don't want to give my job up, unless it's really necessary.* 2 renounce (beliefs, principles). *Will you have to give your religion up in order to marry her?* 3 devote the time of. *All our weekends are given up to gardening.*

give up something 1 stop indulging in. *If you gave up smoking and drinking, your health would improve. Bad habits are not so easily given up.* 2 abandon; no longer try, perform etc. *They've given up the search for survivors. We've given up all attempts to complete the project on time.*

go about 1 circulate, be current. *There's another rumour going about that the President will resign soon.* 2 move or walk about. *Teenage boys tend to go about in groups. Does old Mr Wilkins still go about in those old trousers?*

go about something manage; perform. *Can you help me with this problem? I don't quite know how to go about it. She went about her work of discovering the truth very efficiently.*

go after someone/something try to get. *Jim's gone after another job. They both went after the same girl.*

go along with someone/something agree with; approve of. *Do you go along with the idea of inherited wealth?*

go by someone/something form a judgment from; trust as correct. *You can't go by what George says, he gets confused. Don't go by that clock. It's fast.*

go down 1 (informal) be received. *How does the prospect of working again after the holidays go down? His speech went down very well with the audience.* 2 lose in value; fall. *Shares have gone down again by ten points. The tone of the neighbourhood has gone down a lot since those ugly new houses were built.*

go down with something fall ill with. *Most of my colleagues have gone down with flu.*

go for someone 1 (informal) attack. *He went for him with a knife. The newspapers really went for him over the handling of the crisis, but he wasn't the only one who deserved criticism.* 2 (informal) admire; be attracted by. *Dark men often go for blondes.* 3 (informal) include; apply to. *Listen carefully, because this goes for you all. Does that go for the rest of us too?*

go for something 1 (informal) like. *I don't go for modern art.* 2 try hard to get; strive for. *Ken's going for the tennis championship this year.* 3 be sold for. *'How much did the house go for?' 'It went for far less than I expected.'*

go in for something 1 compete in. *Jack's gone in for the long-jump, but I don't think he has a chance. She went in for a singing competition.* 2 have as an interest. *Peter goes in for collecting antique weapons.* 3 choose as one's career. *Mary's gone in for nursing.*

go into something 1 investigate; examine. *The lawyer said that he would go into the matter very thoroughly. The case will have to be gone into very carefully.* 2 state in detail. *We haven't enough time to go into the history of the case, so perhaps you could summarize the main points.*

go off 1 explode. *The bomb went off without warning.* 2 (of foodstuffs) go bad; get worse; deteriorate. *Don't drink the milk; I think it's gone off. The standard of his work has gone off over the last few weeks.* 3 (informal) fall asleep. *Grandfather's gone off in the chair. Don't wake him!* 4 result. *'How did your party go off?' 'It went off very well actually.'*

go off someone/something lose one's liking or taste for. *I'm afraid I'm going off Professor Blake. He's not as stimulating as he used to be. We've gone right off camping holidays. We've booked in at a hotel, this year.*

go on 1 (informal) continue talking. *I was tired of listening to her complaints, but she went on and on.* 2 continue; resume. *We'll stop there for today, and go on with the discussion tomorrow.* 3 happen; take place. *Will someone please explain to me what's going on here? There are some very queer goings-on in that house! Strange people coming and going at all hours!* 4 (informal) behave. *Mary was going on like a silly school-girl! I've never seen her go on like that before.*

go on at someone (informal) grumble to; reprimand. *Every day he would go on at me about something or other—so I resigned.*

go out 1 cease to be in fashion. *I hope plastic coats will soon go out.* 2 be sent, circulated, announced etc. *Have all the wedding invitations gone out yet?* 3 emigrate. *He went out to Australia about five years ago.*

go over something 1 repeat. *Could you go over the explanation once more, please? The actor had to go over his lines many times before he got them right.* 2 examine; check. *Let's go over these accounts once more. The policeman went over the facts again and again, but couldn't piece them together.* 3 search. *The police went over his room three times, but found nothing.*

go through be accepted, concluded, successful etc. *I hear that the deal went through. Congratulations! The Conservatives are trying to prevent the Bill from going through.*

go through something 1 use up; consume. *I've gone through too much money this week. How many pints of milk do you go through with five children?* 2 search; examine. *The Customs went through all our luggage at the airport.* 3 suffer pain, hardship, loss etc. *Most families went through quite a lot during the war.* 4 discuss; review. *Shall we go through the details of salary now? The pros and cons of the issue have been gone through again and again, but they still haven't reached a conclusion.*

go through with something complete; conclude; endure to the end. *The plan was very daring, and at the last minute, I felt I couldn't go through with it. I don't think we should go through with the deal, after all.*

go up 1 increase in price. *Butter's going up again next week.* 2 be constructed. *There are supermarkets going up everywhere.*

grow on someone appeal more and more to. *I didn't like the song at first, but it grows on you the more you hear it.*

grow up (of people) mature; become adult. *Your children are growing up very quickly now. Mary's beginning to act quite grown up. Bill's at the age when he likes to spend his time with grown-ups.*

hand down something pass on through tradition. *These paintings have been handed down to us through three generations.*

hand something out circulate; offer. *Will you help me to hand out the leaflets at the meeting? Joe is good at handing out advice which nobody ever follows!*

hang about/around (informal) stand waiting idly. *That man's been hanging about here for over an hour—what does he want? Bill's not here at the moment, but if you hang around for a while you should catch him.*

hang back hesitate to come forward. *If you know the answer, say it! Don't hang back so much. Paul hung back from taking part in the discussion.*

hang behind linger, lag behind. *Walk faster! If you hang behind we'll lose you. A few students hung behind after the lecture to talk to the Professor.*

hang on (informal) wait. *If you can hang on a second, I'll look for Bob and tell him you're on the phone for him. Just hang on till I get help!*

hang on to something (informal) retain; not sell or part with. *I should hang on to those shares—they'll be going up again soon. Old Walker should have retired ages ago, but he's hanging on to his job.*

hang out 1 endure; manage. *The besieged soldiers had to hang out for six days without supplies.* 2 (informal) live. *Where's Dick hanging out these days?*

hang up end a telephone conversation (perhaps abruptly). *I'll have to hang up now. I've no more time. We were in the middle of the conversation, when suddenly she hung up on me!*

hang someone/something up (informal) delay (often passive). *I'm sorry I'm late. I got hung up by a friend on the way here. The heavy rain hung up the work on the building site for three weeks.*

have someone down invite to one's house. *Shall we have Mother down for the weekend?*

have someone in get the presence of. *I'm having the electrician in today to fix the light. We had the Robinsons in for supper yesterday evening.*

have something on 1 wear. *Gloria had her new fur coat on again last night.* 2 have something arranged; have an engagement. *Would you like to visit us this evening, or have you (got) something on already? I'll come and see you as soon as I can, but I have a lot on at the moment.*

have someone on (informal) tease; trick. *Uncle George said my old car would fetch a thousand pounds, but I think he was only having me on.*

have something on someone (informal) have proof or evidence against. *The police can't lock him up yet. They haven't got anything on him—only their suspicions.*

have something out cause to be extracted or removed. *Jim's in hospital having his tonsils out. The dentist told me I'll have to have this tooth out.*

have something out (with someone) (informal) argue or discuss to the end. *It's time you had the whole matter out with her. You'd feel much better for it!*

have someone up get the presence of. *Shall we have the Greens up this weekend?*

have someone up for something (informal) summons for; charge with. *If you say things like that, they can have you up for slander! Joe's been had up for drunken driving again.*

head someone off divert; elude. *The thief realised that the police were following him, but he succeeded in heading them off at the junction.*

head someone off something (informal) prevent from talking about. *We tried our best to head Henry off the topic, because we knew he'd reveal confidential information.*

head something off (informal) avoid; divert. *I knew he'd try to head off awkward questions about his past. I've been trying to head a cold off by taking tablets and hot lemon drinks.*

help (someone) out (informal) help. *Who's helping out in the garden this afternoon? I've often helped Bob out when he's been a bit short of money. They've been helped out on occasions by Chris's father.*

hold back hesitate; restrain oneself. *I held back because I wasn't sure of the way he'd react. She was only held back from telling him her real opinion by her fear of him.*

hold something back not reveal; withhold. *Jimmy told me most of the facts of the affair, but I'm sure he's still holding information back. The research findings have been held back long enough! They should be published.*

hold off (usually of weather) fail to occur; be delayed. *If the rain holds off, we can play cricket this afternoon.*

hold someone/something off resist. *The police had difficulty in holding the fans off when the pop-star was getting in the car. The soldiers managed to hold off the enemy attack for three days.*

hold on 1 manage to endure; stand firm. *Hold on until I fetch help!* 2 (informal) wait. *Just hold on a second while I get the car out. I'll run you home.*

hold out 1 manage to endure; resist. *The regiment held out against the enemy until reinforcements were sent.* 2 last; continue to exist. *How long will the rations hold out? Three more days, then we've nothing until the next supplies arrive.* 3 continue to function (of something old or broken). *I hope the engine will hold out until we get the car to a garage.*

hold out on someone (informal) refuse to tell; keep a secret from. *If I thought you were holding out on me, I should be very annoyed.*

hold out for something (informal) use delaying tactics in the hope of getting. *The union has been offered ten per cent, but the leaders are deliberately holding out for twelve.*

hold something over postpone. *Can't we hold the matter over until the next meeting? It's too late to begin a discussion on it now.*

hold up endure. *Old Mr Black holds up very well, in spite of all the trouble and illness he's had.*

hold someone/something up 1 delay; stop. *Sorry I'm late. I was held up by the traffic. This working to rule is holding up production considerably. 'What's the hold-up?' 'There's probably been an accident.'* 2 threaten and try to rob. *The thief held up four employees at gun-point and forced them to open the safe.*

hold with something (informal) approve of. *I don't hold with excessive drinking and late hours. Do you hold with private schools and hospitals?*

hunt something up (informal) find by investigation or research. *I managed to hunt up that quotation in the library. Where did you hunt all those details up?*

hush something up not reveal; prevent from becoming public. *They did their best to hush the whole thing up. The affair was hushed up, don't you remember?*

iron something out solve; resolve. *Have they managed to iron out* *their differences of opinion? There are few problems that cannot be ironed out, if people are prepared to talk about them.*

join in (something) participate in. *Why don't you join in? We're having fun! Ask Brian if he wants to join in the game.*

join up enter the armed forces voluntarily. *I never thought Peter would join up, but he says he's always wanted to be a soldier.*

jump at something (informal) accept with enthusiasm. *Alice would jump at the chance of going to Egypt. It was the offer of a lifetime and she couldn't help but jump at it.*

jump on someone (informal) criticize severely; be suddenly angry with. *The teacher jumped on him for giving in untidy homework. I don't like being jumped on for trivial matters.*

keep `at someone (informal) pester; keep under pressure. *You'll have to keep at Sam if you want your money back!*

keep `at something (informal) persist with. *If you keep at it for long enough, you're sure to find something.*

keep in (informal) stay indoors. *It's best to keep in while it's hailing.*

keep someone in punish by detaining after school. *Johnny has been kept in twice this week for being cheeky to the teacher.*

keep something in (informal) store, have on hand. *We don't keep much beer in as we don't drink it.*

keep in with someone (informal) have friendly relations with. *It's best that I keep in with the Parkinsons—he's my bank manager!*

keep on continue. *Keep on until you reach the traffic lights. Then turn left.*

keep something on continue to maintain. *Will the Jacksons still keep on the big house, now that all their sons have married and moved out?*

keep on at someone for/about something (informal) pester, worry, criticize continuously for/about. *I do wish you wouldn't keep on at me about the money I lost—it wasn't intentional!*

keep out of something not get involved in. *I warned Bill to keep out of it, but he would interfere!*

keep up 1 (of the weather) remain unchanged. *If this storm keeps up the crops will be destroyed.* 2 remain bright and cheerful. *Her spirits kept up in spite of all her troubles.* 3 persevere. *If you can't keep up, then give up!*

keep someone up (informal) prevent from going to bed. *It's getting late. I'm keeping you up, so I'll go now.*

keep something up maintain. *To keep your strength up, eat well and get enough sleep. The country house became too expensive to keep up.*

keep up something continue; maintain. *We've kept up our friendship for over twenty years now. I wish I'd kept up Physics at school. We're having difficulty in keeping up the payments.*

keep up with 1 remain at the same level, position etc as. *Are you* *keeping up with me, or am I reading too fast?* 2 maintain contact, familiarity etc with. *Do you still keep up with Ron and Sheila?*

knock off (informal) stop work. *The men usually knock off at six o'clock.*

knock something off 1 (of money) deduct. *I'll knock you five pounds off if you buy two! How much was knocked off the retail price?* 2 (informal) write, compose etc quickly. *He earns his money writing short stories for women's journals. He's able to knock them off in no time!*

knock someone up 1 awaken by knocking. *I'd like to be knocked up early tomorrow. I've an appointment in London at 9 o'clock.* 2 (informal) make ill by exhaustion. *Bill must be overworked—he looks badly knocked up.*

knock something up (informal) produce quickly. *I'll knock us up a few sandwiches; it won't take long.*

knock up against something (informal) be confronted with. *I didn't expect to knock up against so many difficulties when I started on this project.*

lay something aside (of money) save. *He lays a little aside every week for his old age.*

lay someone off dismiss temporarily because there is no work. *The car factory is having to lay people off again.*

lay off something (informal) stop. *Why don't you lay off smoking for a while until your cough gets better?*

lay something on 1 provide, (of a service) supply. *We can't move into the new house until the gas and electricity have been laid on. The bus company intends to lay on two more buses for this route.* 2 arrange; organize. *Who's laying on the entertainment for the children's party? Has all the food and drink been laid on?*

lay someone up (of illness) cause to stay in bed. *A bad attack of flu can lay you up longer than you think. I've been laid up with rheumatism for a week.*

lay something up store. *Have you got enough supplies laid up for the winter?*

lead someone on 1 (informal) tease. *Don't take any notice of what Uncle Fred says. He's just leading you on!* 2 persuade. *Salesmen do their best to lead people on to buy things they don't need.*

lead up to something prepare the way for; signify. *I know what he's leading up to. Just wait and see if he doesn't ask you for a loan! It all leads up to the fact that he doesn't really want the responsibility.*

let someone down (informal) disappoint; fail. *He won't let you down; he's very reliable. I've had so many let-downs that I've stopped asking people for help.*

let someone off (informal) forgive; allow to go unpunished. *I'll let you off this time, but don't do it again!*

let something off explode. *We're letting fireworks off tonight to celebrate my birthday.*

let on (informal) reveal by telling. *You can confide in Janet. She won't let on if you ask her not to.*

let someone out (informal) release (from something unpleasant). *My flu let me out of attending the meeting. The snow gave me a lucky let-out from coming to work today.*

let up (informal) stop; decrease; slacken off. *I think the rain's beginning to let up. Harry never lets up for a minute—he can't rest until he's found the solution.*

lie in (informal) stay in bed; get up late. *You ought to lie in tomorrow and catch up on your sleep. There's nothing nicer than a Sunday lie-in!*

lie up 1 stay in hiding. *The police suspect that the escaped convict is lying up in the hills.* 2 rest. *The doctor advised me to lie up for a week.*

live something down (informal) get (something unpleasant, disgraceful etc) forgotten, ignored or accepted. *I thought she'd never live down the humiliation, but she did. Such a scandal won't be lived down for a long time.*

live up to something reach and maintain a standard expected of one. *I hope I can live up to the expectations of my parents. He was well known for squandering his money—in fact, he still lives up to his reputation!*

look after someone/something take care of; be responsible for. *If you want to go out, I'll look after the children for you. Bill knows how to look after his own interests.*

look down on someone/something regard as inferior. *Sebastian's a snob: he looks down on people of lower birth than himself. His views are looked down on by his fellow students.*

look in (on) (informal) visit; call (on). *If you're free this evening, why don't you look in (on us)?*

look into something investigate. *The police are looking into the matter very thoroughly. I don't think my complaint has been looked into at all!*

look on watch inactively. *I couldn't stand there looking on while the old lady struggled with her parcels, so I carried them for her.*

look on someone regard. *I've always looked on Fred as someone who's going to be a leader. He's always been looked on as one of the best lawyers in town.*

look out (informal) be careful. *Look out when you're crossing the road!*

look out for someone/something keep a watch for. *I'll look out for Mr Jackson and give him your message. We've been looking out for a new house, but the ones we've seen have all been too expensive.*

look over someone/something (informal) examine. *The boss is looking over two new applicants at the moment. Those accounts need a thorough looking-over : I'm not sure that they're accurate.*

look to someone (for something) turn to; rely on (for help, reassurance, encouragement etc). *If he needs advice, he always looks to his father.*

look up (informal) improve. *The weather's looking up at last. Share prices are looking up again! So is business!*

look someone up (informal) go to visit. *I must look up Uncle George. I've heard he's in bed with arthritis.*

look something up try to find in a dictionary, timetable, map etc. *Can you look up the time of the next train to Brighton?*

look up to someone admire. *John has always looked up to his Uncle Sidney—probably because he's a Judge. It's embarrassing to be looked up to by one's colleagues.*

make off hurry away; escape. *When the police arrived, the thief was making off down the road.*

make off with something steal. *The thief made off with the jewellery and the contents of the safe.*

make out (with) (informal) manage or succeed (with). *How's Peter making out with Shirley? He's been after her for months now.*

make someone out (informal) understand. *David's a puzzle to me. I just can't make him out.*

make something out 1 (of a bill, cheque, form etc) write; fill in. *Would you make out the bill, please? All cheques to be made out to Global Enterprises Ltd.* 2 distinguish (in bad light etc). *I couldn't make the frog out in the dark until I'd almost stepped on it!*

make out that ... claim or assert that ... *You can't make out that I haven't helped you financially—ask my Bank Manager!*

make something over to someone legally transfer to. *For tax reasons, the Duke of Hades has made all his property over to his two sons.*

make up apply cosmetics. *The play starts soon. The actors are already making up.*

make someone up apply cosmetics to. *Have you made up the chorus girls? They're due to go on stage.*

make something up 1 invent. *Don't believe him. He made that story up!* 2 compensate. *How can he make his losses up in such a short time?* 3 mix together. *The chemist made up a red mixture for my cough that tasted like cherry juice.* 4 prepare; pack. *If you won't be in for lunch, the hotel will make a hamper of food up for you to take with you.* 5 complete by supplying what is missing. *Won't you make up the total by contributing £3?*

make up for something compensate for. *I took yesterday afternoon off, so I'm working this evening to make up for it.*

make up to someone attempt to win favour with; be pleasant to (for a reason). *He's really angry with you—you'll have to make up to him for a long time before all is well again.*

make something up to someone compensate someone for something. *He's given me a lot of his time. I'd like to make it up to him at Christmas by giving him a generous present.*

mess about/around (informal) waste time. *Get on with your work and stop messing around!*

mess something up (informal) spoil. *The rain came down and messed up our picnic completely. Bob came in from the garage with his best trousers messed up with oil.*

miss someone/something out omit. *I can't find Mrs Robins on the list. I think we've missed her out. Yes, her name has definitely been missed out.*

miss out on something (informal) not experience; not profit from. *Don't forget to invite Wendy—she's always missing out on these discussions and feels left out.*

mix someone/something up confuse; muddle. *The teacher explained too much at once and mixed us all up. She mixed the story up so much that I couldn't follow it.*

mix someone up in something involve. *Don't mix me up in this —I want nothing to do with your affairs!*

move in settle in; take possession (of a house, office etc). *Our new neighbours have just moved in next door.*

move in on someone/something surround to attack. *The soldiers moved in on the town and attacked at dawn.*

move out (of) vacate (a house, office etc). *Have the Mackintoshes moved out yet next door?*

move up change one's sitting or standing place to make room for someone else. *We'd better move up—here come two more people, and there's lots of room on the bench.*

nod off (informal) fall asleep. *I was just nodding off when the telephone rang.*

open out lose one's reserve or shyness. *Jill soon began to open out when she started work at the factory.*

open up 1 start a business. *A new butcher is opening up on the corner.* 2 (informal) talk frankly. *He decided to open up to the police and tell them everything.* 3 emerge; develop. *New opportunities have opened up for the firm which should not be neglected.*

own up (to something) (informal) confess or admit (to). *You'll win respect if you own up to what you've done.*

pack something in 1 (informal) abandon; stop indulging in. *I've packed gambling in. I've been losing too much money.* 2 (informal) end (a relationship, job etc). *Jim is seriously considering packing his job in. Mary's packed her boyfriend in.*

pack up 1 (informal) cease work. *The workers packed up at 2* *o'clock on account of the rain.* 2 (informal) stop functioning. *We were going up a steep hill when the engine suddenly packed up!*

pass for someone/something be thought to be; be (wrongly) recognized as. *Your accent is excellent: you'd pass for an Englishman any time. She looks just like her younger sister, and she'd pass for 30 easily!*

pass off gradually subside or disappear. *Take this tablet and the pain should pass off within half an hour.*

pass someone off as someone falsely represent as. *He passed his secretary off as his wife. I don't like being passed off as your financial advisor, just to make you look important!*

pass out (informal) faint. *Jane passed out because of the heat and the stuffy atmosphere.*

pass over something avoid; ignore. *That's a subject I would prefer to pass over.*

pay off (informal) succeed; prove to be profitable. *The deal will pay off, I'm sure. The gamble's paid off after all: we're rich!*

pay someone off 1 (informal) pay to keep quiet. *The blackmailer had to be paid off. He was too dangerous.* 2 settle one's debts with. *Has Jones paid off all his creditors yet?* 3 pay and dismiss. *Another ten employees have been paid off at the firm. There's not enough work for them.*

pay something off finish paying for. *I've just paid off my loan from the bank. What a relief!*

pick on someone (informal) single out for criticism, teasing etc. *They always pick on me when anything goes wrong. Poor Joe's always being picked on at school, because he's so small and shy.*

pick someone/something out choose (from among many). *Can you pick your brother out from that group of people? Have you picked out the photographs that you'd like to have?*

pick up 1 (informal) continue. *We can now pick up where we left off.* 2 (informal) improve (in health, business etc). *Henry's been ill, but he's picking up again now. Share prices have picked up recently, I'm glad to say.*

pick someone up 1 (informal) collect. *I'll pick you up on the corner at three; don't be late!* 2 (informal) make casual acquaintance with. *That's the girl Bill picked up at the dance.* 3 (informal) reprimand; correct. *I made a few mistakes and he picked me up for them.* 4 (informal) catch; arrest. *The police picked up the man they were looking for just outside the town.*

pick something up 1 learn. *Where did you pick up your Russian? Statistics isn't a subject that can be picked up in a month.* 2 acquire. *I picked up a bargain today in the sales. Look at this lovely coat for only £8!* 3 become infected with. *Where did you pick up that cold?* 4 collect. *Did you pick the washing up from the laundry?*

pile something on (informal) intensify and make worse; exaggerate. *The news is bad enough—don't pile it on by telling me more. She's always piling on how artistic she is!*

pin someone down cause to define intentions, ideas etc. *We must try to pin the Management down to stating a definite figure, otherwise we'll never get a rise in salary! He's not a man who's easily pinned down.*

pin something down state exactly. *It's difficult to pin down what it is that I don't like about him.*

play along (informal) cooperate. *I'm sure Jack will play along once we've made all arrangements. Play along with them to see what their intentions are.*

play someone along (informal) keep waiting. *They've played him along for long enough. It's time they told him whether or not he'll get the job.*

play something down/up (informal) make to appear less/more important. *Most newspapers either play their stories up or down—you'll never get a neutral report.*

play up (informal) cause trouble. *My rheumatism's playing up again. The children always start playing up when we have visitors.*

play up to someone (informal) flatter to gain an advantage. *Stop trying to play up to Miriam like that. It's so obvious—and you'll get nowhere with her!*

play with something consider (idea, notion, plan, scheme etc). *I played with the idea of going into business, but I don't think I can raise the capital.*

polish something off (informal) finish quickly. *Who's going to polish off the rest of this cream-cake? The rest of the work can be polished off tomorrow.*

polish something up (informal) improve. *The content of the essay's fine: just polish the style up a bit. I just need ten minutes to polish up my appearance before the guests arrive.*

press for something demand. *The workers are pressing for another ten per cent rise.*

press on (informal) continue one's efforts. *Don't be discouraged. Press on and hope for the best!*

press something on someone 1 (informal) force to accept. *I didn't want the money, but he pressed it on me!* 2 underline the importance of. *I need not press the urgency of the matter on you, as I know you are fully aware of it yourselves.*

pull something off (informal) complete successfully. *He pulled the deal off splendidly, as I knew he would.*

pull out 1 (of a vehicle) leave; move away. *The Tyne–Tees express pulled out on the dot.* 2 (informal) withdraw. *I don't like the plan. I'm going to pull out before it's too late.*

pull round (informal) get better (after an illness, shock etc). *The* *operation weakened him, but he'll soon pull round now that he knows he's coming out of hospital.*

pull through recover (from serious accident or illness). *The patient has very serious injuries. He's not expected to pull through.*

pull together (informal) cooperate. *If we all pull together we'll overthrow the oppressors sooner.*

pull up (of a vehicle) come to a halt. *The car pulled up in front of me and I had to brake suddenly.*

pull someone up (informal) stop in order to reprimand, warn, fine etc. *The police pulled him up for overtaking on a bend. I was pulled up again this morning for speeding.*

pull something up improve; bring to a higher standard. *You'll have to pull your knowledge of Africa up for the interview. His English isn't very good, but with a bit more work and practice it could be pulled up before the oral exam.*

push for something demand. *The union leaders are pushing for higher wages and early retirement.*

push off (informal) leave. *Well, I'll have to push off now, so I'll see you later at the club.*

push on (informal) continue. *We're pushing on with our investigation as fast as we can.*

push something on to someone (informal) force or impose on. *They're pushing all the unpleasant, tiresome jobs on to the new junior clerk. It's not fair.*

put someone about (informal) inconvenience. *Jack doesn't mind putting people about, as long as he gets what he wants. I'm tired of being put about by ungrateful people!*

put something about (informal) circulate (a story, rumour etc). *Don't believe it! It's just a rumour that someone has put about.*

put something across communicate. *Try to put your explanation across as simply as possible. His ideas are good, but they aren't always put across very clearly.*

put something away 1 save (money). *He puts a little away every week for his grandchildren.* 2 (informal) eat or drink in large quantities). *I've never seen anyone eat so much! He put away a whole chicken and five bottles of beer!*

put someone away (informal) confine (in a mental hospital or prison). *He's been put away as a dangerous criminal.*

put someone down (informal) snub; criticize; suppress. *You never give me credit for anything—you're always putting me down. Sammy's so cocky that he deserves every put-down he gets.*

put something down as/to something explain as; assign to. *We put his rude manner down to ignorance of our British customs. His behaviour has been put down to an unhappy childhood, but I don't think that's any excuse!*

put in interrupt (by speaking). *'But I object!' he put in, suddenly and unexpectedly.*

put something in 1 spend or devote (time, energy, care etc). *I have to put in an hour's piano practice every day.* 2 install. *We can't move into the house until they've put the heating in.*

put in for something request; claim. *Most of the staff have put in for a wage-rise after Christmas.*

put something off postpone; delay. *The cricket match has been put off until Monday afternoon. Don't put off going to see the dentist if you have toothache.*

put someone off 1 allow (a passenger in a vehicle) to alight. *Could you put me off at the Town Hall, please?* 2 **put someone off (something)** (informal) discourage or deter (from doing something); persuade against. *I wanted to see that new film at the Odeon, but the newspaper review put me off.* 3 (informal) distract. *I don't like music playing when I'm working. It puts me off.* 4 (informal) avoid; evade. *I refuse to be put off, and I ask you, once again, to answer my question.*

put someone on (informal) deceive; cheat. *Old Mrs Carnaby's so innocent and kind—but it's no surprise that people keep putting her on. The new religion turned out to be nothing more than a huge money-grabbing put-on.*

put someone out 1 disturb; upset; inconvenience. *I feel very put out about the whole matter. She's in a bad mood; she must have been put out by something.* 2 knock unconscious. *The other boxer put Jim out in the third round.*

put something out 1 circulate; publish. *A statement has been put out denying all rumours that the firm is having to close down. The police have put out a general call to all public places.* 2 extinguish (flames, a fire etc). *We just managed to put the flames out before any real damage was caused.* 3 dislocate (a part of the body). *I put my shoulder out digging the garden.* 4 cause to be inaccurate. *That one little mistake has put the whole calculation out.*

put someone through connect (on the telephone). *Can you put me through to Mr Brown's office, please?*

put something through conclude; complete; process. *I'd be obliged if you would put my application for a visa through as quickly as possible.*

put up 1 stay temporarily. *He always puts up at the Grand Hotel when he's in town.* 2 stand as a candidate in an election. *Jim's putting up for the Liberals again, but I don't think he'll get in.*

put someone up 1 give accommodation to. *We can put you up if you're staying in town overnight. We were put up by a very old friend of my father's.* 2 nominate as a candidate in an election. *The Liberals are putting Jim up again in the by-election.*

put someone up to (doing) something encourage in. *'Who put George up to the idea?' 'He was put up to it by his brother.'*

put something up 1 build; erect. *Another supermarket's been put up near our house.* 2 increase. *The grocer's put the price of coffee up again.*

put up something 1 offer as a contribution; lend. *He put up a lot of money for the art gallery. When the first loan had run out, he put up another £500.* 2 prepare or provide (food). *Could you put me up a few sandwiches?* 3 advocate; put forward. *He's going to put up another proposal at the meeting.*

put up with someone/something (informal) tolerate; bear; endure. *I can't put up with a lot of noisy people when I'm working. If I were you I wouldn't put up with his behaviour any longer.*

put upon someone (Usually in the passive.) take advantage of; exploit. *Don't let yourself be put upon by that lazy, selfish liar!*

read something up acquire knowledge or information through reading. *I must read up what Roberts has written on the history of India.*

read up on something improve one's knowledge by reading. *I'm going to read up on statistics before the exam.*

reckon on something expect; include in one's calculations. *I wasn't reckoning on having this problem to deal with. We had reckoned on your help.*

rest up have a complete rest. *After the exam, I'm going to rest up for a few weeks.*

ring off close (a telephone conversation). *I'll have to ring off now but I'll ring you back this afternoon.*

roll in 1 (informal) (of people) appear; come in casually. *Peter never arranges a visit. He just rolls in when he feels like it!* 2 (informal) (of money) come in quantity. *Since Fred opened up a business, money's just been rolling in!*

roll on (informal) come soon. (Usually the statement of a wish.) *Roll on Christmas! I'm looking forward to all the good food!*

roll up (informal) (of people) appear; come (to see something). *Visitors have been rolling up in crowds all day to see the exhibition.*

round something off (informal) finish in a satisfactory way. *Let's round off the evening with a snack and a drink over at my place. The excursion was rounded off with a short visit to the zoo.*

round someone/something up (informal) gather together. *Let's round up the whole group and ask them what they think about it. The cowboys are rounding the cattle up.*

rule someone/something out exclude. *That would rule out the possibility of accident and would suggest either suicide or murder. Anyone who has entered for the same competition before is ruled out by the regulations.*

run across someone/something find; meet by chance. *Guess who I ran across in town the other day! Where did you run across this beautiful old vase?*

run after someone 1 (informal) pay excessive attention to. *He's always running after the girls—what's he trying to prove?* 2 (informal) serve. *Michael's a man who likes his wife running after him all the time.*

run away with one (of imagination, temper, feelings etc) control; direct. *Now you're letting your imagination run away with you!*

run away with something (informal) use up. *I'm afraid the research programme is running away with the government loan.*

run someone down 1 (of a vehicle) knock down. *He was almost run down by a bus.* 2 (informal) speak badly of; disparage. *I do wish Jane wouldn't run people down the way she does—I think it's jealousy.* 3 follow and take captive. *Policemen were searching the moors for the escaped prisoner all day. They finally ran him down in a farm-house.*

run someone in 1 (informal) arrest. *The police have run old Sam in again for being drunk and disorderly.* 2 (informal) drive in a car. *I'm going to town, too. If you can wait five minutes, I'll run you in.*

run something in (of a new engine, machine, vehicle etc) use carefully at first. *If you take care to run the engine in properly, the car will give you a lot of pleasure.*

run something off 1 produce quickly. *He's a remarkable writer : he can run off a novel in a week.* 2 print; duplicate. *Can you run me off two hundred copies of this sheet by tomorrow? Has the article been run off yet?*

run out 1 expire. *The contract runs out at the end of the year, and will have to be renewed.* 2 come to an end; be used up. *We'd just reached the motorway when the petrol ran out!*

run someone over 1 (informal) take (in a vehicle). *I'm going to the party, too, so I'll run you over.* 2 knock down (with a vehicle). *The bus ran him over, but he's not seriously hurt. He was run over by a car.*

run over something practice; rehearse. *I'll just run over my speech again—I'd hate to forget it in the middle! Will you run over my part with me? I still haven't got my lines at the beginning of the second act.*

run through something 1 rehearse. *He ran through his lecture in his mind.* 2 read quickly. *Run through this article and tell me what you think of it.* 3 use up. *We run through ten gallons of petrol a week.*

run to something 1 amount to; reach. *The book runs to about three hundred pages.* 2 (informal) provide money for. *My salary doesn't run to buying a new suit every week.*

run something up 1 make; sew quickly. *Can you run me up a*

costume for the fancy-dress ball? 2 accumulate. She runs up bills
everywhere in town. I've run up an overdraft and now the bank's
stopped my credit.

run up against someone/something be confronted with; encounter. Could you help me—I've run up against a few problems. If
Mick runs up against Mac, there'll be trouble!

see about something (informal) deal with; attend to. Have you
been to see about a new washing-machine?

see into something investigate. I took my complaint to the manager; he's going to see into it. It's about time the matter was seen
into.

see someone off accompany to the place of departure. Are you coming to see us off at the station?

see someone out accompany outside. I'll see you out. I'd hate you
to get lost in the building.

see something out 1 endure. It's a terrible film, but we ought to
see it out now because the tickets were so expensive! 2 last. I don't
think these old boots will see the winter out; I'll have to buy new ones.
He's very ill: he may not see the week out.

see through someone/something (informal) recognize to be
false. Jack thinks I believe his story, but I can see through him. I can
see through his scheme—he won't cheat me so easily!

see someone through help. Don't worry about money: I'll see you
through. Will £100 see him through?

see something through persevere with to the end. Now that we've
started the project, we'll have to see it through.

see to someone (informal) attend to. Will you see to that customer,
please?

see to something 1 attend to. I hope you'll see to the matter immediately. 2 fix; repair. The electrician's come to see to the faulty
light-switch. Has the car been seen to yet?

sell out (of something) have no more (of) left to sell. I'm sorry,
but we've sold out. There will be a new delivery tomorrow.

sell out (to someone/something) (informal) yield (to); betray a
cause (to). He sold out to ambition and the desire for wealth. The
new wage settlement was called a sell-out to trade union pressure.

sell up sell one's business, property etc. Why is he having to sell up?
Has he got into debt or is he moving out of the district?

send away for something request or buy by post. I've sent away
for the spring catalogue.

send for someone summon. We're going to send for the doctor. The
fever's getting worse.

send for something request or order by post. She sent for the
'special offer' cookery book.

set about someone (informal) attack physically or with words.

When I told the facts of the matter, he set about me in order to make my story look ridiculous.

set about something begin. *As soon as she got home, she set about preparing lunch. Please help me with this exercise—I don't know how to set about it.*

set someone back 1 delay; hinder. *This hold-up will set us back half an hour. Our trip's only major set-back was when the car caught fire.* 2 (informal) cost. *The new house must have set him back a few thousands!*

set in begin; establish itself. *It's been very cold the last few days: I think the winter's set in already. After pneumonia had set in, there wasn't much hope for his recovery.*

set off begin a journey. *Let's set off nice and early tomorrow, shall we?*

set someone off cause to begin. *Don't mention the war! You'll set Grandfather off reminiscing for hours!*

set something off 1 cause to explode. *The children are setting fireworks off in the garden.* 2 cause to begin. *I accidentally pressed the button and set off the alarm clock.* 3 show to advantage; make look attractive. *The red dress sets her blonde hair off beautifully.*

set on someone attack. *He was passing by the front door, when suddenly their dog set on him.*

set out 1 begin with the intention of. *He set out to cut the grass, but he finished up talking to the neighbour over the garden wall.* 2 begin a journey. *They set out as the sun was rising.*

set to start energetically; apply oneself vigorously. *She set to and finished cleaning the house within an hour. When Billy sets to, he can eat more than his father!*

set up establish oneself in a business or profession. *He intends setting up as a lawyer in the next town.*

set someone up 1 provide with required facilities. *His father will set him up as a doctor when he has completed his training in the hospital.* 2 improve someone's health. *Take a holiday in the mountains. The fresh air will set you up and you'll feel much better.*

set something up 1 erect; place in position. *He sets his vegetable stall up in the market every Saturday morning.* 2 establish; institute. *The government has set up a committee to examine the fishing industry. The whole set-up* (= structure) *of the conference broke down when the three main speakers didn't arrive.* 3 put forward; propose. *He set up the theory ten years ago and scholars have been discussing it ever since.* 4 (in sport) create (a new record). *Wilkins set up a new time in the 200 metres.*

settle down 1 marry and lead a routine life. *George is 35 already. I don't think he'll ever settle down.* 2 establish oneself permanently. *The Browns have lived in several parts of England, but I think they intend settling down in Norfolk.* 3 make oneself comfortable. *She* *settled down by the fire with her knitting and a box of chocolates, and turned on the radio.* 4 **settle down (to something)** apply one-self (to); concentrate (on). *I've been trying to read this book all day, but somehow I can't settle down to it properly.*

settle for something be prepared to accept. *I won't settle for a second-rate job.*

settle in establish oneself comfortably in new surroundings. *The new neighbours seem to have settled in now. How's Richard settling in at his new school?*

settle up (with someone) pay the money owing (to someone). *I owe you some money for the drinks. We'll settle up after lunch.*

settle on something decide on; choose. *We couldn't make up our minds which vase to buy, but we finally settled on the blue one.*

shake someone/something off get rid of; escape from; avoid. *The thief drove as fast as he could in an effort to shake off the pursuing police car. I'm afraid I didn't succeed in shaking off my cold.*

shake someone up upset; disturb. *The sad news has shaken her up pretty badly. She's rather shaken up about the matter.*

show off (informal) display (one's capabilities to others). *She always shows off with her knowledge of literature, if she thinks she can impress anyone. Thomas is a terrible show-off!*

show someone/something off proudly display to advantage. *Andrew is visiting all his friends, taking his new girlfriend with him in order to show her off to them. Jimmy loves showing off his stamp collection to his school-mates.*

show up (informal) appear. *Did Dick show up at the meeting last night? You never know when she's coming: she just shows up when she feels like it.*

show someone up (informal) reveal (something disagreeable) about. *The children always behave badly and show me up! Nobody likes to be shown up in public.*

shut up (informal) stop talking; be quiet. *I wish Gloria would shut up! No one else has a chance to get a word in edgeways.*

sink in (informal) be understood fully. *The teacher explained it to me twice, but I'm afraid it still hasn't sunk in.*

sit back (informal) be inactive; remain in the background. *I'm very annoyed with Tom. He just sits back and lets me do all the work alone.*

sit down to something (informal) accept without protest or complaint. *He seemed surprised when I objected—but surely he didn't expect me just to sit down to it?*

sit in on something attend as a listener or visitor. *When I was do-ing teaching practice, people often sat in on my lessons.*

sit on someone (informal) repress; put in one's place. *I don't like being sat on by anyone!*

sit on something 1 neglect; be inactive about. *I sent up a com-*

plaint, but the committee just sat on it for ages. 2 keep hold of; not part with. *Brian knows I need that information urgently, but he doesn't want me to have it, so he's just sitting on it.*

sit out not take part in. *Most people joined in the dancing. Only a few sat out.*

sit something out attend until the end. *I didn't enjoy the play, but we sat it out.*

sit up 1 stay out of bed until late. *I sat up until midnight, writing letters and reading.* 2 (informal) become attentive. *George was falling asleep in the lecture, but he sat up when the examination results were announced.*

skip over something (informal) pass over quickly. *We can skip over the details and concentrate on the general issues.*

sleep something off (informal) recover from (eg too much food or drink) by sleeping. *Dick got drunk at the party last night so he's sleeping it off now.*

sleep on continue to sleep. *My alarm-clock didn't go off this morning, so I slept on until 10 o'clock.*

sleep on something (informal) postpone (eg a decision) overnight. *I can't make up my mind now, but I'll sleep on it and let you know tomorrow.*

slip up (informal) make a mistake. *These figures aren't correct; I must have slipped up somewhere. Make sure you rehearse your part well—we can't afford a slip-up on stage!*

slow down become slower or less energetic; (of a vehicle etc) decrease speed. *Grandfather has slowed down considerably since the doctor told him to be careful with his heart. The lorry slowed down and finally stopped.*

slow someone down cause to become slower or less energetic. *The doctor's warning has slowed my father down a lot. He's not as intensely active as he used to be.*

slow something down cause to become slower. *The policeman slowed the van down and signalled the driver to stop.*

slow up become less energetic or efficient (eg because of age or illness). *Professor Brown's beginning to slow up; he'll be retiring next year.*

snap at someone speak very abruptly. *When I asked him a question, he snapped at me!*

snap at something (informal) accept immediately. *I'd snap at the chance of going to Canada.*

snap something up grab eagerly. *This antique clock was a real bargain, so I snapped it up. Sarah won't marry poor old Bill; she's waiting to be snapped up by some handsome millionaire.*

sneeze at something (informal) reject; not treat seriously. *It's a chance/offer/opportunity not to be sneezed at.*

soften someone up (informal) persuade. *'Has Tom managed to soften his father up yet? Will he let him go on the fishing trip?' 'Yes, he's been softened up.'*

sort someone out (informal) punish; reprimand. *When your father hears about this, he'll really sort you out!*

sort something out (informal) deal with; make orderly. *Have you sorted out all that trouble you had with the bank yet?*

spell something out (informal) state clearly and explicitly. *He still hasn't understood what you mean; you'll have to spell it out for him.*

spin something out (informal) make to last a long time. *Tom tells some entertaining stories, but he spins them out too long. How do you manage to spin your money out?*

spring up (informal) happen. *Has anything new sprung up this week?*

square up (with someone) (informal) settle a debt (with). *Have you squared up with Alex for the meal?*

square up to someone/something (informal) confront bravely; face. *He squared up to his attackers and managed to fight them off. You'll have to square up to your responsibilities; you can't simply run away from them.*

square something up (with someone) (informal) settle or manage (with). *He said he's got a problem to square up with the manager.*

stamp something out get rid of; suppress. *The police are campaigning to stamp out violence and crime in our cities.*

stand down withdraw (an application); surrender (a chance). *Johnson applied for the post of director, but then he decided to stand down for a younger colleague.*

stand in (for someone) substitute (for). *'I didn't know Polly worked in this department!' 'She doesn't. She's just standing in for a colleague.'*

stand out 1 be very noticeable; be conspicuous. *Your red pullover really stands out in that photograph.* 2 **stand out (from)** be in favourable contrast (with). *Elizabeth's voice really stands out from the rest of the choir.*

stand out for something (informal) try to get (by delaying acceptance etc). *The workers were offered ten per cent, but they're standing out for another five.*

stand up (to something) bear examination (from). *Her story sounds convincing, but I doubt very much that it will stand up to questioning in a court of law.*

stand up for someone/something give moral support to; defend. *I believe that you're innocent of the crime and I'd stand up for you anywhere.*

stand up to someone confront bravely; face. *If that big boy hits you again, stand up to him and hit him back!*

stand up to something resist. *Children's toys don't stand up to much knocking about. They break very easily nowadays.*

step in intervene. *The police had to step in to control the outbreak of rioting.*

step something up increase. *The increased demand for exports will mean stepping production up considerably. Staff efforts will have to be stepped up, too!*

stick at something (informal) persevere. *When he has work to do, he sticks at it until it's finished.*

stick out for something (informal) be resolute in trying to get. *The strikers are sticking out for a higher bonus.*

stick to someone (informal) be loyal to; remain with. *Fred always sticks to his friend, no matter what happens.*

stick to something (informal) adhere to, not change. *Make sure you stick to the same story when you're questioned a second time.*

stick up for someone (informal) defend; support. *Will you stick up for me when I make my protest next week?*

stir something up (informal) provoke (something unpleasant). *Mary's always trying to stir up trouble between Jenny and Anne.*

straighten something out (informal) put right. *We've had a bit of trouble at the factory, but the management and the union will be able to straighten it out.*

swear by something (informal) have a high opinion of; value. *Grandfather swears by rum as the only medicine for a cold.*

take after someone resemble; have a similar character or appearance to. *Margaret takes after her father in being strong-willed.*

take someone down (informal) humiliate. *Margaret has a much too high opinion of herself. Someone must take her down a bit.* Note the expression: *She needs taking down a peg or two.*

take something down write down; record. *The policeman took down all particulars of the accident.*

take someone in (informal) trick; fool. *He's a clever talker—and good at taking people in. I don't allow myself to be taken in by sales talk.*

take something in 1 understand. *This book is difficult to understand, and when I'm tired I can't take in what the author means.* 2 observe; look at. *I was too busy taking in the beautiful furniture to notice who was in the room.* 3 (in sewing) make narrower. *This dress is too big at the waist. I'll have to take it in.*

take in someone give accommodation to. *Mrs Robinson is considering taking in students next year.*

take in something 1 include; cover. *The study of physics takes in many different subjects.* 2 work at (for payment, in one's own home). *She takes in sewing for the neighbours.*

take off 1 (of aircraft) leave the ground. *The plane took off on time.*

It was a smooth take-off. 2 (informal) leave in a hurry. *Janet took off for Morocco immediately term ended.*

take someone off (informal) imitate (for amusement). *Bob's party-piece is taking politicians off. His take-offs are hilarious.*

take something off 1 remove. *Take your coat off and sit down! Who took the knob off the door? Why doesn't the government take the tax off cigarettes?* 2 remove from service. *Some local trains have been taken off, as there was no demand for them.* 3 lose weight. *I took off three pounds last week!* 4 set aside (free time for a holiday). *When are you taking your holidays? I took a week off in March and I'm taking Easter off, too.*

take on 1 (informal) become popular. *I didn't expect pointed shoes to take on, but they have.* 2 (informal) get upset. *I wish she wouldn't take on so!*

take someone on 1 employ. *Is the supermarket taking on any more assistants? No more workers are being taken on at present.* 2 accept as an opponent. *Will you take me on for a game of chess?*

take something on accept; undertake. *Is he willing to take on the responsibility? I'll take the work on, but I can't tell you exactly when I'll finish it.*

take on something acquire. *His writing has taken on a very peculiar style. In the translation, the word takes on a different meaning.*

take someone out invite for entertainment. *Bob takes his wife out to the theatre every weekend, but my husband hasn't taken me out for months!*

take something out 1 (of a contract, licence etc) obtain (for a fixed time). *You'll have to take out a dog licence. How long may the subscription be taken out for?* 2 (of dirt, stains etc) remove. *I need something that will take the grease stains out.*

take something over (from someone) come into control or possession of. *Henry's taken over the running of the family firm from his old father. There's been a take-over in Ruritania—the President's been assassinated.*

take to someone form a liking for. *I didn't take to our new neighbours at first, but now we're good friends.*

take to something 1 form a liking for. *How has Billy taken to his new school?* 2 embark on; start with; form the habit of. *If a man once takes to gambling, it's difficult for him to break the habit. My father has taken to playing golf at the weekends.*

take up improve. *I think the weather's going to take up at last.*

take something up 1 (sewing) make shorter. *That skirt's too long —why don't you take it up a bit? It's been taken up an inch already.* 2 occupy (space). *This big bed takes up a lot of room. Let's put it in the attic.* 3 discuss; examine. *That's an issue we ought to take up at the next meeting. The matter has already been taken up with my* *member of parliament.* 4 accept (an offer etc). *Do you intend to take up his offer of a job?* 5 absorb. *Use blotting paper to take up ink, not your handkerchief!*

take up something 1 begin to practise (as a hobby or interest). *I think I'll take up oil painting in my spare time. She's taken up flower-decoration at evening classes.* 2 begin (duties, work etc). *When does the new man take up his post? He takes up his duties as representative for this area next year.* 3 continue (an unfinished narrative). *She took up the story at the point where the thief had just made off with the jewels.*

take someone up on something 1 question about. *Do you mind if I take you up on this matter of participation? James took the speaker up on a few points.* 2 (informal) accept (an offer, challenge etc). *He said he'd buy me a drink, so I took him up on it and ordered a large brandy.*

take up with someone become friends with; keep company with. *When Philip went to London, he took up with some very strange people from Soho.*

talk someone down silence (by talking so much oneself). *Richard is good at talking his opponents down.*

talk down to someone (informal) address in a patronizing manner. *That lecturer talks down to his students as if they were children.*

talk someone into (doing) something (informal) persuade (by talking). *The salesman tried to talk me into buying an electric tooth-brush. Don't let yourself be talked into doing anything you don't want to do!*

talk someone out of (doing) something (informal) dissuade (by talking). *I'd like to go camping, but my wife's trying to talk me out of it.*

talk someone round (informal) persuade (by talking). *I was against going to China, but Mary eventually managed to talk me round.*

tell someone off (informal) reprimand. *The boss told his secretary off for making private telephone calls from the office. But she didn't like being told off in front of other people, so she gave in her notice.*

tell on someone 1 have a bad effect on. *All this smoking and drinking will tell on his health in later life.* 2 betray; give away the secret of. *Jimmy told on his brother for breaking the vase, so their mother punished them both!*

think about something 1 consider. *It's certainly an offer well worth thinking about. We're thinking about buying a new car before the prices go up.* 2 have as an opinion about; judge to be like. *Would you read through this report and tell me what you think about the style?*

think of something 1 remember. *I know his face, but I can't think* *of where I've met him. Can you think of his name?* 2 give attention to; consider. *John would have liked to accept the offer of a job in Alaska, but he has his wife and children to think of, so he refused it. There are many things which have to be thought of before we finally make up our minds to emigrate.* 3 contemplate as a possibility. *I'd never think of asking someone to lend me so much money! You know we wouldn't think of going without you.* 4 have as an opinion about; judge to be like. *What do you think of my new shoes? Tell me what you thought of the concert.* 5 invent; suggest; imagine. *I'm trying to think of a good example to illustrate my point. Bill says he's thought of a good scheme to make some money.*

think something out work out by careful reasoning. *We should start by thinking out a satisfactory plan. His arguments had obviously been well thought out.*

think something over consider carefully. *When you've thought things over, you'll probably realise that my idea is quite good after all. I made him an offer, but he said he'd have to think it over first.*

think something up invent. *Jack's very good at thinking up excuses for not working. I realised that his story had been thought up on the spur of the moment.*

throw something off discard; get rid of. *Peter has managed to throw off the annoying habit of staring at people in buses. I've been trying to throw off a cold for days.*

throw someone out cause to make an error. *The slightest inaccuracy will throw us out in our calculations.*

throw something out dismiss; reject. *I consider the proposal to be fairly good, but it was thrown out by the Board immediately.*

throw out something 1 radiate; produce (heat, light etc). *The electric fire throws out a lot of heat.* 2 give (a casual or indirect hint, warning, suggestion etc). *He refused to throw out even the slightest hint about who he was bringing to the party.*

throw someone over (informal) reject; end an acquaintance with. *She threw him over for a tall, dark and handsome Arab.*

throw something up (informal) abandon, reject. *She threw up a promising career as a model to get married.*

tie someone down (informal) restrict (in one's actions). *I don't want you to feel tied down by my presence; do go out whenever you like.*

tie in (with something) fit (with). *It all ties in very well. Her story didn't tie in with his—that's why the police were suspicious.*

tie something up 1 (informal) complete. *Are all the arrangements for Saturday tied up now?* 2 (informal) (of money) bind. *He's tied all his money up in stocks and shares and has nothing in the bank to pay his debts with.*

touch something off cause. *An incident in the market-place touched* *off a riot and the police had to intervene. The crisis was touched off by a few undiplomatic remarks on the part of one of the heads of state.*

touch on/upon something mention very briefly. *The President only touched on the issue in his speech.*

touch something up (informal) improve (the appearance of, often by painting, cleaning, adding small details etc). *The kitchen needs touching up in a few places; we'll put a bit of paint on this afternoon. Your essay is quite good: just touch it up a little with a few illustrations and quotations.*

trade on something (informal) take advantage of. *You'll always find someone who's ready to trade on your generosity and never offer any help in return.*

trip someone up (informal) deliberately cause to make a mistake. *In the interview, he tripped me up by asking me what I thought about his book. I later discovered that he's never published one!*

try something on (with someone) (informal) attempt (to gain an advantage) (from). *Don't try it on with me, because you won't succeed! The woman tried it on with the policeman, by saying that she hadn't seen the traffic lights, but it didn't work—he fined her.*

turn someone/something down reject; refuse. *We've had to turn down four applicants already. His book has been turned down by the publishers.*

turn in (informal) go to bed. *Come on. It's time to turn in.*

turn someone in (informal) hand over (to the police). *He was afraid that the farmer would turn him in for stealing chickens.*

turn something in 1 hand in; submit. *Bill's a hard-working student. He turns in two essays every week.* 2 (informal) abandon. *David has a part-time job as mechanic at the garage, but he's having to turn it in, because they want to replace him for a full-time mechanic.*

turn someone off (something) (informal) cause to lose interest (in). *I always enjoyed French at school, but the advanced course in literature turned me right off it! Men with long droopy moustaches turn me right off.*

turn someone on (informal) attract; interest; delight. *Rock music really turns me on. I don't understand how Carol can be turned on by Rod.*

turn on someone attack; criticize. *He beat the dog so much that it turned on him. I didn't expect to be turned on by someone I hardly know!*

turn out 1 result. *How did your bread-baking turn out? We weren't looking forward to the outing, but it turned out to be really enjoyable.* 2 assemble; appear; attend. *Everybody turned out to watch the procession. There was a good turn-out at the meeting.*

turn someone out (of somewhere) (informal) eject (from);

expel (from). *Shhh! You'll get us turned out of the library for talking! If he drinks any more, the landlord will turn him out of the pub.*

turn something out   I empty. *When you turn the cupboard out, you'll probably find the letter.* 2 switch off. *Don't forget to turn out the lights when you leave.*

turn out something   produce; manufacture. *The factory turns out bottles at the rate of several thousand per day.*

turn someone/something over (to someone)   deliver (to); hand over (to). *His family refused to turn him over to the police. Luckily my watch was turned over to the lost property office.*

wait up (for someone)   stay out of bed (until someone comes home). *Don't wait up for me; I may be very late.*

wake up   (informal) realise the truth of something. *I wish she'd wake up! She's so naive!*

walk off with something   (informal) win easily. *We expected Peter to walk off with the prize, but he didn't.*

walk out   (informal) strike; lay down one's work. *There's another strike threatening: some of the workers walked out today. There's some talk of another walk-out up at the factory.*

walk out on someone/something   (informal) abandon. *She treated him badly, but she never thought he'd walk out on her. He's walked out on his job, as well as on his wife.*

warm up   (informal) become lively. *We arrived just when the party was beginning to warm up.*

warm something up   (informal) make lively. *Peter's jokes certainly warmed the party up!*

wash something out   (informal) spoil; ruin. *His plans were washed out by the seamen's strike.*

wear off   (informal) lose in attraction, power, interest etc; disappear. *His enthusiasm for the plan seems to have worn off; he never speaks about it any more. Jimmy rides his new bicycle every day, but as soon as the novelty's worn off, it will be left in the garage.*

wear on   continue; pass. *The snow will melt as the day wears on. The evening wore on and her husband still hadn't come home from work.*

wear someone out   (informal) make tired; exhaust. *Playing with little children really wears me out!*

wear something out   make useless by long or hard wear. *The children have worn their shoes out. They'll have to have new ones.*

wind down   (informal) relax. *You'll be able to wind down a bit, now that all the excitement is over.*

wind something up   (informal) end. *Let's wind up the meeting; it's getting late. Oh, that's all over now—the case was wound up a year ago!*

wink at something   (informal) pretend not to see; ignore; overlook. *You can't expect me to wink at your mistakes all the time.*

work something off 1 (informal) get rid of (surplus energy, weight etc). *Dick's digging the garden. He's trying to work his Sunday lunch off.* 2 repay (a debt or loan) by working. *I shall have worked my debts off by Christmas. Then I can start saving money again.*

work on someone (informal) try to influence (by constant persuasion). *I can't go abroad this summer because I haven't saved up enough money, but perhaps I can work on my father to give me a loan.*

work on something be engaged in work. *He's working on a new project which has to be finished by the end of the year.*

work out succeed. *Don't despair! Everything will work out all right in the end.*

work something out 1 calculate. *Have you worked out what I owe you yet? The sum total of my income can be worked out in one minute.* 2 devise; construct. *We must work out a plan as quickly as we can.* 3 (informal) understand; make sense of. *It's a very strange situation. I can't work it out.*

work out at something amount to. *The car repairs work out at £57.*

work something up 1 stimulate. *Take a brisk walk to work up a good appetite! I can't work up any enthusiasm for the project, I'm afraid.* 2 increase; build. *He's worked up a good business over the last five years. I wish we could work up a little more support for the cause.*

work up to something 1 develop to. *The film works up to an exciting climax.* 2 prepare (to express a wish, suggestion etc). *I didn't know at the time what he was working up to. Then he asked me to marry him!*

wrap something up (informal) make final. *They're going to wrap up the negotiations this week. The agreement was wrapped up at the last meeting.*

write someone off (as something) (informal) regard (as no good). *Six of the applicants for the job were written off immediately. He was written off by his family as a failure, so they were very surprised when he passed all the exams and went to university.*

write something off 1 regard (a debt) as a loss. *There seems to be no hope of ever getting the money back from Harry. I think you can write it off.* 2 regard as without value, not worth repair etc. *The car was completely written off in the accident.* 3 regard as a failure. *The new comedy at the Grand Theatre is a complete write-off. Don't waste your money on tickets.*

write something up 1 write a full account of. *The pupils were asked to write the chemistry experiment up for homework.* 2 review a film, play etc (for publication). *I've been asked to do a write-up of the play for the local newspaper.*

9 Idioms with the verb *TO BE*

general note

Many phrases in English are dependent on the verb TO BE and will not be found without it. Here is a selection of frequently used phrases, with TO BE followed first by *noun* or *adjective phrases*, then with TO BE followed by *prepositional phrases*.

A *TO BE* + noun/adjective phrases

to be the better/the worse for something to be in a better/worse condition because of it. *Your hair will be the better for a good wash!*

to be born under a lucky star to be continually lucky.

to be born with a silver spoon in one's mouth to be born into a rich or influential family.

to be full of oneself to be vain, to have a high opinion of one's own abilities, accomplishments.

to be Greek/double Dutch to someone to be unintelligible to him, to be beyond his comprehension.

to be the making of someone to be the reason for his success. *His unexpected success in the election was the making of Herbert's political career.*

to be neither here nor there to be irrelevant or unimportant. *Bill said he would lend me a little money, but that's neither here nor there. It won't pay off my debts.*

to be no chicken (informal) means to be no longer young (not complimentary).

to be a nobody (informal) to be a person without wealth, influence, interest, importance etc.

to be nowhere (informal) to be in a position of no importance, not showing success or capabilities. *John was nowhere in the examination. He'll have to work much harder if he wants to go to college.*

to be the order of the day to be the course of action which is the trend, which is of continual or frequent occurrence. *Rises in prices but not wages seem to be the order of the day.*

to be a party to something to take part in it, to support it. *Was the king a party to this conspiracy?*

to be a prey to something to be troubled by it, eg doubt, grief, depression.

to be set on/upon something to be determined to get it. *Danny is set on starting his own pop group.*

to be a slave to something to be under the influence of it, eg a habit, a drug.

to be somebody to be a person of wealth, influence, interest, importance etc.

to be worth its weight in gold said of an article which has proved to be extremely useful, or which has given long and efficient service. *My old record player is twenty years old and has never been repaired. It's worth its weight in gold.* The phrase can also refer to a person who has proved his worth to others through loyalty, personal qualities etc.

B *TO BE* + **prepositional phrases**

to be + *AT*

to be 'at it (informal) to be in the action of doing it. *I told Bill to stop talking, but he's at it again!*

to be (hard) 'at it to be hard at work. *Nancy is taking her exam next week. She's been at it all the weekend.*

to be at someone's beck and call to be continually at his disposal to carry out his wishes, orders etc.

to be at one's best/worst to be most/least able. *Graham's at his best when he's working under pressure.*

to be at cross-purposes (with someone) to misunderstand someone (usually a mutual misunderstanding between two people).

to be at a/the crossroads to be at a crisis, a turning-point in one's life, career etc.

to be at daggers drawn (of two people or groups) to be enemies. *Sheila and Karen were good friends until Pete came along. Now they're at daggers drawn.*

to be at death's door to be gravely ill, to be about to die.

to be at (one's) ease to feel relaxed, comfortable in one's surroundings. *Reg is never at ease in his job, because his boss is always criticising him.*

to be at the end of one's tether to reach the end of one's powers, resources, patience, possibilities etc. *I've tried everything possible to find a solution but now I'm at the end of my tether.*

to be at the helm to be in command, to be the leader.

to be at home in/on a subject to be fully acquainted with it, to be knowledgeable about it. *I won't join your discussion as I'm not really at home in astrophysics.*

to be at home with someone to be on friendly, familiar terms with someone. *He gave me such a sincere welcome that I was at home with him at once.*

to be at large to be free (often used to refer to an escaped criminal or a criminal before arrest). *The train robbers are still at large.*

to be at loggerheads (with someone) to be in a state of quarrel or dispute. *Steve is always at loggerheads with the rest of the class.*

to be at a loose end to be bored, not to know how to occupy one's time.

to be at a loss (to do something) to be very puzzled, to be unable to decide (about it). *Sylvia is at a loss to know exactly how best to deal with Ted.*

to be at a loss for words to be so surprised, shocked etc that one doesn't know what to say.

to be at one to be agreed, to be in harmony.

to be at pains to do something to take great trouble to do it.

to be at sea to be confused or uncertain.

to be at sixes and sevens (of persons) to be in a muddle, to be confused; (of things) to be in disorder.

to be at the top of the ladder/tree to be as high as possible in one's profession, to be very successful.

to be at one's wits' end to be greatly perplexed, not to know what to do next.

to be + IN

to be 'in (informal) 1 at home, at one's office, place of work etc. 2 the short form of 'in season' or 'in fashion'. *When will plums be in this summer? Long skirts and coats will be in again this winter.* 3 (of a player in a game) not yet beaten. *Kelly has been caught out, but Randall is still in.* 4 (of a fire) still burning. *Is the fire still in or shall I put on some more coal?*

to be in the air (of a plan, a decision etc) to be uncertain, to be not definite. *It's still in the air whether or not Max will accept the offer.*

to be in a bad way to be in an unsatisfactory situation or condition (eg a person who is ill, a business which is losing money).

to be in the bag (informal) (of a plan, project etc) to be certain, decided, won, settled etc. *Smith is optimistic about getting the contract. In fact, he's pretty sure that it's in the bag already.*

to be in the balance to be undecided, indefinite. *It's still in the balance whether or not we can control the world's growing population.*

to be in someone's good/bad/black books (informal) to be in someone's favour/disfavour. *I can't ask my father for any more money—I'm in his black books at the moment!*

to be in the chair to be the chairman of a meeting.

to be in the clouds to day-dream, to think unrealistically.

to be in clover (informal) to be living in pleasant, easy circumstances.

to be in someone's clutches to be in someone's power, under someone's influence.

to be in the dark to be ignorant (of a matter), not to be informed. *I had no idea that Keith was leaving the country. He doesn't tell me his plans, so I was completely in the dark.*

to be in deep water to be in (dangerous) difficulties (e g financially).

to be in the ˋdog-house (informal) to be in disgrace or in someone's disfavour.

to be in the doldrums (informal) to be in low spirits, depressed.

to be (down) in the dumps (informal) to be depressed, in low spirits.

to be in easy circumstances to live a comfortable life financially.

to be in one's element to be in a position where the surroundings, conditions, people etc are extremely agreeable to one.

to be in ˋfine/ˋgood fettle to feel in a good physical or mental condition.

to be in a fix/mess/scrape (informal) to be in difficulties.

to be in a flat spin (informal) to be in a state of nervous panic, not knowing what to do.

to be in a flutter to be in a state of nervous excitement, often because of some small unexpected difficulty. *My Aunt Jane was in a flutter last night when she thought she'd missed the last bus and wouldn't be able to get home.*

to be ˋin for something (informal) to be due to receive it, to be going to experience it (either pleasant or unpleasant, e g trouble, a surprise, a shock).

to be in someone's good graces to be in his favour, to be liked or favoured by him.

to be in good hands to be in good care. *I'm not worried about leaving the children with Aunt Jane, as I know they're in good hands.*

to be in hot water (informal) to be in trouble.

to be in keeping with something to correspond, match, fit with it. *Unkindness is not in keeping with John's character.*

to be ˋin at the ˋkill to be present at someone's downfall (e g when someone is punished, discovered etc).

to be in the know (informal) to know details, to have information about a matter which others do not share, to be better informed than others. *I'll ask John's secretary exactly what went on at the meeting. She wasn't present herself, but it's her job to be in the know.*

to be in the limelight to receive much attention or publicity, to be the centre of interest.

to be in one's line (informal) (of a subject) to interest or concern one. *Opera is not much in my line. I prefer a film or a play.*

to be in the money to be earning or to have a lot of money.

to be in the pink (informal) to be in good health, to be feeling very well.

to be in 'Queer Street (GB) (informal) to be in debt, trouble, difficulty.

to be in raptures (about/over something) to be extremely delighted (by it), to be very enthusiastic (about it). *My mother is in raptures over her new stove.*

to be in a rut to be in a state of life which brings no change, eg a boring job, a fixed way of life, a monotonous routine.

to be in the same boat (as somebody) (informal) to be in the same position, in similar circumstances (as someone else).

to be in (the) seventh heaven to be very happy, to be elated.

to be in the soup (informal) to be in difficulties.

to be in a stew (informal) to be confused or nervous because of difficulties.

to be in the swim (informal) to know what is going on, to take a part in current happenings.

to be in a temper to be in a bad temper.

to be in a tight squeeze (informal) to be in a difficult situation, either in a financial or in a personal matter.

to be in a whirl to be in confusion, to be excited.

to be (well) 'in with someone (informal) to enjoy his favour, to maintain a friendly relationship which brings advantages. *Jim should get the promotion, as he's well in with his boss.*

to be + OFF

to be 'off 1 no longer to be showing at the cinema or theatre. 2 (of food in a restaurant) no longer available.

to be off the beam (informal) to be on the wrong track, to have misunderstood.

to be off colour to be unwell.

to be off-hand (with someone) to be curt, abrupt in one's behaviour (to him).

to be off one's head (informal) to be crazy.

to be off the map (of a place) not shown on the map, remote, obscure.

to be off the rails (informal) (of a thing) to be in a state of confusion, disorder, to be badly organised; (of a person) crazy.

to be off the record (of a piece of information) to be unofficial, secret, not for general circulation. *If you need to know the truth of the affair, I can tell you, but remember, it's strictly off the record.*

to be off one's rocker (informal) to be crazy.

to be off to a good/bad start to start something well/badly.

to be + *ON*

to be 'on to be showing at the cinema, theatre, on TV or radio. *What's on at the Odeon?*

to be on the air to be in the action of broadcasting or being broadcast on radio or television.

to be on the alert to be watchful, ready for any emergency.

to be 'on at someone (informal) to criticize, find fault with him. *His wife is always on at him for reading the paper at the breakfast table.*

to be on the ball (informal) to be alert, well-informed, to work intelligently at a task.

to be on the beat (of a policeman) to be on regular patrol duty through the streets of a town.

to be on the bench to be a magistrate or a judge.

to be on the bottle (informal) to be drinking large quantities of alcohol, to be a habitual drinker.

to be on call (usually of a doctor) to be available for duty.

to be on the cards (informal) to be possible or likely. *It's on the cards that John will drop by to see us this evening.*

to be on the carpet (informal) 1 to be reprimanded (usually by one's employer). 2 to be under consideration or discussion.

to be on the dole (informal) to receive unemployment benefits from the state.

to be on the dot to be punctual.

to be on edge to be nervous, worried or irritable.

to be on good/bad terms with someone to be friendly/unfriendly with someone.

to be on (one's) guard to take great care (in order to defend oneself).

to be on one's high horse (informal) to assume a haughty tone (often because one is offended or wishes to show a superior attitude).

to be on the hop (informal) to be hurrying about continually.

to be on the job to be doing a job of work, to be completing or working on a job, project, task etc.

to be on one's last legs (informal) (of a thing) to be in a bad state of repair, shortly before collapse; (of a person) to be very ill or old, about to die.

to be on the level (informal) to be honest, sincere.

to be on the look-out/the watch to be looking out for some expected person or happening (in order to be prepared or give warning).

to be on the make (informal) to be trying to make money, be successful etc.

to be on the mend (informal) to be recovering after an illness.

to be on the move to be moving about, in a frequent state of movement.

to be on parole (of a prisoner) to have been released from prison for a short time on condition that he will not do wrong or try to escape control.

to be on patrol (eg of soldiers, motorised police) to be on look-out and control duty.

to be on the prowl (eg of a wild animal, a thief) to prowl around.

to be on the right/wrong side of forty to be less/more than forty etc years old.

to be on the road to be a tramp, a wanderer, a traveller.

to be on the rocks (informal) to be failing, to be in trouble (eg a marriage, a project, a financial situation).

to be on the run to be evading pursuit, especially from the police.

to be on the shelf (informal) to be without a partner, to have not been chosen out.

to be on show (eg of anything in a shop-window, at a museum or exhibition) to be exhibited to the public.

to be on tenterhooks to be in a state of nervous suspense.

to be on to a good thing (informal) to have discovered something to one's advantage, something pleasant or profitable. *You'd be on to a good thing if you could make sea-water drinkable.*

to be on one's toes (informal) to be prepared, alert, ready to act.

to be on tour (eg of a circus, a theatrical company) to travel round staying at different places, institutions, countries etc, often to give performances.

to be on the trot (informal) to be busy, to have many things to attend to.

to be on the up and up (informal) to be improving.

to be on velvet to be in a favourable state.

to be on the verge of doing something to be just about to do something.

to be on the wane to be gradually growing less, becoming less important, decreasing.

to be on the (water-)wagon (informal) to have stopped drinking alcohol.

to be on the wing (of a bird) to be in the action of flying.

to be + *OUT (OF)*

to be 'out can mean many things according to context. Here are some examples: *Mrs Wood is out,* not at home. *The miners are out again,* on strike. *Is Smith out or is he still playing?* out of the game. *High heels are out this spring,* out of fashion. *The book is out at the moment,* on loan to someone, not in the library.

to be out at (the) elbows to be poorly dressed, to be wearing shabby clothes.

to be 'out for something to make an effort to get it. *I'm out for all the facts I can get.*

to be out for the count (in boxing) to be knocked out.

to be 'out of something to have no more of it. *I must go to the shops. I'm out of sugar and butter.*

to be out of bounds (to/for someone) to be outside the permitted area or limit. *The local bars are out of bounds for the soldiers.*

to be out of one's depth (with something) to be engaged in a task or work which is too difficult; not to understand. *Derek is out of his depth with the new computer.*

to be out of funds to be without money.

to be out of luck to have bad luck.

to be out of one's mind/senses to be mad.

to be out of place to be inappropriate, awkward.

to be out of the question (of a suggestion, idea etc) not to be able to be considered, to be impossible.

to be out of the running not to be in a competition, to have no further chance (after being eliminated). *Now that White is out of the running, there's only Black who has a chance of promotion.*

to be out of sorts to be (slightly) unwell.

to be out of the wood to be out of trouble or difficulties.

to be out to do something to have it as one's aim. *Jack is out to win the championship.*

to be + *UP*

what's 'up? (informal) what's the matter?

to be 'up can mean many things according to context. Here are some examples: *Is John up yet?* out of bed. *Time's up!* the allotted time has expired. *The game is up,* the plan has been uncovered and success is impossible. *His colour was up,* he became angry. *His blood was up,* his passion, strong feelings were roused.

to be up and about to be out of bed again after an illness.

to be up against something to have (a difficulty, problem etc) to deal with.

to be up in arms (about/over/because of something) to be in strong protest. *The students are up in arms about the government's plan to close their college.*

to be up before a/the judge, magistrate etc. to appear in court to be tried for a misdeed.

to be up-and-coming to show promise of success (in one's career etc.). *Tom has been up-and-coming for quite some time now. He should get a promotion fairly soon.*

to be up and doing to be actively engaged in something.

to be 'up for (an offence) to stand trial for (an offence eg theft, murder). *Doreen is up for theft at the juvenile court next week.*

to be up to the mark to have reached the required standard; to be clever. *Annie's good at English and History, but she's not quite up to the mark in Mathematics.*

to be up to the neck in something to be in great trouble, difficulty, debt etc.

to be up the pole (informal) 1 to be in a difficult situation; 2 to be entirely mistaken.

to be up the spout (informal) (of a person) to be in a difficult situation; (of a thing) to be useless or broken.

to be up someone's street (informal) to be a subject to his liking or interest. *I enjoy a good tune, but symphonies and concertos are not really up my street.*

to be 'up to something to be in the act of doing it. *'What's Bill up to at the moment?' 'I don't know. He's always up to something—usually up to no good.'*

it's 'up to someone (to do something) it is his decision, responsibility, duty to do it.

to be up to doing something/'up to it to be capable of doing it. *'I don't feel up to doing this translation, as my Spanish is rather rusty.' 'No, I don't really feel up to it, either.'*

to be up a tree (informal) to be in difficulties, in confusion.

it's all 'up with someone his hopes, plans etc have ended in failure.

to be well 'up on a subject to know a lot, to be knowledgeable about it.

to be + *UNDER*

to be under age to be younger than a required age. *Terry can't join the navy yet—he's under age.*

to be under a cloud to be under suspicion or in disfavour.

to be under the doctor to be having treatment from a doctor.

to be under lock and key to be safely locked up.

to be **under the sod** (informal) to be dead.

to be **under someone's thumb** to be under his control or influence.

to be **under the weather** to be unwell.

to be + other prepositions

to be **above (doing) something** not to do it because pride, self-respect or moral sense will not permit the action.

to be **'after someone/something** to be in pursuit of or in search of him/it.

to be **down in the dumps** (informal) to be depressed, in low spirits.

to be **down in the mouth** to be depressed.

to be **down on one's luck** to experience a period of bad luck.

to be **for (doing) something** to be in favour of (doing) it.

to be **of age** to have reached the age of 18 or 21 (depending on the law of individual countries) when one is regarded as adult for purposes of law. *Randolph cannot inherit his uncle's money until he is of age.*

to be **within an 'inch of doing something** to be very near to doing it.

to be **within the law** to have the law on one's side, not to commit illegal actions.

Idioms with common verbs

general note

This chapter deals with idioms which are centred around certain common verbs. Chapter 5 listed typical nouns that are the grammatical objects of certain verbs. In contrast, this chapter gives the idiomatic uses of the most commonly used verbs in English, when they are followed by all types of words, not only nouns as objects. Minor verbs which are not found in either Chapter 5 or Chapter 10 are listed in Chapter 11.

break

to 'break someone to ruin someone, usually either financially or emotionally.

to break an appointment to fail to keep it.

to break the 'back of something (of work) to have completed the bigger or most difficult part of it.

to break the bank to win all the money which a gambling house has.

to break bounds to go where one is not allowed to go.

to break cover to come out of a hiding place.

to break one's/someone's fall to lessen the force of a fall, to weaken its effect by standing or putting something in the way of the person falling.

to break fresh/new ground to start work on something (eg a project, research) that has not been done by anyone before.

to break someone's heart to make him sad, bring him to despair.

to break a horse (in) to discipline it so that it can be ridden properly and well.

to break the ice to say or do something which makes a stiff, awkward atmosphere friendly, eg when making conversation with strangers, when people are formal and reserved.

to break the news (to someone) to make it known. The news

can be either good or bad. If it is bad news, it is broken to someone in a way which may lessen the shock.

to break prison/goal to escape from prison.

to break a record to make a new record, e g an Olympic/World record by achieving something which nobody else has achieved before.

to break short a conversation/meeting/discussion to end it before time.

to break someone's spirit/will to force him to be meek, to subdue him.

to break a strike to end the strike by forcing the workers to give in.

bring

to bring someone to book (for something) to make him explain his actions or conduct.

to bring something 'home to someone to cause him to understand or realise it fully.

to bring home a charge/accusation to prove its truth.

to bring the 'house down/to bring down the house 1 to receive great applause or approval from an audience; 2 to cause great laughter in an audience.

to bring something to light to disclose it, make it known, discover it.

to bring something into line to cause it to conform, suit one's plans etc.

to bring something to mind to recall it.

to bring something into play to make use of it, put it in action.

to bring up the rear to form the end of a line, to be the last.

come

to come apart to break into pieces.

to come clean (informal) to tell the truth, admit wrongdoings.

to come a cropper (informal) 1 to have a fall; 2 to meet with sudden failure.

to come 'down in the world to lose one's social standing or position.

to come down to earth to return to reality, to give up plans and ideas which cannot be realised.

to come in handy/useful (for something) to be of future use (for something).

to come into fashion (e g of clothing, hairstyles) begin to be popular.

to come into force (e g of a law) to have (legal) power, to be binding.

to come into a fortune to inherit a lot of money.

to come into (some/a lot of) money to inherit, receive, win etc
money.

to come into one's 'own to receive the praise, fame for one's
talents, abilities, achievements which one deserves.

to come into play to begin to operate, be active.

to come of age to become adult in law, ie 21 years of age in some
countries, 18 in others.

come 'off it! (informal) stop talking nonsense or exaggerating.

to come off second best to lose, eg in a competition, an argument.

to come off/through with flying colours to complete something
very successfully.

to come out in spots/a rash to suddenly develop spots or a rash
on one's body.

to come out tops/on top (informal) to do something with the
most successful result.

to come over (all) queer/funny/dizzy (informal) to feel suddenly ill, strange, dizzy.

to come to blows (with someone) to start fighting.

to come to fruition (eg of plans, ideas) to ripen, mature, be
realised.

to come to no good (informal) to reach a bad end.

to come to grief to meet with disaster, to fail, to be ruined.

to come to a head to reach a crisis.

to come to light to become known, to be discovered.

to come to little/nothing to be uninteresting, unsuccessful, unimportant etc.

not to come to much to be uninteresting, unsuccessful, unimportant etc.

to come to pass (formal, old use) to happen.

to come to a 'pretty pass to reach a stage of great confusion, difficulty etc.

to come to one's senses to act or react normally after being foolish
or strange in one's behaviour.

do

to 'do someone (informal) to cheat him, get money from him.

to do one's best to try as hard as possible.

to do something by/in fits and starts to do it impulsively, not
with method; to stop and start it many times.

to do the 'dirty on someone (informal) to play a mean trick on
him, to treat him unfairly.

to do someone 'down (informal) 1 to cheat him; 2 to speak badly of him to others.

to do someone a favour/a good turn to do something to help him.

to do the food to prepare or cook it (eg meat, fish, cabbage).

to 'do for someone (informal) 1 to clean the house or cook for him, to work as his housekeeper or daily help; 2 to ruin him.

to do one/someone good to be of advantage or benefit to oneself/ him.

to do one's hair to comb it.

to do the honours to act as host or hostess.

to do someone 'in (informal) to kill him.

nothing doing (informal) no (in answer to a request).

to do the room(s), the house etc to clean it.

to do the sights (informal) to make a sight-seeing tour of eg a town.

to do a subject to study it (at school, university etc).

to do a sum to solve it.

to be 'done to a 'turn (of food) to be cooked properly, to taste very good.

to do the trick (informal) to serve the purpose, accomplish the aim.

to do 'well out of something to get personal (often financial) advantage or benefit from it.

to do someone/oneself 'well (informal) to provide well for him/ oneself with comforts, good food etc.

to do wonders (with something) to produce good or unexpected results (from it).

fall

to fall between two stools 1 (of a person) to miss two opportunities because one hesitated in choosing either of them; 2 (of a plan etc) not to suit either of two situations.

to fall 'down (on the job) to fail (to carry out a task successfully).

to fall flat (eg of a joke, a performance) to be a failure, unsuccessful.

to fall in line (with someone/someone's plans etc) to agree to act according to his plans, wishes etc.

to fall in love (with someone) to begin to feel passionate love (for him).

to fall on one's feet to be fortunate; to be successful in getting out of a difficulty (through good luck, not good management).

to fall out of love (with someone) to stop loving (him) passionately.

to fall out of use to be used no longer, eg a word in a language.

to fall 'over oneself (to do something) to be extremely eager (to do it).

to fall a prey/victim to someone/something to become the
victim of him/it. *To fall a prey to someone's clever plans.*

to fall short of someone's hopes/expectations to be or do less
than he hoped/expected.

to fall to the ground (of a plan) to become useless, ineffective; to
fail.

get

to get back on one's feet to recover (e g financially) after an illness,
a loss etc.

to get someone's `back up to annoy him.

to get the `better of someone to defeat him.

to get `clear of someone/something to get away from him/it
(that causes difficulty or annoyance); to become free of him/it.

to get down to brass tacks (informal) to pay attention to the
essential facts.

to get down to business to start the work that must be done, to
pay attention to the essential thing, e g in a discussion, at a meeting.

to get drunk to become drunk.

to get `even with someone to have one's revenge on him.

to get a girl into trouble (informal) to make her pregnant (when
she is not one's wife, and without meaning to).

to get hold of the wrong end of the stick (informal) to completely misunderstand something.

to get into hot water to get into trouble (for which one can be
punished).

to get into a mess to get into a difficult, unpleasant or disorderly
situation.

to get into a scrape to get into a difficult or awkward situation (for
which one can be reprimanded).

to get it into one's head (that . . .) to be convinced (that . . .), to
have a fixed idea about something (even if other people do not
share that opinion.

to get mad (at someone) (informal) to become angry (with him).

to get a `move on (informal) to hurry.

to get off lightly/cheaply to receive only slight instead of severe
punishment.

to get `on in the world to be successful socially or in one's career.

to get on someone's nerves to irritate him.

to have got out of bed on the wrong side (informal) to be bad-
tempered, in a bad mood.

to get the sack to be dismissed from one's job.

to `get there (informal) to be successful in one's aim.

to get to 'grips with something (e g of a problem) to confront it seriously, to begin to occupy oneself with it.

to get to the point to reach the essential thing one wants to say.

to get told 'off (for something) (informal) to be scolded (for having done something).

to get under one's skin 1 to irritate one; 2 to (romantically) interest one.

to get up steam to become excited, enthusiastic, full of energy (e g when relating something).

to get the upper hand to be in the strongest position.

to get 'wind of something to hear a rumour of it, to hear some news indirectly.

to get the 'wind up (informal) to become alarmed or frightened about something that might happen in the future.

not get a word in edgeways to be unable to say anything because another person talks all the time.

give

to give chapter and verse for something to be able to prove it, to produce evidence that it is correct or true.

to give chase (to someone/something) to pursue (him/it).

to give someone the cold shoulder to treat him in a cold or abrupt manner.

to give countenance to something (formal) to give one's favour, support to it (e g a project).

to give (a) false colouring to something to describe it in a false way.

to give the 'game away to betray a secret, with or without intention.

to give loose rein to something to leave it unchecked; to have a loose control on it (e g feelings, actions, ideas).

to give someone a piece/bit of one's mind (informal) to scold him, to tell him what one thinks of his conduct.

to give rise to something to cause, be the cause of it.

to give someone the slip to escape from or avoid someone who is looking for one.

to give someone to understand that ... to lead him to believe that ...

to give up the ghost (informal) to die.

to give vent to something to show it (e g feelings, anger, grief).

to give way (to someone/something) to yield (to him/it).

go

to go against the grain to be opposed to one's feelings, wishes, ideas.

to go ahead to begin.

to go behind someone's back to do or say something expressly without his knowledge.

to go berserk to become wild with fury.

to go broke (informal) to become penniless; to run out of money.

to go bust (informal) to become bankrupt.

to go dutch (with someone) to share expenses.

to go easy (with/on something/someone) to treat (it/him) gently.

to go for a song to be sold for much less than the true value.

to go halves (with someone) to share something or the costs of something in equal parts.

to go haywire (eg of a plan) to become totally disorganised; to lose control; to become wild.

to go it alone (informal) to act alone, without help or support.

to go mad to become mad.

to go native to adopt the customs, dress etc of a foreign country in which one is living, to live like a native of that country.

to go off the beaten track to leave the usual road which everyone knows; to do something unusual.

to go off the ˈdeep end to show anger or annoyance.

to go off one's head to become very excited and act in a crazy way.

to go on the dole to start to draw money from the government when one has no work.

to go on the pill to start taking pills as a contraceptive.

to go one better (than someone) to improve on his achievement, to be still better than him.

to go out of one's ˈway to do something to try very hard, to do everything possible to do it (often to help someone).

to go out on the town to go out and enjoy oneself in the town.

to go phut (eg of a machine) to break down, collapse.

to go scot-ˈfree to go unpunished.

to go through fire and water (for someone) to do anything at all for someone, no matter how difficult.

to go to the dogs (informal) to reach a state of ruin, collapse, uselessness etc; to deteriorate.

to go to great expense (to do something) to spend much money or energy.

to go to great lengths/trouble/pains (to do something) to try hard (to do it).

to go to one's head (eg of success, money) to make one behave in a conceited, haughty, over-confident manner.

to go to law to take up court proceedings against someone.

to go to rack and ruin to reach a bad, useless condition, a ruined state.

to go to town (on something) (informal) to do something thoroughly.

to go to the wall to be treated worst because one is the weakest.

to go too far to go beyond the limits of accepted behaviour.

to go up the wall (informal) to become very angry or annoyed.

to go the whole hog (informal) to do something thoroughly, completely, not only one part of it.

have

to have a brush with someone to have an argument or an unpleasant encounter with him.

to have clean hands to be innocent.

to have the face/cheek to do something (informal) to do it although it may be annoying or inconvenient for others.

to have the field before one/to oneself to have a full opportunity of showing what one can do; to be unopposed; to be working alone.

to have a flutter (informal) to gamble in a small way.

to have 'had it (informal) not to be going to get any more of something, eg money, a second chance, luck.

to have it 'out with someone (informal) to have a frank discussion or argument with someone until an understanding is reached.

to have no backbone to have no courage, to be easily disheartened.

to have one's 'sleep out to continue sleeping until one wakes naturally.

to have 'other fish to fry to have more important business to attend to.

to have too many irons in the fire to have too many interests, or jobs of work to do at the same time, for any of them to receive sufficient attention.

hold

to hold one's ground not to give way, to keep the advantage which one already has.

to hold one's head high to bear oneself proudly.

to hold something/someone in check to keep a control on it/him.

to hold something in one's head to remember it without writing it down.

to hold someone in high/low esteem/regard to have a high/low opinion of him.

to hold oneself in readiness (for something) to be prepared (eg for an emergency).

to hold a job down informal, to keep the job by showing oneself capable.

to hold one's own to maintain one's own position (eg in an argument), to defend one's own point of veiw.

to hold one's sides with laughter to laugh very heartily.

to hold one's tongue/peace to be quiet, not to give one's opinion or criticism.

to hold true to continue to be true.

to hold someone up to scorn/ridicule to expose him to scorn etc.

keep

to keep the 'ball rolling (informal) to keep the conversation, the action etc going without stopping.

to keep body and soul together to manage to live, survive.

to keep something dark not to reveal it to anyone, to keep it secret.

to keep one's 'fingers crossed (for someone) to hope for good luck, success.

to keep a good table to provide excellent food for oneself and for one's guests at all times.

to keep house (for someone) to be his housekeeper.

to keep someone in the dark (about something) to keep it secret from someone, not to tell him about it.

to keep in touch (with someone) to maintain contact (with him), by visiting, writing etc.

to keep open house to be ready and willing to entertain all comers to one's house at all times, to be hospitable to all visitors.

to keep 'pace with someone/something to advance or make progress as fast as another person, to be as good or as fast as someone.

to keep the 'pot boiling (informal) to earn enough money to buy one's food.

to keep a sharp 'look-out (for someone/something) to watch carefully for him/it.

to keep oneself to oneself to live without the company of others.

to keep something to oneself not to reveal it to others, to keep news, knowledge etc secret.

to keep 'track of/'tabs on/a 'tab on someone to keep oneself well informed of where he is, what he is doing etc.

to keep up appearances to make a good outward impression, eg by dressing well, in order to hide what one does not wish others to know, eg that one has, in fact, little money.

to keep up with the Joneses to compete with one's neighbours and friends in material possessions (car, colour TV etc) which are status symbols.

to keep the wolf (away) from the door to manage to provide enough money, food, clothing etc, for oneself and one's family, although one is poor.

keep your 'hair on! (informal) control your anger!

keep your 'shirt on! (informal) control your anger!

lay

to lay something bare to discover and reveal it (eg the plan of another person), although it was intended to be kept secret.

to lay down one's arms to surrender.

to lay down the law to say with an authoritative tone what must be done.

to lay down one's life to be killed (for a friend, a country etc).

to lay great/little store on/by something to value it very much/ very little.

to lay it on thick (informal) to praise someone/something too much.

to lay someone to rest (formal) to bury him.

to lay someone under a/the obligation/necessity of doing/to do something to make it obligatory or necessary for him to do it.

to lay waste to destroy (eg a city in war-time).

make

to make a'mends (for something) to compensate for damage, injury, insult, wrongdoing etc.

to make oneself at home to act with as much freedom as if one were at home.

to make a 'bee-line for something/somewhere to go there directly and quickly.

to 'make believe to pretend.

to make the best of a bad job/bargain to accept failure or something disappointing without complaint.

to make one's 'blood boil (informal) to make one angry.

to make (both) ends meet to manage with the money one has, even if it is not much.

to make a 'break for it to attempt to escape by running away as quickly as possible.

to make bricks without straw to try to do something impossible.

to make a clean 'breast of something to confess it (a wrong-doing).

to make do and 'mend to manage to continue to use old things (usually household articles) instead of buying new ones.

to make someone feel at home to treat him so well in one's home that he feels as free and comfortable as if he were in his own home.

to make oneself `felt to use one's authority, power.

to make `free with something to use it without asking permission, as if it were one's own.

to make a `go of it/something to be successful.

to make someone's `hair stand on end to shock or frighten him.

to make a `hash of something to spoil it, do it wrong.

to make haste to hurry.

to make hay while the `sun shines to make full use of the opportunity of doing something, as long as one has the chance.

to make headway to make progress.

to make heavy `weather of something to find it difficult, troublesome.

to make a `living as/at/by to earn money as.

to make or mar to bring either success or failure.

to make one's mark to do something noteworthy, which people will remember.

to make merry to enjoy oneself; to celebrate with food, drink, singing, dancing etc.

to make `mincemeat of someone (informal) to show one's superiority either physically or with words, arguments etc over another person.

to make one's `mouth water to cause one to have a strong desire for something (eg food or drink) by talking about it, thinking about it, or seeing it.

to make a mountain out of a molehill to treat something as difficult when in fact it is not difficult.

to make much ado about nothing to make a great fuss about a small thing.

to make a `name for oneself to become famous.

to make neither head nor `tail of something not to be able to understand it.

to make no `bones about it/doing something be frank, truthful, direct; not to hesitate.

to make room (for something) to allow enough free space (for it).

to make oneself scarce (informal) to go away or keep out of the way.

to make a `scene (about something) to have a violent argument or quarrel.

to make short `work of something to finish something very quickly (eg a piece of work, food, drink).

to make a song and `dance about something (informal) to become annoyed or upset about a very small matter.

to make up for lost time to work harder, hurry etc after losing time.

to make a virtue of necessity to do something as if it were a virtuous action when it is in fact a necessary action.

play

to play 'ball (with someone) to cooperate, act together in friendship or partnership.

to play the 'ball, not the 'man to kick the ball, not the opponent, ie to play fair by attacking the right thing.

to play one's 'cards well to make clever use of one's opportunities.

to play it 'cool (informal) to be relaxed and calm, or to give that impression to others.

to play a double 'game to do one thing openly and a different thing secretly.

to play something down to make it seem unimportant.

to play fast and loose (with someone) to behave inconsistently towards him, without caring about his feelings.

to play for time to try to gain extra time before acting.

to play the game to act fairly, observe the rules honestly.

to play 'havoc with something to ruin it (eg one's health).

to play into someone's hands to do what he hopes one will do, to act in such a way that he gains an advantage.

to play the man to act bravely.

to play on/upon words to make puns.

to play 'one person off against a'nother to gain a personal advantage by making two other people oppose each other.

to play second 'fiddle (to someone) to be in a less important position under someone else.

to play something 'up/'down to make it seem important/unimportant.

to play with edged tools to manage, or interfere with, a matter that requires delicate treatment.

pull

to pull a 'fast one (informal) to deceive someone, play a trick on someone.

to pull someone's leg (informal) to make fun of him by telling him something which is untrue but which he believes, to make harmless fun.

to pull one's punches to attack or criticise less severely than one could.

to pull one's 'socks up (informal) to improve one's achievements by working harder, to make a greater effort.

to **pull strings** (informal) to use private influence in order to gain an advantage; to use one's good connections (i e influential people one knows).

to **pull someone up sharp/short** to stop him suddenly (e g while talking).

to **pull one's weight** to do one's fair share of the work.

to **pull the 'wool over someone's eyes** to trick or deceive him.

put

to **put all one's eggs in one basket** to risk everything (e g all one's money, time, energy) on only one thing instead of on several different things.

to **put someone at his ease** to make him feel comfortable, free from restraint.

to **put something 'by for a rainy 'day** to save for future times of need.

to **put the cart before the horse** to try to do something in the wrong order; not to understand the proper order of something.

to **put the cat among the pigeons** to say or do something that causes a disturbance, alarm, argument etc.

to **put one's 'foot down** (informal) to make an objection, be firm about a matter one will not tolerate any longer.

to **put one's 'foot in it** (informal) to make a blunder, say something which one should not have said.

to **put someone in mind of something** to remind him of it.

to **put someone in the picture** to tell him exactly what the situation is.

to **put oneself in 'someone's/someone 'else's shoes** to imagine oneself in his situation, try to see things from his point of view.

to **put someone in his (proper) place** to correct or criticise someone who has become over-confident.

to **put someone on his guard** to warn him.

to **put out one's feelers/a feeler** to test the opinions of others by listening carefully or by asking questions, so that one knows how to act oneself.

to **put something right/to rights** to correct it, put it in good order again (e g a mistake, a situation).

to **put someone right/straight** to correct his mistake or misunderstanding.

to **put the 'screw on someone** (informal) to put a lot of pressure on him, thus forcing him to do something.

to **put one's shoulder to the wheel** to make a great effort, to work hard.

to put a 'spoke in someone's wheel (informal) to hinder or prevent him from making progress, to cause an obstruction.

to put someone through his paces to test his capabilities, to see what he can do, especially if he is new to a job etc.

to put to sea to start on a sea voyage.

to put someone to shame to make him feel ashamed.

to put someone to the sword (formal, old use) to kill him with a sword.

to put something to the vote to take a vote on it.

to put two and two together to draw a conclusion from what one hears, sees, finds out etc about a situation or person.

see

to see the 'back of someone (informal) to see him for the last time (with relief); to get rid of him because he causes annoyance etc.

to see for oneself to find out about something in order to be sure or convinced about it oneself, without relying on the word of others.

to see how the 'land lies to find out the exact position, situation or circumstances, so that one knows how to act or proceed.

to see how the 'wind blows (informal) means to find out how the situation is or is likely to be, what people or a person is thinking and how this will influence future events.

to see life/the world to get to know different aspects of life and people, different countries, experiences etc in order to widen one's own range of experience, knowledge etc.

to see the light 1 to be revealed; 2 to understand.

to see something through rose-coloured spectacles to have a very favourable opinion of it because one is prejudiced and wants to see only the good things.

to see one's way (clear) to doing something to see how to manage to do it, to be ready to do it.

set

to set the 'ball rolling (informal) to start something.

to set one's 'cap at someone to make a direct effort to attract him.

to set fire/(a) light to something to cause it to burn.

to set one's '(own) 'house in order to organise one's own life and affairs before criticising the life and affairs of others.

to set a match to something to use a match to cause it to burn.

to set someone's mind at ease/rest to free him from worry by removing his doubts, fears, suspicions etc.

to set someone's `teeth on edge` (of a noise) give him an unpleasant sensation.

to set the `Thames on fire` or usually **not/never set the** `Thames on fire` (not/never) to do something brilliant or extraordinary.

to set up `house (with someone)` to start living in a house and establish a household (e g after living in one room or lodgings).

stand

to stand on ceremony to pay great attention to correct rules of behaviour and etiquette, so that one's behaviour is formal and stiff.

to stand `clear (of something)` to move away (from it) so as not to be in the way or in danger.

to stand someone a drink/meal etc to pay for his drink etc.

to stand firm/fast not to give way, to be resolute.

to stand a good chance (of doing something) to have good prospects (of doing it), of something happening etc.

to stand one's ground to maintain one's position (e g in an argument).

to stand someone in good stead to be of great advantage to him later in life, in a time of difficulty in the future etc.

to stand in one's own light to act in a way which is disadvantageous to oneself.

it stands to reason that ... it is obvious to reasonable people that . . .

to stand to win/lose etc to be in a position to win/lose etc.

take

to take the bull by the horns to undertake to solve a problem or difficulty without hesitating.

to take someone/something by `storm` to attack something fiercely and take captive; to overcome someone with one's persuasions, passion etc.

to take the cake/biscuit (informal) to surprise everyone by one's conduct, i e by being the best, the worst, the strangest etc.

to take a dim `view of something` (informal) to have a bad opinion of it, to show resentment or disappointment at someone's behaviour etc.

to take someone `down a peg or two` (informal) to lower his pride, because he has been acting over-confidently.

to take something for granted to regard it as certain to happen or as perfectly true.

to take someone for granted to be so used to his presence that one forgets to be careful, sympathetic, sensitive etc about him.

to take a gamble (on something) to do something knowing that it is a risk or may be unsuccessful.

to take a/the hint to understand what is meant and act on it, without it being said directly.

to take something in good part to accept criticism or rebuke without personal resentment.

to take something in hand to manage or control it.

to take something into account to regard, to consider it.

to take someone into a secret to share a secret with him.

to take it from someone that . . . to believe him when he says something which one may have cause to doubt.

to take it into one's head to do something to decide to do it (often without much thought).

to take it 'out on someone (informal) to blame him or treat him badly without a real reason, only because one feels disappointed or badly treated by another person oneself.

to take a lot of doing to be difficult to do or to take a long time to do.

to take (holy) orders to become a priest.

to take the rough with the smooth to endure without complaint unpleasant things that come with (or after) pleasant things.

to take sides (with someone) to defend one of two people in an argument, disagreement etc.

to take things/it easy (informal) not to worry about problems, to be relaxed.

to take to one's bed to stay in bed when one is ill.

to take something to heart to be affected by it emotionally, to feel it deeply.

to take to one's heels to run away.

to take something/someone to pieces (informal) to skilfully criticise and destroy his argument, conduct etc.

to take someone unawares/by surprise to approach him unexpectedly or when he is unaware of one's presence.

turn

to turn one's back on/upon something/someone to abandon it/him.

to turn someone's brain to disturb him mentally.

to turn the corner (informal) to pass or overcome the most difficult part of something, the most critical point of an illness etc.

to turn a deaf ear (to someone) not to take notice of him; to refuse to listen to him.

to turn one's 'hand to something to undertake it, to deal with it.

to turn someone's head   1 cause him to lose his sense of judgment and become vain or conceited; 2 to attract him.

to turn one's `nose up at something (informal) to treat it with
dislike, to refuse it because one feels it is inferior.

to turn over a new leaf to completely change one's behaviour or
views for the better, i e to improve oneself and start again.

to turn the scale(s) (in someone's favour) to decide (favourably)
the result of an undecided matter.

to turn the tables (on someone) to reverse the situation, so that
the other person is now less successful than oneself.

to turn tail to retreat (in a cowardly manner).

to turn something to (good/ill) account to make (good/bad)
use of it.

11   Idioms with less common verbs

general note
Chapter 10 dealt with idiomatic phrases which centre around certain common verbs. In this chapter, idioms with verbs which are used less frequently are listed in alphabetical order.

to affect ignorance (of something) to pretend not to know (about it).

to be asking for trouble (informal) to say or do something which will cause oneself trouble because it provokes the anger of others.

to be barking up the wrong tree (informal) to be making a mistake, a wrong assumption, a complaint or accusation against the wrong person.

to beat the air to make efforts that are in vain.

to blow one's own trumpet to praise one's own successes, good deeds etc.

it (all) boils down to . . . it means . . .

to buck one's ideas up (informal) to improve oneself, one's work, conduct.

to buckle to/down to something (informal) means to begin it (eg work) seriously.

to burn one's boats/bridges to commit oneself to a course of action which cannot be reversed or changed later.

to burn a hole in one's pocket (of money) not be able to stop oneself spending all one's money.

to burn the candle at both ends to use up a lot of one's daily energy by being busy very late and very early, thus damaging one's health.

to burn one's fingers to learn not to do something again through having suffered through doing it once.

to burn the midnight oil to work or study until late into the night.

to butter someone ‵up (informal) to flatter him hoping to gain an advantage.

to buy a pig in a poke to buy something one had not seen before which turns out to be useless.

to call the tune to be the most important person in a situation, and thus to decide what is to be done and how.

to cap someone's joke/story to tell a joke/story which is better.

to catch someone napping (informal) to discover him not doing what he should be doing.

to catch someone red-handed to discover him in the act of a crime.

to chop and change (informal) to change one's ideas, actions, choice etc very frequently.

to clip someone's wings (informal) to limit him so as to slow him down in his plans.

to cross the Rubicon to take a decisive step forward from which one can no longer go back.

to curry favour (with someone) to try to win favour by flattering him.

to cut a long story short to tell someone only the outcome or result of a matter and not all the details leading up to it; to relate briefly.

to cut it fine (informal) to leave oneself with only a minimum of time in which to do something.

to cut one's coat according to one's cloth to adjust one's wishes to one's means, usually one's financial means.

to cut someone off with a shilling to disinherit him, to leave him very little money in one's will.

to cut the ground from under someone's feet to leave him in a weak position by saying or doing something to destroy his argument.

to draw a blank not to find what one was looking for.

to draw in one's horns to manage with less money, spend less and adjust one's needs accordingly.

to drive someone to drink (informal) to cause him so much annoyance, trouble, difficulties etc that one forces him to find comfort in alcohol.

to err on the 'safe side to be intentionally inaccurate in order to avoid taking a risk, usually by providing too much or too many instead of too little or too few.

to feather one's nest to profit dishonestly in order to provide oneself with more comfort; to enrich oneself.

to feel someone's pulse to find out his secret opinions by asking questions which test him.

to feel one's way to proceed with care.

to fight 'shy of something/someone to try to avoid it/him.

to fish for compliments/information to try to get it by indirect questions.

to fish in troubled waters to try to get a personal advantage from a disturbed or troubled situation.

to flog a dead horse to waste one's time or energy by doing something which has already been done, decided etc.

to fly in the face of someone/something to defy him/it openly.

to fly off the handle (informal) to become furious, to lose one's self-control.

to follow in someone's footsteps to take up the same career, lead the same kind of life as him (eg one's father, uncle etc).

to follow the crowd to do, think, act the same as everybody else does, without being critical or thinking about it oneself.

to force someone's hand to compel him to reveal his aims, plans etc.

to gild the lily to spoil the beauty of something by unnecessary decoration.

to hand out bouquets (to someone) to give him praise or compliments.

to handle someone with kid gloves to treat him very carefully, so as not to hurt his feelings.

to harp on the same string to talk repeatedly about the same problem, sorrow etc until it becomes tiresome to others.

to haul someone over the coals to scold or reprimand him severely for a wrongdoing.

to hear something over/through the grape-vine to hear something through an unofficial source, through gossip.

to hide one's light under a bushel to be too modest about one's own talents, capabilities and not show them to advantage.

to hit below the belt to fight or argue unfairly.

to hit the nail on the head (informal) to pick out and state the exact reason for something, the correct explanation or real point at issue.

to hold out the olive branch to show someone that one is willing to make peace or be friendly again after a quarrel etc.

to iron out differences to smooth over an argument or quarrel.

to jog someone's memory (informal) to remind him of something which he has forgotten.

to join forces (with someone) to unite, come together, work together, cooperate etc with him.

to jump on the band-wagon to join a new undertaking or enterprise at the beginning because it looks like being successful, or because it is fashionable to do so.

to kill two birds with one stone to accomplish two things with only one effort.

to knock someone off his perch (informal) to defeat him, bring him down from his secure position.

to know where the shoe pinches to know about hardship or suffering through one's own experiences.

to know which side one's bread is buttered to know what is most advantageous for one.

to laugh up one's sleeve (at someone) to be secretly amused (at him); to be secretly scornful (of him).

to lead a charmed life to pass through danger or difficulties without injury, again and again.

to lead someone a dance (informal) to cause him more exertion or trouble than necessary.

to lead someone a `dog's life to cause him to have a miserable, worried life.

to lead someone up the garden path to mislead, deceive someone.

to leave much to be desired to be unsatisfactory.

to leave someone in the lurch (informal) to desert him when he is in difficulties and expects help.

to leave well alone not to interfere with something.

let by-gones be by-gones to let things that are past and gone remain untouched and forgotten, especially if these things were unpleasant or involved a quarrel between people.

to let sleeping dogs lie not to do anything that will stir up unnecessary trouble.

to let something drop (of a matter, issue, argument etc) to abandon it, not continue to occupy oneself with it.

to let the cat out of the bag to give away a secret, to make it known before it should be made known.

to let the grass grow under one's feet to waste time by not doing a job of work immediately, or by not taking an opportunity immediately.

to look after number one (informal) to look after one's own interests first, to do what is best for oneself.

to look someone up and down (informal) to inspect him critically.

to `lord it (over someone) (informal) to domineer, show one's importance.

to meet one's Waterloo to be totally defeated.

to meet someone half-`way to make a compromise with him, to agree mutually in part.

to mend one's ways to improve one's behaviour, attitudes etc.

to mince (one's) words not to speak frankly because one wants to be polite.

to mind one's own business not to interfere with the affairs of others.

to mind one's p's and q's to be careful what one says or does so as not to make a bad impression; to be very polite.

to move heaven and earth (to do something) to try everything possible to accomplish a purpose.

to name the day to fix the date of something (eg a wedding).

to nip something in the bud to stop or destroy it in the early stages of development so that it cannot have a bad influence or effect in the future.

to pat someone on the back to congratulate him on something (used also in *to give someone a pat on the back*).

to pick a quarrel (with someone) to intentionally try to begin a quarrel.

to pick holes (in something) to find fault with it, to criticise it (often unnecessarily).

to pip someone to/at the post (informal) to defeat him, to gain advantage over him, by a small margin, at the last moment etc.

to pluck at someone's heartstrings to try to arouse sympathy by telling him about one's sadness and sorrows.

to plumb the depths (of something) to try to find out the truth (of a problem, difficulty, mystery etc).

to pocket one's pride to hide one's feelings of humiliation and do something which one is really too proud to do (also used in *to put one's pride in one's pocket*).

to pour oil on troubled waters to try to settle a quarrel or bring calm to a troubled situation by using soothing words.

to quarrel with one's bread and butter to quarrel with the source of one's income (usually one's employer).

to rain cats and dogs to rain heavily.

to rest on one's laurels to be satisfied with one's successes and not to try for more.

to ride a hobby to tire other people by continually referring to one's own favourite subject.

to ring a bell (informal) to seem familiar, to remind one of something or someone.

to ring the changes to provide variety by doing things or arranging things in as many different ways as possible, so as to avoid monotony.

to rise to the occasion to cope with a situation adequately, even if one was not expected to do so.

to rob Peter to pay Paul to take from one to give to another, both being in equal circumstances, thereby not altering or improving the situation.

to roll one's sleeves up (informal) to prepare oneself to start working.

to rub someone up the wrong way (informal) to irritate, annoy him.

to rule the roost to be in control, to dominate (as the cock does in the hen-house).

to run in the blood to be characteristic of the members of a family (usually a certain feature of character, behaviour, ability etc).

to run with the hare and hunt with the hounds to support two opposing sides at the same time, thus trying to gain advantages from both sides by being on good terms with both sides.

to sail under false colours to pretend to be what one is not, in order to deceive for one's own advantage.

to save one's bacon (informal) to escape danger, injury, trouble or reprimand; to manage to avoid failure.

to send someone packing/to send someone about his business to tell him to go away because he is annoying.

to separate the wheat from the chaff to distinguish the good from the bad, the useful from the worthless etc.

to sit on the fence not to take sides, to stay neutral by not supporting either side.

to sit tight (informal) to remain firm in one's purpose or opinion, to be resolute, not to waver.

to skate on thin ice to do or say something which requires great care or tact, because it could easily be misunderstood, cause trouble etc.

to smell a rat (informal) to suspect that something is wrong.

to speak volumes (for/against something) to be supporting evidence for or against it.

to spill the beans (informal) to tell a secret, let out information, news etc before one should do so.

to split hairs to make distinctions that are too small to be important or of value.

to steal someone's thunder to attract attention to oneself, thus getting the praise or admiration which someone else would have had.

to steer clear of something to avoid it because it will bring trouble or danger.

to stick around (informal) to stay in a place and wait.

to stick at nothing (informal) to let nothing prevent one from accomplishing a purpose, even if it may necessitate dishonesty, danger etc.

to stick one's 'neck out (informal) to say or do something (usually criticism or advice which was not asked for) which might cause trouble.

to stick out a mile (informal) to be obvious.

to stick to one's guns (informal) not to allow oneself to be influenced in one's point of view, to be firm and resolute.

to stretch a point to do more than is usual, to make an exception to a rule, usually in order to help someone.

to strike while the iron is hot to take advantage of an opportunity while it presents itself.

to sugar the pill to make something unpleasant seem pleasant.

to talk shop to talk about one's special occupation with someone, although this subject may well exclude others from the conversation.

to talk through (the top of) one's hat to talk foolishly, ignorantly.

to tell someone where to get 'off to tell him (sharply, angrily) what one thinks of his behaviour, advice etc.

to tempt Providence to take dangerous and unnecessary risks.

to throw in the towel (informal) to accept defeat.

to tie someone's hands to restrain him from action, to limit his possibilities.

to tighten one's belt to spend less money, cut down on unnecessary things in a time of financial difficulty.

to tread on someone's toes to upset someone, hurt his feelings, usually by criticising.

to upset the apple-cart to spoil a plan or something which was well organised.

to want 'jam on it (informal) to want everything, not to be satisfied with something which is already good, but to want still more or something still better.

to wash one's dirty linen in public to quarrel over or discuss in public personal or family matters which should be kept private.

to wash one's 'hands of something/someone to withdraw one's involvement in it/him so as to be no longer responsible for it/him.

to wear the trousers to be the partner in a relationship with most influence or the stronger will, who makes the decisions.

to weather the storm to survive a crisis, overcome difficulties.

to wet one's whistle (informal) to have a drink (usually to refresh oneself).

to whistle for the wind to spend one's energy on ridiculous or impossible projects.

to wipe the 'floor with someone (informal) to triumph over him, to completely defeat him in an argument etc to show oneself to be superior.

to wipe the slate clean to put right what is wrong and begin again.

12

Idioms from special situations and categories

general note

This chapter has two parts, both of which present idioms to the learner in special groups for easier learning and reference.

Part A groups idioms around particular situations or subjects. These sections introduce the student to words and phrases which are typically found and used in conversation in these situations or on these subjects. It often happens that even an advanced student cannot follow a simple conversation on an every-day subject such as 'motoring', because he does not know some of the phrases English speakers use when talking about motoring. Even if the student can understand what the word means, he cannot use it himself unless he practices it carefully. For example, if a motorist talks about 'jacking up' his car, 'nosing in', going up the hill 'in bottom', or asking another motorist 'How many do you average?', the learner may not understand the important points of a story or conversation. In order to help him to do this, idiomatic phrases are listed together which are often found in the subjects of *motoring, telephoning, buying and selling, health, business and finance, politics, work and industry*.

Part B groups idioms around the special categories of *animals, colours, parts of the body* and *time*, ie groups of idioms which include the words eg *horse, bird; red, blue; head, arm; day, year*. This gives the learner a quick and easy way of looking a phrase up, and it also provides an opportunity of learning idioms systematically.

A Idioms from special situations

banking

You **open** and **close a 'bank account**. You **put money into an account**, ie you deposit money at a bank, or you **draw money** `out (of an account).** You can have a `current account** for money that you want to use at any time. Money which is kept in a bank **at interest**, and which cannot be drawn out without notice, is kept in a `savings/de`posit account.** A `joint account** is one that belongs to two people, e g a husband and wife.

the rate of interest (or **interest rate**) the amount of money charged by the bank, or paid by the bank for the loan or use of money. It is expressed as a percentage. *He gets 7% interest on his money at the City Bank, but the rate of interest for loans is much higher, 11%.*

If you pay for something by cheque and the **cheque bounces** (informal), it means that you do not have enough money in the bank to cover payment of the cheque.

If the bank **dishonours a cheque**, it refuses to pay money on it because the customer has not enough money in his account to cover it.

To **cross a cheque** means to draw two parallel lines across it. This means that payment can only be made through a bank. **A crossed cheque** can therefore only be paid into a bank account. If you want to have cash for the cheque, the word *self* or *cash* must appear on it.

You **make out a cheque to someone (for an amount of money).**

business

The financial and commercial part of London, including the Stock Exchange and the banks, is referred to as **The City. A City man** is, therefore, a man who is engaged in commerce or banking and finance. **Wall Street** is the American money market.

A falling market means that prices for a certain commodity are dropping or getting lower. When prices are improving we talk about **a strong market.**

Shares can **drop** or **fall** or **slide** when they lose in value. They can **rise**, **soar** or **rocket** when they increase in value. **Shares are looking `up** means that the value is getting higher after a period of low value. If shares **touch bottom**, they fall very low indeed, and they **bottom `out** if they stay very low for a long time. Shares are **at par** when they sell at their nominal value, i e original price. Shares can also be **above** or **below par.** If the prices of shares does not go up or down, we say they **stay put.** If you have money **tied up in shares**, your money will only become available if the shares are sold.

A business **runs at a profit** or **runs at a loss**, i e it makes or loses money. If a business makes neither a profit nor a loss, it **breaks even**. When business is improving, we say it is **picking up**. We **put money into** a business, industry etc.

Prices or orders may **slump**, ie fall suddenly. A business **slump** means a business depression, a period of little business activity.

to make a `go of a business** to build up a good business. You **open `up a business and **close `down a business**. If you deal in business and trade you are **in business**.

We say that a company's **finances are in good/bad shape**, ie the company has a lot of money/not enough money behind it.

a sleeping partner (US **a silent partner**) a person who provides a percentage of the capital of a business but who does not have a part in the management of the business.

a `take-over the change of ownership or control of a company.

a merger the joining of two or more companies into one.

to go/be bankrupt (informal **to go bust**) to become/be insolvent, ie not able to pay debts.

bad debts debts which are not expected to be paid.

sharp practice(s) business dealings which are not honest.

to talk business to talk about business.

on business for the purpose of doing business, ie not for pleasure.

buying and selling

to buy something on hire purchase/on the HP/(informal) **on the never-`never** to buy it **on credit** and pay for it by weekly or monthly instalments, called **deferred payments**.

You can **pay cash** for an article or **pay by cheque**.

to take goods on approval to buy goods which you can return if you are not satisfied.

a `good/`bad buy something that is well worth/not worth the money you paid.

to shop a`round to compare prices at different shops before buying.

to go `window-shopping only to look at goods on display in the shop windows, not to buy goods.

to shop with (a particular shop) to buy regularly from a particular shop.

to buy a pig in a poke to buy something which you have not seen before buying it and which is not what you wanted to have.

to buy in bulk to buy large quantities of an article, usually cheaply.

to buy `in to buy a large quantity in advance.

to run up an account/a bill (with a shop/firm) to buy a number of things on credit. If you are allowed to do this regularly, you **have an account (with a shop/firm)**, which you **open** (begin) or **close** (end). When you buy goods in this way, you **charge them (up) to your account.**

to settle an account to pay a bill.

a `shop-walker` a person who shows customers to the right counters or departments in a big store.

a `shop-lifter` a person who steals from shops whilst pretending to be a customer, i e during business hours. (Verb: **to `shop-lift`.)**

to set up shop to start a small retail business.

to keep a shop to be a shopkeeper, to own a shop.

to pay through the `nose for something to pay more money than the object is worth.

to buy goods in/at the sales to buy them at special times of the year when all goods are reduced in price in order to clear old stock.

to be `in/`out of pocket to have/lack money (e g through a sale or business deal).

to do a roaring trade to do good business and make high profits.

to run a business on a `shoe-string` to spend very little to maintain it.

to sell something `off` to sell the remaining stock of an article cheaply.

to sell `out of something to have nothing left of a particular article. If an article **sells like hot cakes** it **sells well,** i e many people buy it.

to put something up for sale/auction to offer it for sale/for auction.

to be up for sale/auction to be offered for sale/auction.

if an article **goes for a song** it is sold very cheaply, under its proper value.

an article can **fetch a price** or **go for a price.** *The house fetched/ went for £20,000.*

to bring something under the hammer to sell it by auction. Goods or property therefore **come under the hammer.**

to sell someone up to sell his goods or property forcibly as payment for bad debts.

when prices rise or increase they **go up.** A shopkeeper **puts up** or **brings down** his prices.

to sell `cut price` to sell below the normal price (of other shops).

to knock money `off (goods)` to sell (them) for less than the normal price on the label, often because of a small defect in the goods. A shopkeeper may also **knock something off** for a customer who buys a large quantity.

ready money/ready cash/hard cash money which is available for use.

`paper money` bank notes.

to make money/to be `raking it in/to be making a bomb/

fortune/packet/pile/(informal) to earn a lot of money from business.

to raise money to get money together for use.

to raise the wind (informal) to obtain ready money quickly by any method.

to be in the money to be making/to have a lot of money, usually through business.

health, illness, death

If a person is in good health, we can say of him:
he is **in good/robust health**; he **is/looks the picture of health**; he **feels well**; he **feels on top of the world**; **he's never felt better**; he **is in the pink**; he's **in good shape** (ie physically fit).
If a person is not in good health, we can say of him:
he's **not feeling well**; he's **not feeling himself**; he's **not feeling (quite) up to the mark**; he's **feeling (rather/somewhat) under the weather**; he's in **poor/ill health**; he's **in bad/poor shape**.

to take a turn for the better/worse means that in the course of an illness one's condition has become better/worse.

if a man's **health is failing**, his condition is becoming worse.

if a man's **health is picking 'up**, his condition is improving.

he's doing well; he's on the mend; he's over the worst his condition is improving after illness.

to get 'over an illness to recover from it completely.

to play havoc with one's health to ruin it.

to feel/be/look worn 'out exhausted, very tired.

to feel/be/look washed 'out pale and tired.

to feel/be/look run 'down weak and tired because of illness, overwork, tension etc.

to run/be running a temperature one's body temperature is higher than normal.

to fall ill (with a disease) to become ill (with it).

to go 'down with/be 'down with a disease to get/have it.

to catch a disease to get/become ill with it.

to be laid 'up (with a disease) to be forced to stay in bed or at home (because of it).

to 'throw off/'fight off (a cold or minor illness) to get rid of it.

to come 'round/'to to regain consciousness after a blow or an operation.

to bring someone 'round to revive him, to bring him back to consciousness.

to go on the sick (informal) to report to your place of work that you are ill; you **send in a doctor's note** to prove this.

The most plain and sensible way of talking about death is to use the verb **to die** and the adjective **dead**. Some other expressions are:

to pass away (a 'polite' expression) to die.

to breathe one's last (literary, formal, old-fashioned) to die.

to depart this life; **to go to meet one's Maker** (formal, from the language of the Church) to die.

to go the 'way of all 'flesh (biblical, literary, old-fashioned) to die.

to kick the bucket; **to 'snuff it**; **to peg 'out** (very informal, humorous) to die.

to be pushing up (the) daisies; **to be six feet 'under** (very informal, humorous) to be dead.

to die by one's own hand to commit suicide.

to come to an untimely end (formal) to die young.

to die before one's time to die young.

to die a natural death to die by ordinary or natural causes.

to die/meet a violent death to die by violence, e g murder.

If somebody is gravely ill and is expected to die, we can say:

he's **far 'gone**; there's **no 'hope for him**; he's **not long for this world**; he's **on his 'death-bed**; he's got **one foot in the grave**.

holidays and travel

you **go on holiday** (US **vacation**) **by air, by boat, by train, by car** etc.

you **go on a journey/trip/excursion/outing**; you **make a journey/trip/excursion**; you **have an outing**; you **make/do a sight-seeing tour**.

if you **go on a conducted/guided tour,** you go on a coach/bus tour with a guide. It also means to look round buildings, museums etc **(to do the sights)** with a guide.

to go on a cruise to make a journey by passenger ship.

you **make/go on a world trip**; you **travel round the world**; you **make/go on a round-the-world tour**.

if you **make/go on a round trip** through a country, you travel around the country and return to the starting point.

to go to the seaside to go on holiday or a trip to the coast.

to go down to the sea/country to pay a visit to the coast/country.

to go touring to travel round a country or countries by car or coach. **to tour the Continent** means to travel round Europe, not including Britain.

you **set 'off on** a journey, you **set 'out on** a venture.

to break the journey to stop somewhere on the way to somewhere else. If you do not break the journey, you **travel non-ˈstop** or **travel ˈthrough.**

to travel over land to travel through a country or countries by bus and train, not by air or boat.

a ˈglobe-trotter a person who travels a lot through many countries of the world, usually staying in each country only a short time. (Verb: **to trot the globe, to ˈglobe-trot.**)

a package holiday a holiday made with a group of people booked through a travel organisation, where the price includes the journey there and back, accommodation, meals and (sometimes) excursions.

a journey in a plane leaving an airport at a regular time and travelling a regular route is called a ˈ**scheduled flight.** A journey in a plane that is hired for a group is called a ˈ**charter flight.**

people on holiday are called ˈ**holiday-makers.** People on day excursions to the seaside by bus or train are called **day-ˈtrippers.**

a ˈcoach-party a group of people travelling on an organised journey or excursion by private bus.

to stop ˈoff/ˈover (at/in a place) to break a journey for a short period to stay at a place (noun: a ˈ**stop-over**).

you **stay the ˈnight/stay overˈnight/make an overnight ˈstop (at/in a place).**

to put ˈup (at a hotel) to stay there to sleep and eat.

a ˈboarding-house a private house which takes in guests for **full board** (a bed and 3 meals per day) or **bed and breakfast.**

to get ˈin (at a hotel) to be able to book accommodation there.

to put someone up to provide a bed and food for him.

a five-star hotel a luxury hotel.

you **travel/go/book ˈfirst class;** ˈ**second class** (by train) is often called ˈ**tourist class** (by boat) or eˈ**conomy class** (by plane).

to book a passage (to somewhere) to reserve a cabin on a boat.

to book a crossing to reserve a ticket for a short boat journey across a stretch of sea, e g the crossing from Dover (in England) to Calais (in France).

a ˈboat-train the train which takes people to and from the boat for a particular crossing, e g the boat-train from London to Dover.

a ˈboarding-card/-pass a card allowing you to get on a boat or plane.

a ˈlanding-card a card allowing you to get off a boat.

to book ˈthrough (to a place) to reserve tickets for all parts of the journey, all the way there.

you book **a single ticket** (GB); **a one-way ticket** (US); **a return ticket** (GB); **a round-trip ticket** (US).

when you **cross a border/frontier** to enter a country you must **pass/go through customs.**

to hitch a ride; to thumb a lift; to 'hitch-hike (informal) to stand at the road side and to ask a car-driver or lorry-driver for a ride by giving a sign with your thumb. Someone who does this is a **'hitch-hiker.**

when you **go camping** you **put up/pitch a tent.**

to break (up) camp to pack up your camping tent, to take it down.

to sleep in the open to sleep out of doors.

to go on holiday **'off season** to go at the cheapest and least popular times of the year.

to travel light to travel without much **luggage** (US **baggage**).

to live out of a suit-case to change places and hotels so often that you are always packing and unpacking your suitcase.

a busman's holiday holiday or leisure time which is spent doing the same thing as one does when one is working.

a rubberneck (US, informal; a term of mockery) the kind of tourist or sight-seer who constantly turns his head so as to see as much as possible.

motoring

an **'L-plate** (learner's plate) the sign which a learner must fix to any car he drives before he has passed his driving test. It has a capital 'L' in red.

when you buy a new car you must first **run it 'in. To run 'in a car** means to drive it carefully for a certain distance or length of time.

it is not good **to rev 'up the engine** (US **to gun the motor**), ie to increase the speed of revolutions of the engine too much (by pressing **the accelerator** too hard and too fast).

in order **to drive off** you must **put the car in gear.** You drive off **in first** or **in bottom (gear).** Then you **change into second, then third (gear).** When you drive fast you are **in fourth** or **in top (gear).** When you **change down**, you change into a lower gear. If you are **not in gear** the car will not move: you are **in neutral (gear).** In order to drive backwards, you must be **in reverse (gear).** You **put the car into reverse.**

to put one's 'foot down (ie on the accelerator) to increase speed and drive fast. In other words, **to speed 'up** or **to get 'speed up.**

to slow down to reduce speed.

you must **give way** (US **yield**) when another car **has the right of way**, ie you must let the other car pass (or **over'take**) or drive off before you.

if you have to stop suddenly, you **jam on the brakes.** This may be necessary if another car **cuts 'in** in front of you.

you **pull 'in** or **pull into the side** when you stop your car at the side of the road. A stopping place at the side of the road is a `pull-in.

you **pull** `out when you move away from the side of the road, or move from behind another vehicle to overtake it.

to back a car to reverse it. You **back** `in/`out/`up. Alternatively, you can **nose** `in/`out/`up, ie you drive forwards carefully.

to bear right/left to follow the road that branches to the right or left.

to take a right/left turn means **to turn** `off to the right or left at a crossroads or junction.

to hog the road to drive in the middle of the road, not allowing cars behind to pass. Such a driver is called a `road-hog.

on the **motorway** (US **super highway**) you can use the `slow **lane** (inside lane) or the `fast lane (outside lane). On a very wide road there may be **three-** or even **four-lane traffic.**

a dual `carriageway (US **divided** `highway) a fast road with two lanes in each direction.

a `trunk road a main road (GB).

a `by-road a road which is not used much, a side-road.

a `by-pass a wide road passing around a town or an area of heavy traffic.

a `fly-over (US **overpass**) a road or bridge which crosses above another road.

an underpass the section of a road which passes under another road.

a bottleneck a narrower part of a wide road where the traffic is held up.

where two roads come together to form one, the traffic from the minor road must **filter** `in, ie move carefully into the main stream of traffic.

when the road is so full of cars that you can only drive very slowly or not at all, you are **caught/stuck/held up in a** `traffic jam. This happens in **the** `rush hour, the time in the morning and evening when the traffic is heaviest because people are driving to and from work.

the hard shoulder the hard surface at the side of the motorway where you can stop in an emergency.

cat's eyes the rows of reflecting studs which light up to mark the middle of the roadway in the darkness.

a dead end a road which does not lead anywhere. It is not **a** `through road.

a car park (US `parking-lot) is a place to leave (ie **to park**) your car for a short time.

if you want to **change the wheel** of your car, you must **jack the car** `up. You use a device called **a jack** to raise the wheel off the ground. When the wheel is changed, you **jack** `down the car.

if you want to **fill up with petrol** for the car, you go to a ˋ**petrol**/ ˋ**filling**/ˋ**service**/(US) ˋ**gas station**.

if you want to **have repairs done to your car,** you take it to a ˋ**service station** or (GB) **a garage**.

a big accident where many cars have run into each other is called a ˋ**pile-up**.

if you **have a smash**, you have quite a bad accident. If you **have a knock/bump**, you have a small accident. A car can **smash/ knock/bump/run/back into** another car.

if you **hit an oncoming car**, ie an approaching car, you have a **head-on colˋlision.**

if your car is very badly damaged and cannot be repaired, you **write the car** ˋ**off**, it is called a ˋ**write-off** (US you **total the car**, it is **totalled**), ie it has no value.

if you do not claim money from the insurance company because of accident, you receive **a reduction in premium** called **a no claims bonus.**

if you have **third party insurance,** an insurance company pays for damage to a person in addition to the person insured.

if a car **does/averages 25 (miles) to the gallon,** the driver can travel 25 miles (on average) using one gallon of petrol. The driver **gets 25 to the gallon.**

the running costs (of a car) the costs which the driver pays in order **to run the car,** ie to keep and look after his car. If you **run two cars,** you own and use two cars.

you put **luggage** (US **baggage**) in the **boot** (US **trunk**). The engine is under the **bonnet** (US **hood**).

politics and government

(The following expressions are relevant to politics and government in Great Britain.)

Great Britain is a **constitutional monarchy**, where the **Monarch** (the King or Queen) is **the Head of State.**

the Commons *The House of Commons* or Lower House of Parliament. It represents the whole population which is entitled to vote. A member of the Commons is called a **Member of Parliament** (an **MP**). He **represents a constituency,** the voters of which **elect him to Parliament.**

the Lords *The House of Lords* or Upper House of Parliament. All members have the title *Lord*, but the House has limited political power.

a bill a draft of an *Act of Parliament*, ie a law which has not yet been passed by Parliament. A bill must **pass through the first/ second/third reading** in the Commons, ie it must be presented, discussed and amended three times. If the **bill is adopted/ passed**, ie accepted by the Commons, at the third reading, it is **sent up** to the Lords (or **sent down** to the Commons if it was introduced by the Lords). When the bill is passed, it is said to have been **put through the Commons/Lords**. If a bill is not accepted, it is said to be **thrown 'out/defeated/rejected**.

the Speaker the officer in the Commons who directs the debates and keeps order.

a back-'bencher a less important member of the Commons, ie he **sits on the 'back-benches**, ie the seats furthest away from the Speaker's chair.

a front-'bencher a more important member of the Commons, eg a minister or ex-minister. Therefore, **the 'front-benches** are the seats nearest to the Speaker.

a cross-'bencher a member of **the 'cross-benches**, ie an independent member who does not vote regularly for either one of the two main parties in the Commons.

the Cabinet the group of **Ministers**, headed by **the Prime Minister**, who direct the administration and policy of the **government in power**.

the shadow Cabinet the group of ministers of the **Parliamentary Opposition** (the **government in opposition**) ie of the party which is not in power.

the 'right wing/'left wing (of a political party) those parliamentary members of the party whose views are more extreme (conservative or socialist) than the views of the majority. Such a member is called **a right-'winger/left-'winger**.

a candidate for a political office **stands for/runs for/puts up for election**.

a general election occurs when all the voters in the country, in the different constituencies, vote for their particular Member of Parliament from among a group of candidates, each of whom represents a political party. The candidate who gets the most votes **gets 'in** (informal), or **gains office** (formal). The leader of the party that has gained the most Members of Parliament is asked by the Head of State to **form a Government**.

a local election occurs when the people who live in (part of) a town or district elect a **councillor** for their **district/borough/ town council**. These councils make up the country's administrative system of **local government**, which deals with local matters of education, health, transport, etc.

the political party which governs the country is said **to be in office/ to hold office**. To be **out of office** means not to be in power.

a `bye-election an election held in one constituency while a government is in office.

telephoning

Other idiomatic expressions for **to telephone someone** are:

to ring someone; to ring someone up; to give someone a ring; (GB).
to phone someone; to phone someone up; (GB).
to make a call to someone; (GB and US).
to call someone; to call someone up; to give someone a call; (US).

you make a call from a **public telephone** or `coin-box or `telephone kiosk/box/booth** (GB) or from a `pay phone** (US).
a trunk call a long distance call, made by an **operator** who works at a **switchboard**, with charges according to distance.
to reverse charges; to make a reversed charge call to charge the cost of the call to the person you telephone.
a `party line; a `shared line a telephone line which is shared by two or more people (who have their own telephones).
a `hot line a direct line between heads of governments.
when you telephone someone you may not **get `through**, ie you may not get a connection. This may be because **the line is engaged** (US **the number is busy**), ie someone is already speaking from the number. The telephone may be **out of order**, ie it is not working because of a mechanical fault. You may have a **poor/ bad line**, ie you cannot hear clearly because of interference (crackling, buzzing etc). You may have a **crossed line**, ie hear other people having a conversation. The line may **go dead**, ie the connection may be lost. You may **be cut `off**, ie the line may be interrupted and the connection lost.
to be on the phone 1 to have a (private) telephone. *Are the Jacksons on the phone yet?* 2 *There's Mr X on the phone for you*, means 'Mr X is waiting on the telephone to speak to you' 3 to be speaking on the telephone. *I'll take a message for her. I'm afraid she's on the phone at the moment.*
to hang up/ring off to end a telephone call by replacing the receiver.
in an organisation with many telephones, the `**switchboard operator**` will give you the number you wish to speak to. He will **put you `through to the extension** or will **connect you with** it.
to take a/the call to speak to the person who is **on the line/phone.**
if you have no time to take the call, you can **ring/phone/call someone back (later).**

to hold the line; to hold ʼon to wait while the person at the other end goes away from the telephone for a short time.

work and industrial relations

a man is ʼ**wage-earning,** ie a ʼ**wage-earner** if he receives money for his work every week.

a man is ʼ**salary-earning,** ie a ʼ**salary-earner** if he receives money for his work every month.

a man is **self-emʼployed** if he works for himself, ie without an employer.

a man is **a freelance** if he has no regular employer but works independently wherever he can, eg a writer or a journalist. (Verb: **to freelance.**)

to work in the field to work outside, usually travelling from place to place, not in an office. Salesmen or market researchers work in the field.

a white-ʼcollar worker a worker who does an office job.

a blue-ʼcollar worker a manual worker, eg in a factory.

to be on the board to belong eg to the directors of a company or to the governors of a school.

the men who work **on the shop floor** are the manual workers in the factory, not the management or the clerical staff.

a shop-ʼsteward a man chosen by his fellow workers to represent them in their **trade union.**

to do/work overtime to work after the usual hours for extra pay.

to be on overtime to do overtime regularly for a longer period of time.

to be on ʼdouble time to receive double the hourly payment for working at difficult times, ie on Sundays or at night.

to be on ʼpiece-work to receive payment for the number of pieces produced, not for the length of time you work.

ʼ**time-work** manual work paid for by the hour or day.

to be on shifts/on ʼshift work a **shift** is a group of workmen who start work as another group finishes. The ʼ**day-shift** is the group of workmen who work in the day-time, the ʼ**night-shift** works through the night. The **shift** can also be the period of time which the men work, usually eight hours. Thus: **to be on the ʼnight-shift/to be on nights** and **to be on the ʼday-shift/to be on days.**

to knock ʼon/ʼoff (informal) to begin/finish work. *What time do you knock on? When is knocking-off time?*

to clock ʼin/ʼon/ʼout/ʼoff Workers in a factory must *clock in/on* when they arrive and *clock out/off* when they leave. These times are recorded by an automatic *clocking-in* machine.

if you want to have a wage or salary increase you (as an individual) **put in for a rise** or (as a group) **make a 'wage-claim**.

to fire someone; to give someone the sack to dismiss him from employment.

to strike; to go on strike; to come out (on strike) to refuse to work. *The railwaymen are coming out next week*. Workers can **strike for** higher wages, better working conditions etc.

a 'sit-in a protest action by the workers. They **sit 'in/stage a 'sit-in/stage a sit-down strike** in the factory, ie they stay in the factory and refuse to move until their demands are considered by the employers.

the workers may agree **to go to arbitration** ie to have their claims etc judged by an independent **arbitrator** who is appointed by the government.

to lock someone 'out (of the employers) to refuse to let the workers enter their place of work until they agree to proposed conditions of work and pay (noun: **a 'lock-out**).

a 'work-in a take-over by workers of a factory that is threatened with closure.

a man who offers to work when the regular workmen are on strike is called **a 'black-leg** (verb: **to 'black-leg**).

a picket a group of workers (usually members of a trade-union) who are on strike, who gather outside their place of work to persuade other workers to join their strike. They **form a 'picket line** (verb: **to picket**).

when strikers refuse to handle goods, materials, a cargo etc they **black** the goods, the cargo etc.

the hard core (of the strikers) the decisive, controlling group which is often the most extreme.

a closed shop a place of work (factory, firm, workshop) or a trade or profession which is only open to members of a particular trade union.

(to be on) a 'go-slow; to go slow. This is another kind of protest action. Workers work more slowly than usual and do not do overtime. If this happens in the public services, eg the postal service, the delivery of letters will be delayed.

(to be on) a work-to-'rule; to work to 'rule. Another form of protest. The workers follow strictly the rules which are laid down for the job. This leads to a considerable slowing down in the pace of work. A union can **order a work-to-'rule**.

to make someone redundant (of an employer) to end a worker's employment because his work is no longer needed. For example, if a factory closes down the workers are *made redundant*.

to lay someone 'off. Employers lay workers off at a time when trade is bad and there is not enough work for them, ie the workers are temporarily dismissed from work. (Noun: **a 'lay-off.** A worker **is laid 'off.**)

to be on 'short time to work less than usual because there is not enough work.

to be/go on the dole (informal) to receive money weekly from the state when you have no work. (Other expressions: **to be on/to receive unemployment benefit/social assistance/**(US) **welfare.**)

B   Idioms from special categories

ANIMALS

(i) Idioms containing animal names

to make an 'ass of oneself (informal) to behave in a foolish way so that one is laughed at.

to make a 'beast of oneself (informal) to eat large quantities of food, leaving little for others.

to have a bee in one's bonnet to be continually occupied with or obsessed by one idea.

to make a 'bee-line for something to take the quickest and most direct way towards it.

to kill two birds with one stone to achieve two aims with only one effort.

birds of a feather flock together people of similar character or interests like to share or will be found in each other's company.

to take the bull by the horns to decide to face a problem or difficulty instead of avoiding it.

to have butterflies in one's stomach to feel physical discomfort in one's stomach because of nervousness.

to play cat and 'mouse with someone (informal) to delay a decision etc purposely in order to make him feel very uncertain or insecure.

to let the cat out of the bag (informal) to reveal a secret.

to rain cats and dogs to rain very hard.

to put the cat among the pigeons/canaries (informal) to say or do something which causes trouble, disturbance, argument, surprise etc.

to be/have no/not enough room to swing a 'cat in/round (informal) to be/have very little space.

to lead a cat-and-'dog life (informal) (of two people who live together) to live a life full of quarrels.

to count one's chickens before they hatch/are hatched to be over-optimistic, over-confident (about something in the future).

to wait till the 'cows come home (informal) to wait for a very long time (referring to something which is never likely to happen).

a dog in the manger someone who prevents others from using, enjoying or having something that is of no use to him.

to go to the dogs (informal) to slowly decline into a very bad state or condition, (of persons) morally or physically, (of a country etc) economically etc.

to lead/give someone a 'dog's life (informal) to make life continually difficult for him.

to be top dog (informal) to be the most powerful person.

to let sleeping dogs lie to avoid following a course of action, or mentioning a subject, which could cause trouble.

to do the 'donkey work (informal) to do the most unpleasant or least important part of a task, often heavy work or routine work.

to have 'other fish to fry (informal) to have other, more important tasks to attend to.

a 'pretty kettle of fish (informal) a state of disorder, confusion, difficulty or trouble. (Usually used as an exclamation: *Now 'there's a 'pretty kettle of fish!*)

a fly in the ointment something that causes slight difficulties or a disadvantage, which thus prevents total satisfaction, enjoyment etc.

there are no flies on him (informal) he is very alert, not easy to deceive etc.

to get one's goat (informal) to annoy one greatly.

he can't/couldn't/won't/wouldn't say 'boo' to a goose (informal) he is very timid or quiet by nature.

to cook someone's goose (informal) to spoil his plans, chances etc either intentionally or unintentionally.

(straight) from the horse's mouth (informal) (of news, information etc) directly from the person who knows most about it.

to hold one's horses (informal) to be patient, to wait. (Usually used as an exclamation: *Hold your horses!*)

to flog a dead horse (informal) to waste time or energy on something which is hopeless, useless, unchangeable etc.

to look a gift-horse in the mouth to show dissatisfaction or find fault with a gift. (Usually used in the form *Don't look a gift-horse in the mouth.*)

to have kittens (informal) to be very anxious about something, to be very worried that something might or might not happen.

to be up with the lark to get up very early in the morning.

a/the leopard can't change its spots one cannot change one's character or temperament.

the 'lion's share the largest and best part of something (eg money, work, food).

to **make a 'monkey out of someone** (informal) to make him seem foolish, inadequate etc.

to **buy a pig in a poke** to buy something without having examined it, which turns out to be worth less than one paid for it.

to **make a 'pig of oneself** (informal) to over-eat, to eat large quantities greedily.

someone's pigeon (informal) his responsibility, decision, concern etc.

to **smell a rat** (informal) to detect something suspicious, to sense that something is wrong.

to **go at a 'snail's pace** to travel, work etc very slowly.

to **have a 'whale of a time** (informal) to enjoy oneself very much.

a wolf in sheep's clothing a person who pretends to be a friend but who is really only hiding his unfriendly, selfish intentions.

to **keep the wolf from the door** to be able to provide one's family with enough food etc in difficult times.

(ii) Idioms containing words related to animals

to **bark up the wrong tree** (informal) to direct one's complaints, wishes, suggestions etc to the wrong person.

his bark is worse than his bite he is outwardly bad-tempered, angry etc but he does not carry out his threats.

a feather in one's cap (of one's own actions, achievements) something to be proud of.

to **show the white feather** to show fear and cowardliness.

to **feather one's nest** to provide oneself with money etc for the future by securing advantages, even if dishonestly.

to **make the 'feathers/'fur fly** (informal) to make trouble, to cause quarrels.

to **draw in one's horns** (informal) to spend less money.

to **hold the reins** to be in control, to be the most influential person behind a scheme etc.

to **keep a tight 'rein on someone/something** to control him/it firmly, allow only a little freedom.

to **clip someone's wings** (informal) to check his behaviour, activities, by limiting his possibilities, money etc.

to **take someone under one's wing** to give him protection, security.

COLOURS

black

to **beat someone black and blue** to hit him so that he has many bruises.

to have something in black and white to have it in writing.

black can mean 'angry', eg **a black mood, a black look, to be/go black in the face**. **to be in someone's black books** means that he is angry with you.

black can mean 'unhappy', eg **a black day, a black outlook**.

a ˈblack-leg, to black—see *Work and Industrial Relations* (Chapter 12).

to ˈblack-ball someone to prevent him from doing something (eg joining a club or group) by voting against him.

a ˈblack-out 1 a sudden loss of consciousness or memory; 2 a loss of electric light due to power failure.

a ˈblack-list a list of persons who are considered to be dangerous, undesirable, unreliable etc. (Verb: **to ˈblacklist someone**.)

the black sheep (of the family) a person of whom the family is not proud.

to be not so black as one is painted to be not so bad as people say one is.

black magic witchcraft.

to sell/buy goods on the black market to do so against the law, and in private.

a black spot a place on a road where accidents often happen.

to be in the black (of one's money) to be in credit; to have more assets than liabilities, ie not to be in debt. (See *red* below.)

black ice (on a road) ice that is very dangerous to traffic because it is almost invisible.

to be dressed in black (ie clothes) to be in mourning when eg a member of one's family has died.

blue

in a blue mood; to feel blue; to have the blues to be sad or miserable.

out of the blue unexpectedly.

a bolt from the blue something unexpected.

to blue one's money to spend all one's money wastefully.

a blue pencil a censor. (Verb: **to blue-pencil something**.)

blue blood aristocratic origin. (Adjective: **blue-blooded**.)

a true blue a loyal member of the British Conservative Party.

once in a blue moon rarely or never.

a blue film an obscene or pornographic film.

a blue book (GB) a government report.

a blue-ˈcollar worker a manual or factory worker, not an office worker (*a white-ˈcollar worker*).

brown

to be in a brown study to be thinking deeply about something, and not easily distracted.

to be browned `off (with something) to be bored, tired or irritated (by it).

brown paper strong paper used for wrapping parcels.

green

a green belt an area of fields and woodlands around a town.

a `green room the room in a theatre where actors can spend time when they are not on stage.

to have green fingers to be good at gardening.

to give someone the green light to give him permission or approval to start doing something.

to be green to be too trusting; to be easily deceived through lack of experience; to be inexperienced or new to something.

grey

to turn grey to become grey-haired.

`grey matter the brain; intelligence.

pink

to be pink to have mild left-wing political views.

to be in the pink to be and to feel very healthy.

to see pink elephants to have had too much to drink; to be drunk.

red

to see red to become suddenly angry.

to see the red light to recognise danger.

red tape too much attention to official regulations and papers, e g in government departments, which slows down people and processes.

red meat beef and mutton, i e not pork, veal or poultry (*white meat*).

a `red-head a person with red hair.

a red `letter day an important or joyful occasion in one's life.

a red herring an unimportant or irrelevant matter which is introduced into a discussion to distract attention from the important matter which is being discussed.

to catch someone red-`handed to catch him in the act of doing something, often a criminal offence.

to put out the red carpet (for someone) to welcome him (eg an important visitor) in a special way.

to paint the town red to celebrate wildly and noisily in public places.

to be in the red to owe money to one's bank. (Also **to go into the red, to get out of the red**.) (See **black** above).

white

a white lie a small lie which does no harm and perhaps spares someone's feelings.

a white elephant a useless possession which is often expensive or difficult to get and a trouble to keep.

a white paper (GB) a government report.

white coffee coffee with milk.

white meat pork, veal or poultry, ie not beef or mutton (*red meat*).

the white flag the symbol of surrender.

a white-'collar worker an office worker, not a manual or factory worker (*a blue-'collar worker*).

to show the white feather to show fear or cowardice.

to whitewash someone/something to try to make him/it appear to be better than he/it is by covering up faults.

PARTS OF THE BODY

arm

to keep someone at arm's length to avoid becoming too friendly with him.

to be up in arms (about/over something) to protest strongly, be angry (about it).

to welcome someone/something with open arms to welcome him/it with enthusiasm.

back

to do something behind someone's back to do it without his knowledge or when he is not present.

to break the 'back of something (usually of a job or some kind of work) to finish the greater or most difficult part of the work.

to be glad to see the 'back of someone to be glad that he has left or gone away.

to take a back seat to play an unimportant or a less important part in something than before.

to put one's `back into something to work very hard at a task, usually with energy and enthusiasm.

to get/put someone's `back up to make him angry, annoyed or nervous.

to have one's back to/against the wall to be in a position where you are forced to defend yourself.

bone

a bone of contention a subject of disagreement or argument.

to have a `bone to pick with someone to complain to him about something he has said or done which did not please you.

to make no `bones about (saying/doing) something to say/do it openly and without hesitation or pretence, although it may not be pleasant.

brain

to beat/rack one's `brain(s) (about something) to think very hard or for a long time to try to find a solution to a problem.

to pick someone's brains to talk to him about a matter or problem in order to get to know and later use his knowledge or ideas on that matter.

to have something on the brain to think repeatedly or constantly about it.

a `brain-wave a good thought, idea or suggestion which comes unexpectedly or suddenly.

breast

to make a clean `breast of something to tell the truth about or confess to something which you tried to hide previously.

chest

to get something off one's chest to admit or tell something to someone which was worrying one and which one did not want to talk about previously because it was unpleasant.

ear

to play music by ear to play it from memory.

to have a good `ear for something (eg music, the pronunciation of foreign languages) to be able to discriminate sounds and tones accurately.

to be all ears to listen eagerly or curiously.

to be up to the `ears in something (eg work, problems) to be very busy or to have a lot of trouble with it.

to be wet behind the ears to be young, inexperienced, innocent etc.

to be within earshot to be within range of hearing.

elbow

`elbow grease** hard work.

`elbow room** enough room to move freely in; enough opportunity for one's abilities.

within `elbow reach not far away, close to one.

eye

to see eye to eye (with someone) (on something) to have the same opinion as someone about something.

with an eye to doing something with the intention/aim of doing it.

to have one's eye on something/someone to watch it/him closely, usually out of interest or suspicion. It also means to want or desire something.

it's all my eye (informal) it is nonsense, lies, stupid talk.

to be all eyes to look intensely, curiously or carefully at something which interests or surprises one.

to have an `eye for something (eg fashion, colour, beauty) to be a good judge of it or to have a good sense of appreciation for it.

an `eye-opener something surprising, unexpected which reveals the truth about something or someone.

to keep an `eye on something/someone to observe it/him continually and carefully. It also means to look after it/him when someone else is not there.

face

to lose face to be humiliated, to lose one's good reputation or the respect of others.

to keep a straight face not to laugh although you find something very funny, to hide amusement.

to say something to someone's face to say it openly and directly to him even if it is unpleasant.

on the `face of it as it seems to be from the facts.

in the `face of in the presence of (eg difficulties) or in spite of (eg danger).

to pull a face to show dislike or discontent by the expression on one's face.

finger

to twist someone round one's (little) finger to get him to do what one wants him to do.

to have a finger in the pie to be concerned with the matter.

to have a finger in every pie to be concerned with many matters, often for personal gain.

one's fingers are all thumbs one is clumsy or unskilled.

to have something at one's 'finger-tips to have a thorough knowledge of or familiarity with a subject or a skill.

to put/lay one's 'finger on something to point out or find out exactly the reason for something that is wrong.

to keep one's 'fingers crossed to hope that the best thing will happen.

to keep one's fingers 'crossed for someone to wish him luck in a matter or difficulty.

to put the 'finger on someone (informal) to betray or inform against a criminal.

to burn one's fingers to suffer because of rash words or actions.

foot/feet

to foot the bill to pay the bill, often for another person.

to put one's 'foot in it to say something foolish or tactless without thinking; to blunder.

to put one's best foot forward to do one's best, work one's fastest etc.

to put one's 'foot down to insist on something, to be firm in an objection or a protest against something.

to fall on one's feet to have luck which gets you out of a difficult or unpleasant situation.

to be rushed off one's feet to be extremely busy or overworked.

to feel/find one's feet to begin to show one's abilities, to become self-confident.

to stand on one's own two feet to be independent and self-confident.

to vote with one's feet (informal) to cause something not by voting for it but by direct action.

hair

keep your 'hair on! calm down! don't get angry!

to let one's 'hair down to have a carefree time, to relax and enjoy oneself, after being formal and correct in behaviour.

one's 'hair stood on end one was very frightened.

to make someone's 'hair stand on end to greatly frighten him.

to a hair (of describing) exactly.

not to turn a hair not to show fear, to remain calm.

to split hairs to talk or argue about irrelevant or unimportant differences and details.

to escape by a hair's breadth to escape very closely, narrowly.

hand

to be at hand to be very near, close to one.

to have something in hand (eg a job, a problem, a situation) to have it under one's control and to be working on it.

to take something in hand to deal with it, to take control of it.

to be/get out of hand to become out of control.

to have time/money in hand to have it spare, left over to be used.

to live from hand to mouth to live without saving money, spending it as soon as it is earned.

to keep one's 'hand in to keep in practice.

to have one's 'hands full to have a lot of work, to be fully occupied.

to win hands 'down to win very easily.

to give someone a good hand to applaud him after a good speech, performance etc.

to be (quite) a handful (eg of a child) to be unruly, difficult to manage or control.

to be hand in 'glove with someone to be in close co-operation or relationship with him, to work towards the same ends or aims.

to be an old hand to be experienced at something.

to get the upper 'hand of something/someone to win an advantage over it/him.

to eat/feed out of someone's hands to do everything which he wishes willingly, without protest.

to do/say something off-'hand to do it without previous thought or preparation.

head

to have a good 'head for something (eg figures) to be naturally good at something which requires logic or precise thinking.

to lose one's head to panic, lose control or act in a confused way.

to keep one's head to remain calm, not to panic.

one can't make head or 'tail of something one can't understand it at all, ie the matter is unclear or too difficult to understand.

to come to a head to reach a crisis.

to be head and shoulders a'bove someone to be superior in skill, ability or intelligence to him.

to put an idea into someone's head to give him an idea or suggestion to think about.

to be/go off one's head to be/become mad.

to keep one's head above water to keep out of debt, out of difficulty etc.

to have a good 'head on one's shoulders to have a lot of common sense and practical ability.

to talk over someone's head to talk about things which are too difficult or specialised for him to understand.

to put our/your/their 'heads together to consult together in order to solve problems, work out ideas etc.

heart

to take something to heart to be greatly affected or influenced by it (eg advice, news).

to have a heart-to-heart 'talk with someone to talk openly to him about personal matters.

to know/learn something by heart to know it/to get to know it from memory.

someone/a man/a woman after one's own heart a person one likes or approves of because he shares one's likes, dislikes, tastes, opinions etc.

to have one's heart 'set on something to want it very much and to aim at getting it.

to lose heart to become discouraged.

to have one's heart in one's mouth to be very nervous or frightened in anticipation of something.

leg

to pull someone's leg to tease him by telling him something which is untrue.

not to have a leg to 'stand on (in an argument) to be unable to convince, persuade, defeat etc; to be in a weak position.

to stretch one's legs to walk around in order to get physical exercise; also to go for a leg-stretcher (informal).

to be on one's last legs (informal) to be very weak, close to death.

to be on its last legs (informal) it is close to collapse or total breakdown.

neck

to stick one's `neck out to say something with the risk that it may cause trouble or criticism for oneself.

to be neck and neck to be equally good in competition for a first place; to be side by side in a race.

to breathe down someone's neck to put him under pressure by continually observing him closely or constantly demanding something from him.

a pain in the neck (informal) an irritating, tiresome person.

nose

to pay through the nose to pay more money for something than it is worth.

to turn one's `nose up at something to reject it because you think it is not good enough.

to look down one's `nose at someone not to have respect for him; to think he is inferior to oneself.

to poke one's nose into someone's/someone else's business/affairs to interfere with matters which do not concern one.

to keep one's nose to the grindstone to work hard all the time without resting.

to be as plain as the nose on your face to be very clear to see or guess; to be very obvious.

shoulder

to give someone the cold shoulder to ignore him or to treat him in an unfriendly way.

to rub `shoulders with someone to come into (social) contact with him.

to be/come straight from the shoulder (of a criticism, rebuke etc) to be direct, open, frank.

toe

to toe the line to do as someone tells you to do, to obey orders in spite of personal wishes.

to be/keep on one's toes to be/keep alert, prepared for difficulties.

to tread/step on someone's toes to hurt his feelings.

tongue

to hold one's tongue to be silent, to keep quiet, to say nothing.

to have one's ˈtongue in one's cheek; to say something tongue-in-ˈcheek to say something which is not meant to be taken seriously.

to have lost one's tongue to be too shy to speak.

to have something on the tip of one's tongue to be on the point of remembering and saying it.

to make a slip of the tongue to make a mistake when speaking, sometimes without noticing.

a ˈtongue-twister a long word, phrase or sentence which is difficult to pronounce quickly and correctly, because of a particular succession of sounds.

tooth/teeth

to have a sweet tooth to enjoy eating sweet things.

to fight tooth and nail to fight or argue fiercely.

to do something by the skin of one's teeth just to manage to do something.

to get one's ˈteeth into something (eg a job, work, learning) to put much effort into it.

TIME

(i) Expressions with the word **time**

to take one's time (over/about something) not to hurry over it.

to be pressed for time to be obliged to hurry.

to be behind time to be late.

to be on time to be punctual.

to be in ˈtime for something to come at the right time to do or get it. *You're just in time for tea!*

to do something in ˈno time to do it very quickly.

from time to time occasionally; sometimes.

at times occasionally; sometimes.

at ˈall times always.

time and again; time after time repeatedly; often.

behind the times old-fashioned; out of date.

now's the/your time! now is the right opportunity, chance for you to do something.

to be in good time to be early, to have time to spare.

in time after a certain expected length of time has passed. *You'll learn how to do it in time.*

in times gone ˈby in the past, in past times.

at the `best of times even when conditions are favourable. *I can't speak French well at the best of times, but I'm even worse when I'm tired!*

it's about time! This is said about something that should have happened or been done earlier, but which was delayed. *The train's arriving at last. It's about time, too! I'm cold and tired!*

it's high time (one did something) This is said when something must be done without more delay. *It's high time you stopped sitting about at home and went out to look for a job!*

for the time `being for the present time, until something else is arranged.

in the nick of time just before it would have been too late. *He just managed to jump on to the last bus in the nick of time.*

to have an easy `time of it (informal) to lead a comfortable life without worry or hard work; to do something which does not require effort.

to have a good time to enjoy oneself.

to have the time of one's life (informal) to have a lot of fun, a very pleasant experience.

to have a bad time (informal) to have an unpleasant or painful experience.

to kill time to do something in order to make time pass more quickly. It may be something which is useless or boring.

to do/serve time (informal) to be in prison, to serve a prison sentence.

to serve one's time to work as an apprentice, to do one's service in the army etc for a fixed number of years.

to sing in time to sing in the correct rhythm.

to keep/beat time to move hands or feet to the rhythm of the music.

to keep good/bad time (of a clock) to show the time correctly/incorrectly.

to pass the time of `day with someone to exchange greetings or a few friendly words with him.

time's up! there is no time left, no more time allowed.

to make the best of one's time to use the time available to the best advantage.

to bide one's time to wait patiently for a favourable opportunity.

to waste time to spend time uselessly.

to work against time to work quickly in order to finish something within a given period of time.

to talk against time 1 to talk quickly in order to say everything within a given period of time; 2 to keep on talking until after a certain length of time has passed.

time flies! time is passing very quickly.

time is money money is to be made in the time available and so one should not waste either.

to keep up with the times to accept and adapt oneself to modern changes, ideas, opinions etc.

(ii) Expressions with the word **day**

an `off day` a day when one cannot do one's best work etc.

this day week today in exactly a week's time.

day `in, day `out every day without exception.

the other day a few days ago.

to a/the/this day (of a date) exactly. *I can tell you to the day when I shall have paid off my debts. Two years ago to this day I asked Miranda to marry me.*

by day during the hours of daylight.

`some day` at some future time.

one of these (fine) days/one (fine) day at some future time (used when one makes a prophecy or a promise which will be realised in the distant future).

to call it a day to stop doing something. *I've been painting the bathroom all the afternoon, and I'm going to call it a day now.*

it's all in a day's work it is part of the normal routine, and therefore something which you accept because you expect it, even if it is not pleasant.

to win/carry the day have a victory, to win the battle, game etc.

to lose the day to be defeated.

to have seen better days to have been better in the past (said about things which are old or in bad repair, or about people who were richer, more powerful or happier in the past).

to have had its day to be no longer in fashion or in demand.

to make a `day of something to spend the whole day enjoying oneself, to make something pleasant last the whole day.

(iii) Expressions with the word **night**

night after night for many nights following each other.

all night long through the whole night.

to have a `night out to go out for an evening of entertainment.

at/in the dead of night during the time near the middle of the night).

to have a good/bad night to sleep well/badly.

a `nightcap a drink which is taken before going to bed.

to be on nights to work regularly during the night, (on the night shift).

a `night-bird a person who likes to stay out/up late at night.

(iv) Expressions with the word **hour**

at the eleventh hour when it is almost too late, at the latest possible time.

the 'small hours the hours of the morning between midnight and dawn.

after hours during the period after normal business hours.

out of hours during the period before or after normal working hours.

a bad quarter of an hour an unpleasant time or experience.

(at) an un'earthly hour either very late or very early, when the time is not convenient.

to keep good/early/regular hours means to do something (eg get up and go to bed, start and finish work etc) at a good/early/regular time.

to keep bad hours to get up, go to bed, start and finish work etc at late, irregular hours.

(v) Expressions with the word **minute**

in (half) a minute soon.

to the minute exactly.

up-to-the-minute (adjective) the most modern or most recent.

the minute (that) as soon as. *I'll tell him the minute he arrives.*

to do something at the last minute to do it at the latest possible time or opportunity, although it could have been done before.

to have a minute to be available to do something.

(vi) Other expressions of time

at any moment very soon. *I'm expecting him at any moment.*

on the spur of the moment without hesitating, quickly, on impulse, spontaneously. *Acting on the spur of the moment, he said he'd take the job.*

a month of Sundays a long time. *She insists on painting the house herself in her free time, even if it takes her a month of Sundays.*

one's Sunday best one's best clothes.

to be out of date to be out of fashion, not modern.

to bring something up to date to give it the qualities of modern standards, ideas, design etc.

a blind date an arranged social meeting with someone you do not know.

all the year round at all times of the year, throughout the whole year.

to be (getting) well on in years to be (getting) old.

to look young for one's years to appear to be younger than one is.

not to look one's age to appear to be younger than one is.

to burn the midnight oil to study or work late into the night.

to be in the autumn of one's life to be elderly, going towards old age.

to see daylight to suddenly understand a problem or situation.

the morning after the night before This refers to feeling ill in the morning because you were drunk the night before, ie you have a hangover.

every now and then occasionally, not very often.

once in a blue moon very seldom.

once in a while occasionally, sometimes.

(just) for this once only for this one time or occasion.

at once immediately; without delay.

once more one more time; again.

13

Idioms of comparison

general note

Modern English uses many short comparisons in order to make language vivid and clear. Some of these comparisons may seem very strange to the learner because they are unusual or unpredictable. Such an example is *as cool as a cucumber*. The connection between *cool* and *cucumber* is not obvious, yet every native English speaker will naturally put the two words together. Most comparisons are used with adjectives, and follow the pattern *as cool as a cucumber*, ie *as* + Adjective + *as* + (*a/the*) + Noun (as in List A below). A second set of comparisons includes verbs following the pattern *to swim like a fish*, ie Verb + *like* + (*a/the*) + Noun (as in List B). List C gives other commonly used comparisons which do not follow a set pattern.

One of the difficulties for the learner will be exactly how and when to use these comparisons. Some comparisons are used in typical situations and are therefore easy to remember and use correctly. Others can be used in many different situations and apply to many things. Secondly, the learner must know which comparisons are used to refer to people and which to refer to things. In order to give the learner some help with these difficulties, special indication is made where necessary.

Some adjectives have more than one possible comparison; indeed, some have as many as six or seven different comparisons. In such cases, the most popular or most frequently occurring comparisons appear first and indications of differences in usage are given if there are any.

A Comparisons with adjectives

as black as the Ace of Spades   **as black as coal**
as black as soot   These three are used of

something *dirty*, for example, a child's face, hands, clothes etc after play.

as black as pitch
as black as midnight
as black as ink
These three are used of something *dark*, for example, a room, a cellar, a road or street without light.

as black as jet
Used purely descriptively of hair or an object.

as blind as a bat
Often used jokingly about someone whose eye-sight is bad.

as blind as a beetle
as blind as a mole
These two do not occur often.

as bold as brass
Used of persons and means 'impudent', 'cheeky'.

as bold as a lion
Here *bold* means 'brave'.

as brave as a lion
as bright as silver
Used to describe shiny objects.

as bright as noonday
as bright as day
These two have the sense of 'light', 'not dark' as eg a room, the weather.

as brittle as glass
as brown as a berry
Used of people who have a tanned skin after sunbathing.

as busy as a bee
Used of persons.

as changeable as the weather
as changeable as the moon
These two are used of a per-

son who changes his mood or opinion about something often.

as cheerful as a lark
as clear as a bell
Used of a tone or someone's voice.

as clear as crystal
Used of water, eg a pool, the sea at a shallow point. It can also mean 'obvious' when referring to a situation, problem etc.

as clear as the nose on your face
This means 'obvious', easy to recognise or see through, eg a situation, someone's intention etc.

as cold as charity
as cold as a frog
as cold as a stone
These three are used of a person who shows no emotions or little feeling.

as cold as ice
Used of things, substances, people's hands or fingers etc. Also, of the temperature of a room.

as cool as a cucumber
Used of a person who remains calm at a time of difficulty or danger.

as cunning as a fox
as dark as pitch
Used of a dark room, a dark night etc.

as dead as a doornail
as dead as mutton
These two are slang expressions used of a person.

as deaf as a post
as different as chalk from cheese

Used of two people who are very different in appearance or character

as drunk as a lord
as dry as a bone
as dry as dust
as dry as a stick
These three are used of a substance, e g soil, sand etc. The second is used to describe a boring book, speech etc. The third is used of a thirsty person.

as dumb as a fish
Used of a stupid person.

as dumb as a statue
Used of a person who says nothing.

as easy as ABC
as easy as pie
as easy as anything
These three are used of a task or problem which is easy to accomplish or solve.

as fair as a rose
Used of a beautiful woman, in poetic style.

as fat as butter
as fat as a pig
These two are used of a fat person. The first is more complimentary than the second.

as fierce as a tiger
as firm as a rock
Used of a person or a thing. With persons, it means 'resolute'.

as fit as a fiddle
Used of a person who enjoys excellent physical health.

as flat as a board
as flat as a pancake
These two may be used of very flat countryside, or any flat surface. They are also used (informal, uncomplimentary) of a woman's flat figure.

as fleet as (a) deer
Used of a person or an animal, with *fleet* meaning 'swift'.

as free as (the) air
as free as a bird
These two are used of a person or an animal, with *free* meaning 'not restricted'.

as fresh as a daisy
Used to describe how someone looks or feels.

as gay as a lark
as gaudy as a peacock
as gaudy as a butterfly
These two are used of the extremely colourful way in which someone dresses.

as gentle as a lamb
as good as gold
Used of a well-behaved child, or an orderly person.

as good as a play
Used of something unintentionally amusing.

as graceful as a swan
Used of someone's movements, often a ballet dancer.

as grasping as a miser
Used of someone who is always trying to get more money and who keeps it for himself.

as grave as a judge
Used of a person, with *grave* meaning 'solemn'.

as greedy as a wolf
as greedy as a pig
as greedy as a dog
These three are used of a person who eats more than he needs.

as green as grass

as gruff as a bear
Used of an ill-tempered person.

as happy as a king
as happy as a lark
as happy as the day is long
as hard as a stone
as hard as nails
These two are used of hard substances, or of unsympathetic person.

as harmless as a dove
as harmless as a kitten
These two are used of persons.

as heavy as lead
as hoarse as a crow
as hot as fire
Used of the heat or temperature of something or of someone's face, cheeks etc.

as hot as pepper
Used of food which is seasoned with sharp spices.

as hungry as a hunter
as innocent as a dove
as keen as mustard
Used of a person who is very critical and exact in his expectations or demands on others. It also means 'eager to do something'.

as large as life
Used of a person, meaning 'as he really is, without doubt'. *We had just been talking about Jim's disappearance, when quite suddenly, there he stood in front of us, as large as life!*

as light as a feather
Used of a thing which has very little weight. It can also refer to persons, ie women of fragile build.

as light as a cork
Used of a thing. As a slang expression, it refers to persons and means 'mentally deficient, stupid'.

as light as a butterfly
Used of a person's personality, ie light-hearted, not solemn.

as light as air
as light as thistledown
These two are used of things which have little weight.

as like as two peas in a pod
as like as two beans
These two are used of two persons or things which are very much alike in appearance or character.

as loud as thunder
Used of noises, someone's voice etc.

as mad as a hatter
as mad as a March hare
These two are used of a mad or peculiar person.

as merry as a cricket
Used of a person's mood or personality.

as mute as a fish
as obstinate as a mule
Used of a person or animal.

as old as the hills
Used to describe a story or tale which everybody already knows; also used of a person or a thing.

as pale as a ghost
as pale as death
These two are used of the colour of a person's face, usually because of shock or illness.

as patient as Job (the name of an uncomplaining man in the Bible)

as patient as an ox
as plain as a pikestaff
as plain as the nose on your face
  These two are used of obvious situations and people's intentions which are easy to recognise or see through.
as playful as a kitten
as plentiful as blackberries
as plump as a partridge
  Used of a person.
as poor as a church-mouse
as poor as Lazarus (the name of a beggar in the Bible)
as pretty as a picture
as proud as a peacock
  Used of the way a person dresses, acts, speaks etc.
as proud as Lucifer (a name of the Devil in the Bible)
  Used of a person's personality.
as quick as lightning
  Used of a person. It can refer to a physical action, eg running, or to a mental process, eg seeing through a problem or situation.
as quiet as a lamb
as quiet as a mouse
  These two are used of a person, often of a baby or small child who is quiet when necessary.
as red as a beetroot
as red as fire
  These two are used of a person who blushes or becomes flushed with anger, embarrassment etc.
as red as blood
as red as a cherry
as red as a rose
  These three are used to describe the special colour of things.
as regular as clockwork
  Used of actions and things which happens regularly, or to persons who do things regularly.
as rich as Croesus (Croesus was a very rich king)
as ripe as a cherry
as round as a barrel
  (informal) Used of a fat person.
as round as a ball
as round as a globe
as round as an apple
  Used of the shape of things.
as salty as a herring
as sharp as a razor
as sharp as a needle
  These two are used of a thing or of something hurtful, cruel etc that a person says.
as silent as the grave
as silent as the dead
  These two are used of a person, or a thing, or a place.
as silent as the stars
  Used of a thing or a place.
as silly as a sheep
as silly as a goose
  These two are used of a person.
as slender as gossamer
  Used of a thing or a person.
as slippery as an eel
  Used of a thing or of a sly person.
as smooth as velvet
  Used of a thing which is soft to the touch.
as smooth as butter
as smooth as oil
  These two are used to describe soft, creamy substances.

as sober as a judge
Here, *sober* means 'solemn'. Informally, it also means that a man is not drunk.

as soft as butter
as soft as down
as soft as wax
These three are used of a thing. Whichever is used depends on the likeness of the substance to butter, down or wax.

as sound as a bell
Here, *sound* means 'healthy' or 'in good condition'. Used of a person or a thing (eg a machine).

as sour as vinegar
Used of the taste of something.

as steady as a rock
Used of a person or a thing.

as timid as a rabbit
as tough as leather
Used of a thing, often food, eg a piece of hard meat which is difficult to cut or chew; also used of a physically strong person.

as tough as nails
Used of a person with a strong will.

as tricky as a monkey
Here, *tricky* means 'clever',
'crafty'. Used of a person or an animal.

as true as steel
Here, *true* means 'loyal', 'reliable'. Used of a person.

as ugly as a scarecrow
Used of a person.

as vain as a peacock
as warm as toast
Used of the way someone is clothed warmly in winter, or of a pleasantly warm room.

as watchful as a hawk
as weak as a kitten
as weak as a baby
These two are used of a person.

as wet as a drowned rat
Used of a person whose clothes have got very wet.

as white as snow
Used to describe the cleanliness or purity of the colour white.

as white as a sheet
Used of the colour of the face of a person who has turned pale after a shock or fright.

as wise as an owl
as wise as Solomon (King Solomon in the Bible)

as yielding as wax
Used of materials, substances.

B   Comparisons with verbs

Here is a short list of comparisons using verbs. They are used often, but in *informal speech* only.

to be off like a shot to run or walk away very quickly.
to come down on someone like a ton of bricks to reprimand or criticise him severely and sharply.
to drink like a fish to drink large quantities of alcohol.

to eat like a horse to eat large quantities of food.

to fight like cat and dog (of people) to disagree or argue violently.

to fit like a glove (of clothing) to fit very well.

to get on like a house on fire (of people) to be very friendly and to enjoy each other's company. It also means to make fast progress with something, eg a task, piece of work etc.

to go like the wind to move very fast, eg a car, a person running.

to live like `fighting cocks (of people) to live very well, on the best food etc.

to run like a hare to run very fast.

to sing like a bird/lark/nightingale (of a woman's voice) to sing very sweetly.

to shake/tremble like a leaf to shake/tremble with cold or fear.

to sleep like a log to sleep very deeply.

to smoke like a chimney to smoke large quantities of cigarettes.

to spend money like water to be extravagant, to spend money often, quickly or in large amounts.

to spread like wildfire (of news, a rumour etc) to spread quickly.

to swear like a trooper to use swear-words frequently.

to swim like a fish to swim very well.

to take to something like a duck to water to get used to something new quickly and easily; to enjoy something new immediately, eg a new job or task, some skill which has to be learnt.

to work like a Trojan to work very hard, with great energy.

C Miscellaneous comparisons

(to be) like a bull in a `china shop used of a careless, clumsy person who may cause damage through lack of skill or care.

(to be) like a bear with a sore head to be angry, annoyed by something.

(to be) like a dog with two tails to feel very proud and happy about something.

(to have) eyes like a ferret to have vicious, cruel eyes.

(to be) like a fish out of water to feel uncomfortable, ill at ease in one's surroundings, situation.

(to have) a hide like a rhinoceros used of an insensitive, crude person, who is not affected by criticism, insult etc.

(to have) a memory like an elephant to have a very good memory, especially for things which happened a long time ago.

(to have) a memory like a sieve to have a bad memory, to forget things often and easily.

(to be) like a red rag to a bull to be a cause of anger, dispute, argument.

(to be) like water off a duck's back used of criticism, warnings, advice, reprimands, sharp words etc which have no effect on the person for whom they are intended.

to have as many faces (= phases) **as the moon** used of a person who is deceitful and insincere.

to go at a 'snail's pace to walk or to progress with something (eg work) very slowly.

as the 'crow flies used to describe the distance from one place to another measured as a direct line across the country, ie not the distance by eg road.

to look as if/though one has been dragged through a hedge backwards to look very untidy or disorderly in one's clothes, hair etc.

a very hot room is said to be **like an oven.**

a person who runs around busily, walks briskly, works hard etc is said to be **like a whirlwind.**

14   Proverbs

Proverbs and proverbial expressions are still very much alive in every-day English, and our daily conversation would seem rather dull without them.

We owe many proverbial sayings to the Bible, to Shakespeare and to other major authors of the past. These sayings or quotations have been readily accepted by the people and handed down to the present day because they have a universal value. Proverbs express in few words a truth which relates to everyday experience. We can find proverbs which fit any human situation and this gives them general application. Proverbs are used to give a word of advice or of warning, or a wise general comment on a situation, and they do this in a precise, poignant style which makes them easy to remember and use.

There are many hundreds of proverbs and proverbial sayings, some in much wider use than others. Here, we list and explain some of the expressions which are particularly common because of their wide general application among all classes of people.

For the learner some proverbs are more easily understood than others. The proverbs which have a metaphorical quality, whose meaning must be transferred from the literal plane to the metaphorical plane, are not so easy to the foreign ear. On the other hand, many proverbial sayings say directly what they mean in straightforward language. Two examples will make this clear. *A burnt child dreads the fire* is, of course, true and easily understood in its literal meaning. But the metaphorical meaning of this proverb has a much wider application which extends far beyond the literal meaning. It is applied to any situation in which one has been hurt, disappointed, deceived etc. It says generally that one is always careful to avoid the repetition of a painful experience. Easier to understand are the proverbs which are to be understood

literally only, such as *The more you have, the more you want*, or
If you want a thing well done, do it yourself.

The proverbs are listed alphabetically according to the first
main word (ie not **a** or **the**). Reference is also made to other proverbs which are parallel or opposite in meaning.

1 **absence makes the heart grow fonder** If people are parted for
a time, they tend to appreciate each other more. (See also No 68)

2 **actions speak louder than words** People can say many things,
because talking is easy, but what really matters is what one *does*,
not what one *says*. (See also Nos 35, 72)

3 **all good things come to an end** No pleasure lasts for ever.

4 **all's fair in love and war** All tactics are allowed, fair or unfair,
when fighting *for* someone (ie love) or *against* someone (ie
war).

5 'all's well that 'ends well' (Shakespeare) If the final result is
good, previous failures are forgotten, as the end result is most
important.

6 **all roads lead to Rome** There are many ways of reaching the
same aim or obtaining the same results.

7 **all that glitters is not gold** Appearances can be deceptive. One
should not judge the value of things by their pleasing appearance.
(See also Nos 12, 17, 34)

8 **all work and no play makes Jack a dull boy** It is not wise to
concentrate only on working and not to allow time for relaxation.
Without proper leisure time, the worker and therefore the work
will suffer.

9 **as you 'make your bed, so you must 'lie in it** Each person
must bear the consequences of his own actions and take full
responsibility for them, even if the consequences are unpleasant
or harmful to him.

10 **a bad workman always blames his tools** One tries to cover up
one's lack of skill or to excuse one's failure by putting the blame
on the tools at one's disposal. For example: if one cannot drive
well, one may blame the engine, the gears or the brakes of the car,
but not one's own ability to control the car.

11 **barking dogs seldom bite** People who often lose their temper
and shout in a loud voice are not really to be feared because they
are usually harmless. We may say of such a person: *His bark is
worse than his bite*.

12 **beauty is only skin deep** Inner qualities, not outward appearance, show the true nature of a person. (See also Nos 7, 17, 34)

13 **beggars can't/mustn't be choosers** When we are not in a position to choose we should be thankful for any offer which is made
to us, even if it is not exactly what we would like. (See also No 40)

14 **better late than never** It is better to do something, even if it should have been done earlier, than not to do it at all.

15 **better the devil you 'know than the devil you 'don't know** A danger or unpleasantness which we have already experienced is preferable to a danger or unpleasantness which we haven't experienced.

16 **a bird in the hand is worth two in the bush** It is better to be content with what we have or can easily get, than to reject it in the hope of getting something better, as this may never happen.

17 **clothes do not make the man** Inner qualities, not outward appearance, show the true nature of a person. (See also Nos 7, 12, 34)

18 **cowards die many times before their deaths** (Shakespeare: Julius Caesar) If a man is a coward, he will be afraid of every bad experience and will feel fear when it is not necessary.

19 **a creaking gate hangs long** A person of poor physical health often lives to reach an old age and does not die suddenly.

20 **cross the stream where it is shallowest** Find the simplest way of doing things; don't make difficulties for yourself.

21 **cut your coat according to your cloth** We should not be too ambitious and should not want things which are beyond what we have. For example, we should adjust our spending to our income.

22 **'do as you would be 'done by** Treat others as you would wish them to treat you. If you treat someone unfairly, you must expect that person to treat you unfairly, too.

23 **don't count your chickens before they hatch/are hatched** Do not be sure of success until all difficulties have been overcome.

24 **don't cross a bridge until you 'come to it** Don't create difficulties until they arise; don't worry about things before they happen.

25 **don't have too many irons in the fire** It is better to concentrate on one thing and do it properly than to attempt too many things at the same time.

26 **don't make a mountain out of a molehill** Don't treat unimportant things as if they were important.

27 **don't put all your eggs in one basket** It is risky to concentrate all one's hopes, chances, money etc on only one thing, for if this one thing is lost, there will be nothing left.

28 **don't put the cart before the horse** We should deal with things in the right order and should not start from the wrong end.

29 **the early bird catches the worm** Only early or prompt action will bring success. If we want something, we should not wait until it may be too late. (See also No 36)

30 **every dog has his/its day** Every person will have success or good fortune some time.

31 **every why has a wherefore** There is a reason behind every-thing, even if it not obvious.

32 **everything comes/all things come to him who waits** If a person waits long enough and tries hard enough he will have suc-cess in the end.

33 **an eye for an eye and a tooth for a tooth** (The Bible) This saying from the Old Testament justifies revenge, saying that a wrongdoing can be avenged by treating the wrongdoer in the same way. The teachings of the New Testament (eg *Do good to those who hate you*) are opposed to the spirit of this saying.

34 **fine feathers make fine birds** People judge others by appear-ance. It is therefore wise to dress well if we wish to make a good impression. In a sarcastic sense, the proverb means that someone may not be so important or fine as his clothes would suggest. (See also Nos 7, 17)

35 **fine words butter no parsnips** Fine words are no substitute for effective actions. (See also Nos 2, 72)

36 **first come, first served** The man who has arrived, finished etc first has the best chance of success. (See also No 29)

37 **fools rush in where angels fear to tread** (Alexander Pope: Essay on Criticism) Foolish people say and do things too hastily. A wise person avoids rash action.

38 **forbidden fruit is sweetest** The things which we cannot have are the things we want the most; forbidden things are the most attractive and exciting.

39 **give a dog a bad name and hang him** If enough bad things are said about a person, they will ruin his reputation even though they may not be true.

40 **half a loaf is better than none** We should be thankful for what we receive, even though we hoped to receive more. (See also No 13)

41 **help a lame dog over a stile** One should give help to anyone who is in difficulties.

42 **honesty is the best policy** Dishonesty may seem more profit-able for a short time, but in the long run honesty brings more advantages.

43 **if a thing is worth doing, it is worth doing well** A similar proverb is *Never do things by halves* (ie never leave a task un-completed).

44 **if at first you don't succeed, try, try, try again** (For proverbs of similar meaning, see Nos 74 and 83)

45 **it's a long lane that has no turning** Bad or unpleasant things cannot last for ever, they are sure to improve with time.

46 **it's an ill wind that blows nobody any good** Most things that happen will benefit somebody, somewhere, sometime. It will be a really disastrous happening that brings no advantages at all.

47 **it's easy to be wise after the event** It is easy to say what should have been done to avoid failure after the failure has happened.

48 **it's never too late to mend** It is never too late to improve or alter one's behaviour, attitudes, way of life etc in order to lead a better life.

49 **it's no use crying over spilt milk** If one cannot change a bad result, disappointment etc then there is no use making oneself unhappy about it. A similar proverb is: *What's done cannot be undone.*

50 **it never rains but it pours** Misfortunes rarely come alone, but tend to come together or follow each other.

51 **it takes all sorts to make a world** This teaches that one should be tolerant of one's fellow men even if they are different from oneself, as the world is made up of many sorts of people, good and bad, and all have a right to live.

52 **it takes two to make a quarrel** When a quarrel breaks out, two people and not only one are at fault.

53 **learn to walk before you run** One must learn how to do things gradually, as knowledge cannot be gained all at once.

54 **let sleeping dogs lie** Do not stir up unnecessary trouble: eg let past things remain forgotten; leave things alone that you know will cause trouble.

55 **look before you leap** Do not act without considering the possible consequences of the action. Hasty actions may be regretted later.

56 **make hay while the `sun shines** Make use of favourable opportunities when they present themselves. (See also No 78)

57 **many hands make light work** If many people work together to complete a task, it will be completed more quickly and more easily. (See also No 80)

58 **a miss is as good as a mile** Even if one fails only by a narrow margin, one has still failed to do something. Failure is failure.

59 **money talks** People with money are more likely to have influence in certain things than people without money.

60 **more haste, less speed** The more one tries to hurry, the more time one loses, because one is nervous or makes mistakes.

61 **necessity is the mother of invention** If one needs something badly enough, one becomes very inventive in finding out ways of getting it.

62 **never look a gift horse in the mouth** Never criticise or express displeasure at a gift; be thankful that you have it at all. (See also No 13)

63 **a new broom sweeps clean** When a new person takes over a job, he tends to make noticeable changes and carry out the job with thoroughness.

64 **no gain without pain** Nothing can be gained without a certain amount of discomfort, effort or compromise.

65 ˋ**no news is** ˋ**good news** If one is expecting news and hears noth-thing, one may presume that nothing bad has happened, since bad news will usually come quickly.

66 **one good turn deserves another** If a person has received help from someone, it is fair to help him in return.

67 **one swallow doesn't make a summer** One fact does not prove something, as it may be an exception to the rule.

68 **out of sight, out of mind** Absent friends are soon forgotten, as one tends to forget about people if there is no direct contact with them. (See also No 1)

69 **paddle your own canoe** One should rely on oneself and not expect others to help.

70 **practice makes perfect** Only practice and perseverance will bring success. (See also Nos 44, 53)

71 **the proof of the pudding is in the eating** One can only prove something by putting it into action or use.

72 **the road to hell is paved with good intentions** People often have good intentions but fail to put them into practice. It is not enough to intend to do something; it is the doing itself that is the most important. (See also Nos 2, 35)

73 **a rolling stone gathers no moss** A person who constantly changes his work or his home cannot expect to make much money, gain lasting friendship, be relied on etc.

74 **Rome was not built in a day** An important task needs perseverance and patience. It cannot be completed in a short time. (See also Nos 44, 83)

75 **the spirit is willing but the flesh is weak** (The Bible) A person may have a firm intention to do something because he knows it is sensible or good, but he may not do it, because he finds doing other things more enjoyable, attractive, easy etc.

76 **still waters run deep** A person may say little, but he may think a lot and thus have unrecognised abilities.

77 **a stitch in time saves nine** Prompt action will prevent a lot of trouble later.

78 **strike while the iron is hot** Make the most of present opportunities. (See also No 56)

79 **time and tide wait for** ˋ**no man** The forces of nature (eg the passing of time, the action of the sea) are stronger than the forces of man.

80 **too many cooks spoil the broth** If too many people try to do the same thing at the same time, the task will be done badly. (See also No 57)

81 **where one door shuts another opens** If one opportunity is lost, another will present itself some time.

82 **when the cat's away the mice will play** When a person in

authority is not present, the others will take advantage and do things they cannot do when he is there.

83 **where there's a will there's a way** If a person wants something badly enough, he will find a way of getting it. (See also Nos 44, 74)

84 **while there's life there's hope** As long as we are still alive, we can still hope for better times.

85 **the wish is father to the thought** People believe things because they want them to be true; what is merely a wish can soon become a firm opinion.

86 **a word is enough to the wise** A clever or wise person can understand what is meant by a hint alone; long explanations are not necessary for him.

87 **a word spoken is past recalling** Once something has been said, it cannot be taken back, however much it may be regretted.

88 **you can't ˋhave your cake and ˋeat it** You can only choose one of two alternatives, not both. (See also No 90)

89 **you can't make an omelette without breaking eggs** Small sacrifices of some kind must be made in order to attain one's purpose.

90 **you can't run with the hare and hunt with the hounds** One cannot be loyal to two opposing sides at the same time, in order to gain advantages from both. (See also No 88)

91 **you can't teach an old dog new tricks** Old people do not like to be confronted with changes and innovations.

92 **you may lead a horse to water, but you cannot make him drink** You can persuade a person or guide him only to a certain extent, because the final step can only be taken by the person himself. Thus, you cannot ultimately force a person to do what he does not want to do.

93 **ˋyou scratch ˋmy back and ˋI'll scratch ˋyours** A policy of mutual help or promotion: if one person furthers the interests of another, the other will also further his interests in return.

Appendix 1: Contractions

general note

In English there are several recognised contractions of words which are used in conversation and in written texts which reproduce spoken language, e g drama, direct speech in novels and short stories, personal letters etc. It is important that the learner should learn and make use of these contracted forms if he wants his English to sound natural instead of stiff. Contractions when written shorten an expression by omitting one or two letters and by joining two words together. The letters which are omitted are represented by an apostrophe. The words which are joined together are invariably a *pronoun + auxiliary verb*, e g *he'll* (he will), *we've* (we have), or an *auxiliary verb + not*, e g *isn't* (is not), *didn't* (did not).

A   *personal pronoun + auxiliary verb*

I'm	I am	**she'll**	she will
I've	I have	**she'd**	she would; she had
I'll	I will		
I'd	I would; I had	**it's**	it is; it has
		it'll	it will
you're	you are		
you've	you have	**we're**	we are
you'll	you will	**we've**	we have
you'd	you would; you had	**we'll**	we will
		we'd	we would; we had
he's	he is; he has		
he'll	he will	**they're**	they are
he'd	he would; he had	**they've**	they have
		they'll	they will
she's	she is; she has	**they'd**	they would; they had

B *auxiliary verb + not*

can't	cannot	**mightn't**	might not
couldn't	could not	**mustn't**	must not
daren't	dare not	**needn't**	need not
didn't	did not	**oughtn't**	ought not
doesn't	does not	**shan't**	shall not
don't	do not	**shouldn't**	should not
hasn't	has not	**wasn't**	was not
haven't	have not	**weren't**	were not
hadn't	had not	**won't**	will not

C   Other common contractions

here's	here is	**when's**	when is?
there's	there is	**where's**	where is?
that's	that is	**who's**	who is?
that'll	that will	**who'd**	who would?
how's	how is?	**who'll**	who will?
what's	what is?		

Appendix 2: Abbreviations

general note

Abbreviations have always played an important part in the English language, the influence coming mainly from American usage, where the tendency towards short, time-saving forms has been dominant for a long time. New forms are creeping into both the written and spoken language continually. Note that all abbreviations made up of capital letters can be spoken, using the names for the letters. The last letter in such abbreviations always carries the stress; eg MD is pronounced 'em 'dee'.

A   Abbreviations used in writing and note-taking

ca about, approximately
cf compare with
ch(s) chapter(s)
cont continued
diff difference; different
eg for example
enc(l) enclosure; enclosed
et al and others
etc and all the rest
et seq and the following
excl excluding; exclusive
ff following
ibid in the same place
ie that is
incl including; inclusive
l(l) line(s)
loc cit in the place mentioned
misc miscellaneous

NB note well; take special note of
op cit in the work cited (mentioned)
p(p) page(s)
passim here and there; throughout (used when no specific page references can be given)
PS postscript
PTO please turn over
qv which may be referred to at another place
ref reference; refer to
resp respectively
sec section
v verse
viz namely; by name
vol volume

B   Abbreviations of national and international organisations

ABC (US) American Broadcasting Company; Australian Broadcasting Commission

AID (US) Agency for International Development

ASEAN Association of South East Asian Nations

BBC (GB) British Broadcasting Corporation

CBC Canadian Broadcasting Corporation

CBI (GB) Confederation of British Industries

CBS (US) Columbia Broadcasting System

CD *Corps Diplomatique* (Diplomatic Service)

CENTO Central Treaty Organisation

CIA (US) Central Intelligence Agency

CID (GB) Criminal Investigation Department

EEC European Economic Community (the 'Common Market')

EFTA European Free Trade Association

FAO Food and Agriculture Organisation

FBI (US) Federal Bureau of Investigation

GATT General Agreement on Tariffs and Trade

GPO (GB) General Post Office

ILO International Labour Organisation

CARE (US) Co-operative for American Relief Everywhere

IMF International Monetary Fund

IRA Irish Republican Army

KGB (Russian Intelligence Agency)

MI5 (GB) National Security Division of Military Intelligence

NASA (US) National Aeronautics and Space Administration

NATO North Atlantic Treaty Organisation

NHS (GB) National Health Service

NSPCC (GB) National Society for the Prevention of Cruelty to Children

OECD Organisation for Economic Co-operation and Development

OPEC Organisation of Petroleum Exporting Countries

RAF Royal Air Force

RN Royal Navy

TUC (GB) Trades Union Congress

UN United Nations

UNCTAD United Nations Conference on Trade and Development

UNESCO United Nations Educational, Scientific and Cultural Organisation

UNICEF United Nations Children's Fund

UNO United Nations Organisation

UNRWA United Nations Relief and Works Agency

VSO (GB) Voluntary Service Overseas

WHO World Health Organisation

WRAC Women's Royal
Army Corps
WRAF Women's Royal Air
Force
WRNS Women's Royal Naval
Service

YHA Youth Hostels
Association
YMCA Young Men's
Christian Association
YWCA Young Women's
Christian Association

C   Miscellaneous abbreviations

AA (GB) Automobile
Association
A-Level (GB) Advanced
Level (General Certificate
of Education Examination)
a/c account
AD *Anno Domini* (after the
birth of Christ)
am before noon
Apr April
asap as soon as possible
assoc associate; association
asst assistant
Aug August
Av(e) Avenue
BA Bachelor of Arts (first
university degree)
BC before Christ
Bro(s) brother(s)
BSc Bachelor of Science (first
University degree)
C Centigrade
cc cubic centimetres
cert certificate; certified
Co Company
c/o care of; at the address of
C of E Church of England
Cons (GB) Conservative
(political party)
Co-op Co-operative Society
CSE (GB) Certificate of
Secondary Education
cwt hundredweight (50·8 kilo-
grams)
dbl double

Dec December
Dept Department
Dip Diploma
Dip Ed Diploma of Education
Dir Director
DLitt Doctor of Literature
doz dozen
DPhil Doctor of Philosophy
Dr Doctor; debtor
DSc Doctor of Science
E East
ed edited by; edition; editor;
education
ER *Elizabeth Regina* (Queen
Elizabeth)
Esq Esquire (in an address,
appearing after the name
without Mr)
ext external; exterior
F Fahrenheit
f foot, feet; female
Feb February
fig figurative; figure
Fri Friday
FRS Fellow of the Royal
Society
fwd forward
GB Great Britain
GC George Cross
GCE (GB) General Certificate
of Education
GI (US) enlisted soldier (ie
not an officer)
GMT Greenwich Mean Time
GNP Gross National Product

GP General Practitioner (Medical Doctor, not a specialist)
h hour; height
h & c hot and cold (water)
H-bomb Hydrogen bomb
HE His/Her Excellency
HM His/Her Majesty
HMS His/Her Majesty's Ship
H of C House of Commons
H of L House of Lords
hp horsepower (of engines)
HQ Headquarters
hr(s) hour(s)
HRH His/Her Royal Highness
h/w herewith
in(s) inch(es)
Inc Incorporated
IOU I owe you
IQ Intelligence Quotient
I(s) Island(s)
Jan January
JC Jesus Christ
Jnr Junior
JP Justice of the Peace
Jul July
Jun June
kg kilogram(s)
km kilometre(s)
KO knock-out
kph kilometres per hour
kw kilowatt(s)
l left; length; line
Lab (GB) Labour (political party)
lb pound(s) (454 grams)
Lib (GB) Liberal (political party)
LLB Bachelor of Laws
LP long-playing (record)
Ltd Limited
m male; married; metre(s); mile(s); million
MA Master of Arts (second university degree)

Mar March
MB Bachelor of Medicine
MD Doctor of Medicine
mfr manufacturer
mod cons modern conveniences (in a house)
Mon Monday
MP Member of Parliament (House of Commons); Military Police
mpg miles per gallon
mph miles per hour
Mr (either married or unmarried man)
Mrs (married woman)
Ms (either married or unmarried woman)
ms(s) manuscript(s)
MSc Master of Science (second university degree)
N North
NCO Non-Commissioned Officer
NE northeast
no(s) number(s)
Nov November
nr near
NT New Testament
NW northwest
NY(C) New York (City)
NZ New Zealand
ob died
Oct October
OHMS (GB) On His/Her Majesty's Service
O-Level (GB) Ordinary Level (General Certificate of Education Examination)
op *opus* (work); operation
opp opposite
OT Old Testament
Oxon Oxford(shire)
oz ounce(s) (28·35 grams)
P Parking
pa per year

para(s) paragraph(s)
PAYE pay as you earn
PC Police Constable; (GB)
  Privy Councillor; (US)
  Peace Corps
PG Paying Guest
PhD Doctor of Philosophy
PM Prime Minister
pm after noon; per month
PO (Box) Post Office (Box)
POW Prisoner of War
pp by the authority of;
  representing (before a name)
PR Public Relations
Pres President
pro professional
Prof Professor
pron pronounced; pronuncia-
  tion
Prot Protestant
pw per week
QC Queen's Counsel (lawyer)
Qu Queen; Question
RC Red Cross; Roman
  Catholic
Rd Road
Rep Republic; Representative
Rev(d) Reverend
RIP may he/they rest in peace
rpm revolutions per minute
RSVP please reply (on writ-
  ten invitations)
S South
SA South Africa
sae stamped addressed
  envelope
Sat Saturday
s/c self-contained
Sch School
sci science
SE southeast
sec second
Sept September
SF Science Fiction
Sn(r) Senior

Soc Society
sp spelling; special
Sq Square
SRN State Registered Nurse
SS Steamship
St Saint; Street
STD direct dialling (by tele-
  phone)
Sun Sunday
Supt Superintendent
SW southwest
T temperature
t time; ton(s)
TB Tuberculosis
Tech Technical (College)
tel telephone
Thurs Thursday
TNT Tri-nitro-toluene (an
  explosive)
trans translated; translator
treas treasurer
TU Trade Union
Tues Tuesday
TV television
UAE United Arab Emirates
UFO unidentified flying
  object
UHF ultra high frequency
UK United Kingdom
Univ University
US United States
USA United States of
  America
USSR Union of Soviet
  Socialist Republics
vac vacation
VAT Value Added Tax
VC Victoria Cross; Vice
  Chairman/Chancellor/
  Consul
VHF very high frequency
VIP very important person
vs versus; against
VS Veterinary Surgeon
W west

wc toilet
Wed Wednesday
wpm words per minute

wt weight
Xmas Christmas
yr year

Word index

This Word Index lists words of the categories *noun, adjective, verb* and *adverb* which appear as key-words in idioms. *Prepositions* and grammatical words are also indexed where they are dealt with in detail. Page numbers printed in **bold** type indicate that this is where an item has received its fullest treatment. Phrases are indexed for the convenience of the reader where several page references apply. Particular attention is drawn to the following pages which are *not indexed*, as the entries are already alphabetically arranged in their separate parts of the book:

> *Proper name phrases* 65–67
> *Adjectives with prepositions* 101–112
> *Verbs with prepositions and particles* 113–167

Subject index